THE LAW (IN PLAIN ENGLISH)® FOR WRITERS

Other books by Leonard D. DuBoff

Madrona Publishers' Law (in Plain English)® Series

The Law (in Plain English)® for Craftspeople

Business Forms and Contracts (in Plain English)® for Crafts-people

The Law (in Plain English)® for Small Businesses (September 1987)

The Deskbook of Art Law and 1984 Supplement

The Book Publishers' Legal Guide

Art Law in a Nutshell

Law and the Visual Arts

Art Law, Domestic and International

THE LAW

(IN PLAIN ENGLISH)®

FOR WRITERS

Leonard D. DuBoff

Madrona Publishers   Seattle

To Millicent Pollack DuBoff who gave me life
and the desire to do something useful with it.

Published by
Madrona Publishers
P. O. Box 22667
Seattle, WA 98122

10 9 8 7 6 5 4 3 2 1

Library of Congress Cataloging-in-Publication Data

DuBoff, Leonard D.
    The law (in plain English) for writers.

    Bibliography: p.
    Includes index.
    1. Law--United States.   2. Authors and publishers--
United States.   3. Press law--United States.   4. Authors
and publishers--United States--Handbooks, manuals, etc.
I. Title.
KF390.A96D83   1987   349.73'0248   86-33316
ISBN 0-88089-016-9   347.300248

Contents

Foreword

Have you ever wondered how to copyright your work? Or what an agent can do for you? Or when your writing expenses can be deducted from your taxes? Or what, if anything, can be changed on a contract from a publisher?

Unless it is done for purely personal reasons, and intended to remain tucked away in a drawer, every writer will at some time have to become involved with the legal end of writing. Almost any question you may have about the law and writing is discussed in clear and simple language in Leonard DuBoff's *Law (in Plain English)*® *for Writers*. No writer, beginning or experienced, will want to be without this book.

Jean M. Auel

Acknowledgments

The volume of material which has sprouted in the field of publishing and writing law has been increasing in geometric proportions. The process of gathering this material, digesting it and converting it into the project which has emerged as *The Law (in Plain English)* ® *for Writers* has involved a host of friends, colleagues and former students. This book could not have been completed without their very valuable assistance. I would like, therefore, to thank several of my friends and former students from the Northwestern School of Law of Lewis and Clark College: Michele Gold, Alice Bennison, J.D., 1987; Trilby de Jung, J.D., 1985; Georgene Inaba, J.D., 1985; Jim Losk, J.D., 1987; Elizabeth Strance, J.D., 1987; and Nancy Walseth, J.D., 1987, for all of their help and assistance with the researching of the cases, statutes, treatises and articles discussed in the text. In addition, I would like to thank Ellen Kell, of Portland, Oregon, for her special help.

I would also like to thank my colleagues, Professors Larry Brown and Jack Bogdanski, for their extraordinarily valuable assistance with the many changes that have occurred in the area of taxation. In addition, I would like to express my appreciation to William Parkhurst of the accounting firm of Yergen and Meyer for his incisive comments on the tax-related material in this book. I would similarly like to thank my colleague, Dean Stephen Kanter, for his insight into the area of obscenity law and censorship. Professors Bernie Vail and Edwin O. Belsheim of Lewis and Clark Law School and Professor Francis Michael Nevins of the University of Missouri School of Law were kind enough to review my chapter on estate planning and provide me with some very valuable comments.

Dan Levant, president of Madrona Publishers, deserves thanks for urging me to begin this project and for his recommendations and insights into the practical application of the law for writers and publishers. Thanks also to Sara Levant, editor-in-chief of Madrona Publishers, for her helpful and sympathetic editing. Thanks too to Felicia Eth, formerly a literary agent at Writers House, now with St. Martin's Press, for her generous assistance in understanding the present-day real-world nature of author-publisher contracts.

The process of converting a huge collection of notes, interlineations, changes and corrections into a publishable manuscript was artfully performed by Lenair Mulford, Director of Information Services at Lewis and Clark Law School. She has once again worked her magic with the word processor and managed to plow through my numerous drafts, cryptic notes and revisions.

I would like to sincerely thank my children, Colleen Rose DuBoff, Robert Courtney DuBoff and Sabrina Ashley DuBoff for being so understanding about the time I have had to take to closet myself away from them in order to complete this book.

Finally, I would like to acknowledge the invaluable assistance of my partner, in law and in life, Mary Ann Crawford DuBoff for all of her work on this volume. Her extraordinarily useful comments, recommendations and insights are evident throughout this text. Without her encouragement and support, this project could not have been completed.

Preface

The art of writing dates back to the very dawn of civilization. Writers were active in dynastic Egypt, as well as in the emerging civilizations in the valleys of the Tigris and Euphrates. As society became more complex, the problems faced by writers increased and today the successful writer must also be a successful business person.

When I first began to engage in the practice of law, I realized that it was important for clients to carefully evaluate all of the options available to them and then adopt the most prudent course. Later, as a law professor, I taught my students to use this same principal in counseling their clients. Many of my writer clients and students have asked me to recommend a book which would aid them in understanding the legal issues faced by writers. Unfortunately, I was unable to recommend any single volume which would serve this purpose.

More than a decade ago, I was made aware of the fact that publishers had special legal problems and that there was barely any written material available to help them. It was for this reason that I wrote *The Book Publishers' Legal Guide*, which was published by Butterworth Publishers in 1984. After Dan Levant, president of Madrona Publishers, read that book, he reminded me of the plight of writers and urged me to prepare a book for writers—one that would be "user friendly," and so I began work on this. This is the third book in The Law (In Plain English) ® series and it is my hope that it will continue the tradition of being readable, practical, and comprehensive.

THE LAW (IN PLAIN ENGLISH)® FOR WRITERS

1

Organizing As a Business

One of the reasons—perhaps the primary reason—why writers like their work is that they feel they have escaped the stultifying atmosphere of the dress-for-success business world. But they have not escaped it entirely. The same laws that govern the billion-dollar auto industry govern the writer. This being the case, you might as well learn how you can use some of those laws to your advantage.

Any professional person knows that survival requires careful financial planning. Yet few writers realize the importance of selecting the *form* of their business. Most writers have little need for the sophisticated organizational structures utilized in industry, but since writers must pay taxes, obtain loans, and expose themselves to potential liability every time they write and sell their work, it only makes sense to structure the business so as to minimize these concerns.

Every business has an organizational form best suited to it. When I counsel writers on organizing their businesses, I usually go about it in two steps. First, we discuss various aspects of taxes and liability in order to decide which of the basic forms is best. There are only a handful of basic forms: the *sole proprietorship*, the *partnership*, the *corpora-*

tion, and a few hybrids. Then, once we have decided which of these is appropriate, we go into the organizational details such as partnership agreements or corporate bylaws. These documents define the day-to-day operations of a business and therefore must be tailored to individual situations.

What I offer here is an explanation of features of the various kinds of business organizations, including their advantages and disadvantages. This should give you some idea of which form might be best for you.

I will discuss potential problems, but, since I cannot go into a full discussion of the more intricate details, you should consult an attorney before deciding to adopt any particular structure. My purpose here is to facilitate your communication with your lawyer and to better enable you to understand the choices offered.

THE AMERICAN DREAM: SOLE PROPRIETORSHIP

The technical name *sole proprietorship* may be unfamiliar to you, but chances are you are operating under this form now. The sole proprietorship is an unincorporated business owned by one person. Though not peculiar to the United States, it was, and still is, the backbone of the American dream, to the extent that personal freedom follows economic freedom. As a form of business it is elegant in its simplicity. All it requires is a little money and a little work. Legal requirements are few and simple. In most localities, professionals such as writers are not required to have a business license, but, if you wish to operate the business under a name other than your own, the name must be registered with the state and, in some cases, the county in which you are doing business. With this detail taken care of, you are in business.

Disadvantages of Sole Proprietorship

There are many financial risks involved in operating your business as a sole proprietor. If you recognize any of these dangers as a real threat, you probably should consider an alternative form of organization.

If you are the sole proprietor of a business venture, your personal property is at stake. In other words, if for any reason you owe more than the dollar value of your business, your creditors can force a sale of most of your personal property to satisfy the debt. Thus, if one of your published works contains defamatory material, invades someone's privacy, or infringes a copyright, and your contract with your publisher contains a clause whereby you assume sole responsibility for such liability, you may find that you are financially responsible for paying any judgment which is obtained against the publisher.

For many risks, you can get insurance which will shift the loss from you to an insurance company, but there are some risks for which insurance is simply not available. For example, no insurance is available to cover the loss of the only copy of a manuscript. In any case, insurance policies do have monetary limits. Furthermore, insurance premiums can be quite high, and there is no way to accurately predict or plan for future increases in premiums. These hazards, as well as many other uncertain economic factors, can drive a small business into bankruptcy, and that, in turn, could force you into personal bankruptcy if you are the sole proprietor.

Taxes for the Sole Proprietor

The sole proprietor is taxed on all profits of the business and may deduct losses. Of course, the rate of taxation will fluctuate with changes in income. A particularly successful year can leave the sole proprietor no better off financially than in the less successful years, due to the higher tax bracket.

Fortunately, there are ways to ease this tax burden. For instance, you can establish an approved IRA or pension plan, deducting a specified amount of your net income for placement into the pension plan, or into an interest-bearing account, or into approved government securities or mutual funds to be withdrawn later when you are in a lower tax bracket. There are severe restrictions, however, on withdrawal of this money prior to retirement age.

For further information on these tax-planning devices, you should contact your local IRS office and ask for free pamphlets on the Keogh Plan. Or you might wish to use the services of an accountant experienced in dealing with writers' tax problems.

PARTNERSHIP

When a writer agrees to work with another on a book or when a writer and illustrator get together and agree to produce an illustrated manuscript, a partnership may be formed. A *partnership* is defined by most state laws as an association of two or more persons to conduct, as co-owners, a business for profit. No formalities are required. In fact, in some cases people have been held to be partners even though they never had any intention of forming a partnership. For example, if you lend a friend some money to start a business and the friend agrees to pay you a certain percentage of whatever profit is made, you may be your friend's partner in the eyes of the law even though you take no part in running the business. This is important because each partner is subject to unlimited personal liability for the debts of the partnership. Also, each partner is liable for the negligence of another partner and of the partnership's employees when a negligent act occurs in the usual course of business. In effect, each partner is considered an employee of the partnership.

This means that if you are getting involved in a partnership as, for example, when you collaborate with someone on a book, you should be careful in two areas. First, since the involvement of a partner increases your potential liability, you must choose a responsible partner. Second, the partnership should be adequately insured to protect both the assets of the partnership and the personal assets of each partner.

As I have already mentioned, no formalities are required to create a partnership. If the partners do not have a formal agreement defining the terms of the partnership—such as control of the partnership or the distribution of profits—state law will determine the terms. State laws are based on the fundamental characteristics of the typical partnership as it has existed throughout the ages and are therefore thought to correspond to the reasonable expectations of the partners. The most important of these legally presumed characteristics are:

1. No one can become a member of a partnership without the unanimous consent of all partners,
2. All members have an equal vote in the management of the partnership regardless of the size of their interest in it,
3. All partners share equally in the profits and losses of the partnership no matter how much capital they have contributed,
4. A simple majority vote is required for decisions in the ordinary course of business, and a unanimous vote is required to change the fundamental character of the business, and
5. A partnership is terminable at will by any partner; a partner can withdraw from the partnership at any time, and this withdrawal will cause a dissolution of the partnership.

Most state laws contain a provision that allows the partners to make their own agreements regarding the management structure and division of profits that best suits the needs of the individual partners.

Major Items of Agreement

Some of the major considerations in preparing a partnership agreement include the name of the partnership, a description of the business, contributions of capital by the partners, duration of the partnership, distribution of profits, management responsibilities, duties of partners, prohibited acts, and provisions for the dissolution of the partnership.

As you can see, a comprehensive partnership agreement is no simple matter. It is, in fact, essential for potential partners to devote some time to preparation of an agreement and to enlist the services of a business lawyer. The expense of a lawyer to help you put together an agreement suited to the needs of your partnership is well justified by the amount of money you will save in the smooth organization, operation, and, when necessary, final dissolution of the partnership.

The economic advantages of doing business in a partnership are the pooling of capital, collaboration, easier access to credit because of the collective credit rating, and a potentially more efficient allocation of labor and resources. A major disadvantage is that each partner is fully and personally liable for all the debts of the partnership, even if not personally involved in incurring those debts.

A partnership does not possess any special tax advantages over a sole proprietorship. As a partner you will pay tax on your share of the profits whether they are distributed to you or not. You will also be entitled to the same proportion of the partnership deductions and credits. The partnership must file with the IRS an annual information return known as a K-1 form, against which the IRS can then check the individual returns filed by the partners.

THE LIMITED PARTNERSHIP

The *limited partnership* is a hybrid containing elements of both the partnership and corporation. A limited partnership may be formed when one or more parties wishes to invest in a business and, in return, share in its profits, but does not wish to share in any respect in the control of the partnership.

In effect the limited partner is very much like an investor who buys a few shares of stock. Because of the limited partner's passive role, the law limits his or her liability only to the amount invested. In order to establish a limited partnership it is necessary to have one or more general partners to run the business, and one or more limited partners to play a passive role. A general partner will have the same potential liability, duties, and authority as a member of a regular partnership.

In order to form a limited partnership, a certificate must be filed with the proper state office. If the certificate is not filed or is improperly filed, the limited partner could be treated as a general partner. The limited partner *must* refrain from trying to influence the day-to-day operation of the partnership. Otherwise, the limited partner might be found to be actively participating in the business, and thereby held to be a general partner with unlimited personal liability.

This limited partnership might be appropriate if you need economic backing and wish to reward your sponsor with a share of your profits from the sale of your work without exposing the backer to personal liability. A limited partnership can be used to attract investment when credit is hard to get or is too expensive. In return for investing, the limited partner receives a designated share of the profits. This may be an attractive way to fund your business since the limited partner receives nothing if there are no profits, whereas if you had borrowed money from a creditor, that person can sue if you fail to repay.

Another use of the limited partnership is to facilitate reorganization of a general partnership after the death or retirement of a general partner. A partnership, remember, can be terminated when any partner requests it. Although the original partnership is thus technically dissolved when one partner retires, it is not uncommon for the remaining partners to agree to buy out the retiring partner's share—that is, to return that person's capital contribution and keep the business going. However, a practical problem arises if a large cash source is not available, in which case the partners might be forced to liquidate some or all of the partnership's assets to return the capital contribution. If, rather than withdrawing, the retiring partner simply steps into a limited-partner status, he or she can continue to share in profits (which are in some part, at least, the fruits of that partner's past labor), while removing personal assets from the risk of partnership liabilities yet not forcing the other partners immediately to come up with the capital contribution.

THE EIGHT BASICS OF A PARTNERSHIP AGREEMENT

The Name of the Partnership

Most partnerships simply use as names the surnames of the major partners. The choice in that case is nothing more than the order of names, which depends on various factors from prestige to the way the names sound. If a name other than the partners' is used, it will be necessary to file the proposed business name with the state. Care should be taken to choose a name which is distinctive and not already in use. If the name is not distinctive, others can copy it; if the name is already in use, you could be liable for trade-name infringement.

A Description of the Business

In describing their business, the partners should agree on the basic scope of the project—for example, one book or all written work—its requirements in regard to capital and labor, the parties' individual contributions of capital and labor, and perhaps some plans regarding future growth.

Partnership Capital

After determining how much capital to contribute, the partners must decide when it will be contributed, how to value the property contributed, and whether there is to be a right to contribute more or to withdraw any at a later date.

Duration of the Partnership

Sometimes partnerships are organized for a fixed amount of time or are automatically dissolved on certain conditions such as the completion or publication of a book.

Distribution of Profits

You can make whatever arrangement you want for distribution. Although ordinarily a partner does not receive a salary, it is possible to give an active partner a guaranteed salary in addition to a share of the profits. Since the partnership's profits can be determined only at the close of a business year, ordinarily no distribution is made until that time. However, it is possible to allow the partners a monthly draw of money against their final share of profits. In some cases it may be necessary to allow limited expense accounts for some partners.

Not all of the profits of the partnership need to be distributed at year's end. Some can be retained for expansion, an arrangement that can be provided for in the partnership agreement. Note, though, that whether the profits are distributed or not, all partners must pay tax on their shares. The tax code refers directly to the partnership agreement to determine what that share is, which shows how important a partnership agreement is.

Management

The division of power in the partnership can be made in many ways. All partners can be given an equal voice, or some more than others. A few partners might be allowed to manage the business entirely, the remaining partners being given a vote only on specifically designated areas of concern. Besides voting, three other areas of management should be covered. First is the question of who can sign checks, place orders, or enter into contracts on behalf of the partnership. Under state partnership laws any partner may do these things so long as they are in the usual course of business. But such a broad delegation of authority can lead to confusion, so it might be best to delegate this authority more narrowly.

Second, it is a good idea to determine a regular date for partnership meetings. Third, some consideration should be given to the possibility of a disagreement among the partners that leads to a deadlock. One way to avoid this is to distribute the voting power in such a way as to make a deadlock impossible. However, in a two-person partnership this would mean that one partner would be in absolute control. This might be unacceptable to the other partner. If, instead, the power is divided evenly among an even number of partners, as is often the case, the agreement should stipulate a neutral party or arbitrator who could settle any dispute and thereby avoid a dissolution of the partnership.

Prohibited Acts

By law, each partner owes the partnership certain duties by virtue of being an employee or agent of the partnership. First is the duty of diligence. This means the partner must exercise reasonable care in acting as a partner. Second is a duty of obedience. The partner must obey the rules of the partnership and, most importantly, must not exceed the authority that the partnership has vested in him or her. Finally, there is a duty of loyalty. A partner may not, without approval of the other partners, compete with the partnership in another business. A partner may not seize upon a business opportunity that would be of value to the partnership without first telling the partnership about it and allowing the partnership to pursue it.

A list of acts prohibited to any partner should be made a part of the partnership agreement, elaborating and expanding on these fundamental duties.

Dissolution and Liquidation

A partnership is automatically dissolved upon the death, withdrawal, or expulsion of a partner. Dissolution identifies the legal end of the partnership but need not affect its economic life if the partnership agreement provided for the continuation of the business after a dissolution. Nonetheless, a dissolution will affect the business because the partner who withdraws or is expelled, or the estate of the deceased partner, will be entitled to a return of the proportionate share of capital that the departing partner contributed. Details such as how this capital will be returned should be decided before dissolution, because at the time of dissolution it may be impossible to negotiate. One method of handling this is to provide for a return of the capital in cash over a period of time. Some provision should be made so the remaining partners will know how much of a departing partner's interest they may purchase.

After a partner leaves, the partnership may need to be reorganized and recapitalized. Again, provision for this should be worked out in advance, if possible. Finally, since it is always possible that the partners will eventually want to liquidate the partnership, it should be decided in advance who will liquidate the assets, which assets will be distributed, and what property will be returned to its original contributor.

WHAT YOU DON'T WANT: UNINTENDED PARTNERS

Whether yours is a straightforward partnership or a limited partnership, one arrangement you want to avoid is the unintended partnership. This can occur when you collaborate on a work with another person and your relationship is not described formally. Thus, if you work as a ghostwriter or illustrator, or use portions of another person's work, it is essential for you to spell out in detail the arrangements between you and the other person. If you do not, you could find that the other person is your partner and entitled to half of the income you receive even though the contribution was minimal. You can avoid this by making an outright purchase of the other person's work or pay that person a percentage of what you are paid. Whichever arrangement you choose, you will be well advised to have a detailed written agreement.

THE CORPORATION

The corporation may sound like a form of business that pertains only to large companies with many employees—an impersonal monster wholly alien to the world of the writer. In fact, there is nothing in the nature of a corporation itself that requires it to be large or impersonal. In many states, even one person can incorporate a business. There are advantages and disadvantages to incorporating; if it appears advantageous to incorporate, you will find it can be done with surprising ease and with little expense. However, you will need a lawyer's assistance to ensure that you can comply with state formalities and learn how to use the corporate machinery and pay the corporation's taxes.

Differences between a Corporation and Partnership

To discuss the corporation, it is useful to compare it to a partnership. Perhaps the most important difference is that, like limited partners, the owners of the corporation—commonly known as shareholders or stockholders—are not personally liable for the corporation's debts; they stand to lose only their investment. But unlike a limited partner, a shareholder is allowed full participation in the control of the corporation through the shareholders' voting privileges.

For the small corporation, however, limited liability may be something of an illusion because very often creditors will demand that the owners personally cosign for any credit extended. In addition, individuals remain responsible for their wrongful acts; thus, a writer who infringes a copyright or creates a defamatory work will remain personally liable even if incorporated. Nevertheless, the corporate liability shield does protect a writer in situations where a contract is breached and the other contracting party has agreed to look only to the corporation for responsibility. For example, publishing contracts frequently require authors to make certain guarantees and statements of fact. If the publisher will contract with the writer's corporation, rather than with the writer as an individual, then the corporation alone will be liable if there is a breach.

The corporate shield also offers protection in situations where an employee of the writer has committed a wrongful act while working for the writer's corporation. If, for example, a research assistant negligently injures a pedestrian while the assistant is driving to the library to pick up some books for the writer, the assistant will be liable for the wrongful act and the corporation may be liable, but the writer who owns the corporation will probably not be personally liable.

The second area of difference between the corporation and the partnership is in continuity of existence. The many events which can cause the dissolution of a partnership do not have the same result when they occur to a corporation. It is common to create a corporation with perpetual existence. Unlike partners, shareholders cannot decide to withdraw and demand a return of capital from the corporation; all they can do is sell their stock. Therefore a corporation may have both legal and economic continuity. But this can also be a tremendous disadvantage to shareholders or their heirs if they want to sell their stock but cannot find anyone who wants to buy it. However, there are agreements which may be used to guarantee a return of capital should the shareholder die or wish to withdraw.

The third difference is the free transferability of ownership. In a partnership, no one can become a partner without unanimous consent of the other partners unless otherwise agreed. In a corporation, however, shareholders can generally sell their share, or any part of it, to whomever they wish. If a small corporation does not want to be open to outside ownership, transferability may be restricted.

The fourth difference is in the structure of management and control. Common shareholders are given a vote in proportion to their ownership in the corporation. Other kinds of stock can be created that may or may not have voting rights. A voting shareholder uses the vote to elect a board of directors and to create rules under which the board will operate.

The basic rules of the corporation are stated in the articles of incorporation, which are filed with the state. These serve as a sort of constitution and can be amended by shareholder vote. More detailed operational rules— bylaws—should also be prepared. Both shareholders and directors may have the power to create or amend bylaws. This varies from state to state and may be determined by the shareholders themselves. The board of directors then makes operational decisions for the corporation and might delegate day-to-day control to a president.

A shareholder, even one who owns all the stock, may not act against a decision of the board of directors. If the board has exceeded the powers granted it by the articles or bylaws, any shareholder may use the courts to fight the decision. But if the board is acting within its powers, the shareholders have no recourse except to remove the board or any board member. In a few more progressive states, a small corporation may entirely forego having a board of directors. In such cases, the corporation is authorized to allow the shareholders to vote on business decisions just as in a partnership.

The fifth distinction between a partnership and a corporation is the corporation's greater variety of ways of raising additional capital. Partnerships are quite restricted in this regard; they can borrow money or, if all the partners agree, they can take on additional partners. A corporation, on the other hand, may issue more stock, and this stock can be of many different varieties: recallable at a set price, for example, or convertible into another kind of stock.

A means frequently used to attract a new investor is to issue preferred stock. This means that the corporation agrees to pay the preferred shareholder some predetermined amount before it pays any dividends to other shareholders. It also means that if the corporation should go bankrupt, the preferred shareholder will be paid out of the proceeds of liquidation before the common shareholders are paid, although after the corporation's creditors are paid.

The issuance of new stock merely requires, in most cases, approval by a majority of the existing shareholders. In addition, corporations can borrow money on a short-term basis by issuing notes, or for a longer period by issuing debentures or bonds. In fact, a corporation's ability to raise additional capital is limited only by its lawyer's creativity and the economics of the marketplace.

The last distinction is the manner in which a corporation is taxed. Under both state and federal laws the profits of the corporation are taxed to the corporation before they are paid out as dividends. Then, because the dividends constitute income to the shareholders, they are taxed again as personal income. This double taxation constitutes the major disadvantage of incorporating.

Avoiding Double Taxation of Corporate Income

There are several methods of avoiding double taxation. First, a corporation can plan its business so as not to show very much profit. This can be done by drawing off what would be profit in payments to shareholders for a variety of services. For example, a shareholder can be paid a salary, rent for property leased to the corporation, or interest on a loan made to the corporation. All of these are legal deductions from the corporate income.

The corporation can also get larger deductions for the various health and retirement benefits provided for its employees than can an individual or a partnership. For example, a corporation can deduct all of its payments made for an employee health plan while at the same time the employee does not pay any personal income tax on this. Sole proprietors or partnerships can only deduct a much smaller portion of these expenses.

The corporation can also reinvest its profits for reasonable business expansion. This undistributed money is not taxed as income to the individual as it would be if earned by a partnership, which does not distribute it.

Reinvestment has at least two advantages. First, the business can be built up with money which has been taxed only at the corporate level. Second, the owner can delay the liquidation and distribution of corporate assets until a time of lower personal income and therefore lower possible personal taxes.

S Corporation

Congress has created a hybrid organizational form which allows the owners of a small corporation to take advantage of many of the features described above in order to avoid the double taxation problem. This form of organization is called an *S corporation* (formerly a Subchapter S corporation). If the corporation meets certain requirements, which many small businesses do, the owners can elect to be taxed as a partnership. This can be particularly advantageous in the early years of a corporation because the owners of an S corporation can deduct the losses of the corporation from their personal income, whereas they cannot do that in a standard corporation. They can have this favorable tax situation while simultaneously enjoying the corporation's limited-liability status.

Precautions for Minority Shareholders

Dissolving a corporation is not only painful because of certain tax penalties, it is almost always impossible without the consent of the majority of the shareholders. If you are forming a corporation and will be a minority holder you must realize that the majority will have ultimate and absolute control unless minority shareholders take certain precautions from the start. I could relate numerous horror stories of what some majority shareholders have done to minority shareholders. Avoiding these problems is no more difficult than drafting a sort of partnership agreement among the shareholders. I recommend that you retain your own attorney to represent you during the corporation's formation rather than waiting until it is too late.

It is important for you as a writer to determine which form of business organization will be most advantageous for you. This can best be done by consulting with an experienced business lawyer and having your situation evaluated.

2

Keeping Taxes Low

Writers rarely think of themselves as being engaged in a business; many, in fact, go to great lengths to avoid feeling involved in the world of commerce. The IRS, however, treats the professional writer like anyone else in business; thus the writer has many of the same tax concerns as any other business person. In addition, most writers have some special tax problems.

First, generally the professional writer does not work for a fixed wage or salary; as a result, the writer's income can fluctuate radically from one tax year to the next. Second, many tax rules designed to facilitate investment are not useful to writers. Writers can, however, benefit from certain provisions of the Internal Revenue Code to reduce their tax liability. In this chapter I will cover income-tax issues only; estate and gift tax provisions are considered in Chapter 11.

INCOME SPREADING

There are two principal ways of reducing tax liability. First, as I will discuss later in this chapter, there are significant deductions available to writers. Second, writers can spread their taxable income (and thus reduce their tax liability) by using several provisions in the tax code.

Income in Installments and Deferred Payments

One way the writer can spread income is to receive payment in installments. Care must be taken with the mechanics of this arrangement, however. If a writer sells a manuscript for a negotiable note due in full at some future date, or for some other deferred-payment obligation that is essentially equivalent to cash or has an ascertainable fair market value, the writer may have to report the total proceeds of the sale as income realized when the note is received, not when the note is paid off with cash. However, the Internal Revenue Code enables writers who sell property with payments being received in successive tax years to report the income on an installment basis. Under this method, tax is imposed only as payments are received.

For example, suppose you sell a magazine article for $3,000. Ordinarily the entire $3,000 would be taxable income in the year you received it. But if you use the installment method, with four payments of $750 plus interest received annually over four years, income from the sale will be taxed as the installments are received. In either case, the amount of income is $3,000, but under the installment method the amount is spread out over four years. You may be taking advantage of a lower tax bracket than you would be in had you taken the full $3,000 in the year you sold your article.

Writers in high tax brackets may wish to defer income until the future. For example, a writer could agree in a publisher-author contract (discussed more fully in Chapter 4) that royalty payments for a book will not exceed a certain amount in any one year, with excess royalties to be carried over and paid to the writer in the future. This would result in tax savings if, when the deferred amounts are finally paid, the writer is in a lower tax bracket.

There are drawbacks to deferred payments which include the possibility that your publisher may not be willing to pay interest on the deferred sums, or the possibility that the publisher could go broke before you are fully paid. The writer should consider these risks carefully before entering into a contract for deferred payments, because it might be quite difficult to change the arrangement if the need should arise.

Spreading Income among a Family

Another strategy for writers in high tax brackets is to divert some of their income directly to members of their immediate family who are in lower tax brackets by hiring them as employees. Putting dependent children on the payroll can result in a substantial tax savings for professional writers because they can deduct the salaries as a business expense, and they are not responsible for withholding social security from their children's wages.

Your child can earn up to $4,900, in 1987, without any tax liability, taking into account the $3,000 standard deduction and the $1,900 personal exemption. This salary arrangement is permissible so long as the child is under nineteen years of age or, if over nineteen, is a full-time student. Under the Internal Revenue Code of 1986, however, the child may not claim the personal exemption if he or she can be claimed by the parents on their tax return.

There are some restrictions on such an arrangement:
1. The salary must be reasonable in relation to the child's age and the work performed;
2. The work performed must be a necessary service to the business; and
3. The work must actually be performed by the child.

A second method of transferring income to members of your family is the creation of a family partnership. Each partner is entitled to receive an equal share of the overall income, unless the partnership agreement provides otherwise. The income is taxed once as individual income to each partner. Thus, the writer with a family partnership can break up and divert income to the family members where it will be taxed to them according to their respective tax brackets. The income received by children may be taxed at significantly lower rates, resulting in more income reaching the family than if it had all been received by the writer, who is presumably in a higher tax bracket than the children. But the Internal Revenue Code of 1986 stipulates that if a child is under fourteen years of age, and receives unearned income from the partnership, any amount over $500 will be taxed at the parents' highest marginal rate.

Although the IRS allows family partnerships, it may subject them to close scrutiny to ensure that the partnership is not a sham. Unless the partnership capital is a substantial income-producing factor and unless partners are reasonably compensated for services performed on the partnership's behalf, the IRS may, in relying on the section of the Code which deals with distribution of partners' shares and family partnerships, decide to forbid the shift in income. This section provides that a person owning a capital interest in a family partnership will be considered a partner for tax purposes even if he or she received the capital interest as a gift. But the gift must be genuine, and it should not be revocable.[1]*

Incorporating a Family

In the past, some families had incorporated in order to take advantage of the then more favorable corporate tax rates. If the IRS questioned the motivation for such an in-

---

* The numbers that follow a reference to a legal source or the name of a case refer to notes in the back of the book. These will save you money in legal time because they tell your lawyer where to research the case.

corporation, the courts examined the intent of the family members, and if the sole purpose of incorporating was tax avoidance, the scheme was disallowed.

The Tax Reform Act of 1986 reduced the individual income tax rates so that, for most taxpayers, they are substantially in line with or lower than the tax imposed on corporations. There may, therefore, no longer be substantial tax benefit to be derived by incorporating a business. There may, however, be other reasons for incorporating, as, for example, to obtain limited liability as discussed in the preceding chapter. A writer may, therefore, wish to incorporate and elect to be taxed as an S corporation. This will enable the corporation to insulate the writer from personal liability while permitting the business to be taxed as if it were individually owned. If the writer employs a spouse and children, salaries paid to them will be considered business deductions and thus reduce the writer's taxable income. When the spouse and children are made owners of the corporation by being provided with shares of stock in it, then all of the benefits discussed in the preceding section on partnership will be available. Note: Losses derived from passive investment, such as stock ownership, may be used only to offset earnings from passive investments and may not be deducted against other ordinary income. As to the unearned income received from the corporation by a child under fourteen, the same rule applies as unearned income from a family partnership: amounts over $500 are taxed at the parents' highest marginal rate.

QUALIFYING FOR BUSINESS DEDUCTIONS

Up until now we have been discussing the various ways in which writers can spread their taxable income. Another means of reducing tax liability involves making use of deductions. Professional writers may deduct their business expenses and thereby significantly reduce their taxable income. However, as with other artists and craftspeople, writers must be able to establish that they are engaged in a trade or business and not merely a personal hobby. You must keep full and accurate records. Receipts are a necessity. Furthermore, it would be best if you had a separate checking account and a complete set of books for all of the activities of your trade or business. A dilettante is not entitled to trade or business deductions.

Tax laws presume that a writer is engaged in a business or trade, as opposed to a hobby, if a net profit results from the activity in question during three out of the five consecutive years ending with the taxable year in question. If the writer has not had three profitable years in the last five years of working as a writer, the IRS may contend that the writer is merely indulging in a hobby, in which case the writer will have to prove *profit motive* in order to claim business expenses. Proof of profit motive does not require the writer to prove that there was some chance a profit would actually be made; it requires proof only that the writer intended to make a profit.

The Treasury Regulations call for an objective standard on the profit-motive issue, so statements of the writer as to intent will not suffice as proof. The regulations list nine factors to be used in determining profit motive:[2]

- The manner in which the taxpayer carries on the activity (i.e., effective business routines and bookkeeping procedures);
- The expertise of the taxpayer or the taxpayer's advisors (i.e., study in an area, awards, prior publication, critical recognition, membership in professional organizations, etc.);
- The time and effort expended in carrying on the activity (i.e., at least several hours a day devoted to writing, preferably on a regular basis);
- Expectation that business assets will increase in value (a factor that is of little relevance to the writer);

- The success of the taxpayer in similar or related activities (i.e., past literary successes, either financial or critical, even if prior to the relevant five-year period);
- History of income or losses with respect to the activity (i.e., increases in receipts from year to year unless losses vastly exceed receipts over a long period of time);
- The amount of profits, if any, which are earned;
- Financial status (wealth sufficient to support a hobby would weigh against the profit motive);
- Elements of personal pleasure or recreation (i.e., if significant traveling is involved and little writing produced, the court may be suspicious of profit motive).

No single factor will determine the results. The case of *Chaloner* v. *Helvering* provides an example of how the factors are used.[3] Chaloner was a wealthy man who wrote and published several books over a twenty-year period. Very little effort was put into marketing the books and very few were sold. Chaloner made use of secretaries in producing the books but did not detail their duties in any way. On the basis of these facts, the court declared that no profit motive existed and disallowed business expenses for writing and publishing.

In *Howard* v. *Commissioner*, another tax case involving a writer, the court found a profit motive did exist.[4] In this case the writer was married and thus the court held that, like Chaloner, she did not depend on writing for her livelihood. However, the court was persuaded by the facts that the writer devoted substantial time on a regular basis to her writing; she marketed all her products according to industry standards, she maintained separate and accurate records, and she had enjoyed past successes in the literary field. Her expenses were thus fully deductible.

Once you have established yourself as engaged in writing as a business, all your ordinary and necessary expenditures for professional writing are deductible business expenses. This would include writing materials and supplies, work space, office equipment, research or professional books and magazines, travel for business purposes, certain conference fees, agent commissions, postage, legal fees, and accounting fees.

One of the most significant and problematic of these deductible expenses is the *work space deduction*. It is quite common for writers to have their offices at home for a variety of reasons, including the desire to be able to create whenever inspiration strikes, regardless of the hour. The most important reason, though, is probably economic. The cost of renting a separate office is such that not too many writers are willing or able to pay for it. Others, of course, choose to work at home because it enables them to juggle work and family. Whatever the reason, writers who wish to get tax deductions for use of their homes in their business will have to do some careful planning.

Deductions for the Use of a Home in Business

For some time the IRS did not allow deductions for residential offices or studios. This policy was challenged in a case in which a physician managed rental properties as a sideline. The doctor's rental business was run out of an office in his house, and the space was used only for this particular business. When the physician deducted the expenses for the office in his home, the IRS disallowed the deduction. But the court was apparently convinced by the physical set-up of the room that the doctor used it exclusively and regularly as an office in connection with his rental business. The court noted the room had no television set, sofa, or bed.

This decision has been incorporated into the tax code. As a general rule, a business deduction is not allowed for the use of a dwelling that is used by the taxpayer during the taxable year as a residence. Use as a residence is defined as the use of the unit for personal purposes for more than fourteen days of the taxable year. But the statute makes an exception to this general rule in certain circumstances, allowing the taxpayer to take a deduction for a portion of a dwelling unit "exclusively used on a regular basis . . . as a principal place of business for any trade or business of the taxpayer," even if that business is not the taxpayer's primary source of income.

Exclusive and Regular Use

The exclusive and regular use exception applies to any portion of the residence used *exclusively* and *on a regular basis* as the writer's *principal place of business*.

The qualifications for this exception are strictly construed by the IRS and the courts. The requirement of exclusivity means that the taxpayer may not mix personal use and business use; in other words, an office that doubles as a storeroom for personal belongings, a laundry room, or the like will not qualify as an office for tax purposes, and a taxpayer may not deduct such space as an office.

However, there has been a recent liberalization of this rule in some parts of the country where the courts have held that a studio or an office can exist in a room that has a personal use, so long as a clearly defined area is used exclusively for business. It is important to remember that generally the Internal Revenue Service functions on a regional basis. Except for issues that have been reserved for decision by the national office, each IRS office is autonomous and makes its own decisions until the United States Supreme Court or Congress makes a decision that applies nationally. That is why the decision by a lower court in one area may not apply elsewhere.

The requirement regarding regular use means that the use of the room may not be merely incidental or occasional. Obviously, there is a gray area between regular and occasional. Perhaps some writers can use this rule as an inducement to overcome temporary bouts of laziness or ennui. For if you as a writer are planning on deducting any expenses for your office, you must keep working to satisfy the regularity test.

Like the regularity requirement, the rule regarding the principal place of business has been very vague. However, under IRS interpretations, a taxpayer may have a different principal place of business for each trade or business in which that person is engaged. The test requires looking at the particular facts of each case, but generally the key elements are (1) the amount of income derived from the business done there, (2) the amount of time spent there, and (3) the nature of the facility.

Thus it is now possible, for example, for an elementary or secondary school teacher, whose principal place of business (judging by income and time spent) is a school, to also run a sideline business of writing and selling magazine articles out of the home and to claim the home office as the principal place of business for the writing enterprise. A university professor, on the other hand, will have a more difficult time qualifying for the office-at-home deduction. The difference is that, although many professors prefer to write in offices at home, their writing is not a sideline or separate business as it may be for a teacher. For most university professors, writing is an occupational requirement. Accordingly, judicial response to whether professors who write in offices at home can claim a home-office deduction has been mixed.

In *Weissman* v. *Commissioner*, the plaintiff, Weissman, was an associate professor at City College of New York.5 His job required him to prepare and deliver lectures, meet with students, grade examination papers, and, under university bylaws, do an unspecified amount of research and writing. City College provided on-campus offices and library facilities. However, Weissman had to share his office space, and neither the office nor the library contained typing facilities. Additionally, security was poor enough that professors could not safely leave important research and writing materials in their offices. Due to all these problems, Weissman used two rooms at home for his academic writing. Significantly, he spent fifty to sixty hours each week working at home, compared to fourteen or fifteen in his on-campus office.

Although the tax court refused to allow Weissman to claim his rooms at home for tax purposes, the Second Circuit Court of Appeals reversed. The appellate court noted that 80 percent of Weissman's work time was spent on writing and research and that Weissman's use of the office at home was based on practical necessity. The court concluded that Weissman's principal place of business was indeed at his office space at home.

Moskovit v. *Commissioner* provides an example of a professor's home office that did not qualify as his principal place of business.6 In this case, the professor worked for a state university. He was required to teach, meet with students, attend departmental meetings, prepare and grade exams, develop new programs, and research and publish scholarly articles. The university provided a private office and access to secretarial staff. Moskovit maintained an office at home, primarily because it gave him privacy with no interruptions, and was cooler during summer months. Moskovit kept his typewriter and a 2,700 volume library in his office at home.

The tax court held that the focal point of Moskovit's employment was at the university, even though Moskovit spent more time each week at home than at the university. Although this case was not appealed to a federal circuit court as was *Weissman*, it is likely that the decision would have stood. The holding in *Weissman* was based upon a practical necessity to maintain a home office, which was not present in *Moskovit*. In other words, mere desire for uninterrupted privacy or preference for a home environment likely will not suffice to shift the focal point of a professor's employment to his home and thus make an office at home the principal place of business.

When a writer who has another profession—say as a teacher or professor—is employed by someone to do work as a writer, a deduction for the office at home becomes even more difficult to justify. In addition to fulfilling the tests outlined above, the employee's use of the office at home must be "for the convenience of his employer." Necessity is an important consideration in determining whether a writer's office at home is for the convenience of an employer, just as it is in determining whether an office at home is the principal place of business as discussed above.

In *Frankel* v. *Commissioner*, the court considered the deductibility of an office at home for a *New York Times* editor who continuously and regularly used an identified room in his house for business purposes.[7] The court reasoned that the home office was clearly for the benefit of Frankel's employer, since Frankel could not properly perform his job without the office at home unless he were to go on duty twenty-four hours a day and "sleep on an army cot in his employer's office."

The tax court went on to say, however, that there was one additional requirement. The editor-employee—Frankel—must meet with "patients, clients or customers" in the office at home. The court was liberal in its interpretation of which individuals would satisfy this criterion for an editor, finding that writers, political figures, and news sources would be considered clients for purposes of the Internal Revenue Code. Nevertheless, the court found that Frankel did not "meet with" the clients at the home office but, rather, spoke with them on the telephone. It held that he did not satisfy all of the Internal Revenue Code's requirements.

This reasoning may well be applicable to employee-writers who find themselves in circumstances similar to Frankel's. For example, if you are a professional writer who maintains an office at home even though your employer provides work space, it may be necessary for you to meet with "clients" in your home office in order to satisfy the "for the convenience of the employer" test. If, for an editor, clients are writers, political figures, and news sources, your clients might be editors, news sources, subjects of articles, expert consultants, or other people who are involved in whatever you are writing.

It is not clear what impact the *Frankel* case would have for writers engaged by an employer who does not supply any office space, so that the only office available is in the writer's home. The prudent individual will strive to fulfill the *Frankel* criteria even in this situation, by inviting any other people involved in the work to meet with the writer in the office at home.

When the office is in a structure separate from the principal residence, the requirements for deductibility are less stringent. The structure must be used exclusively and on a regular basis, just as an office in the home itself. However, when the office is in a separate structure, it need only be used "in connection with" the writing business, not as the principal place of business.

When writers use a portion of their homes for storage of business materials (as well as for business), the requirements for deductibility of the storage area are also less stringent. The dwelling must be the sole fixed location of the business and the storage area must be used on a regular basis for the storage of the writer's works or business equipment. The entire room used for storage need not be used exclusively for business, but there must be a "separately identifiable space suitable for storage" of the writer's works or work-related materials.

Is the Office-at-Home Deduction Worthwhile?

If a writer meets one of the tests outlined above, the next question is what tax benefits can result. The answer after close analysis is frequently, "Not very many." An *allocable portion* of mortgage interest and property taxes can be deducted against the business. These would be deductible anyway as itemized deductions. The advantage of deducting them against the business is that this reduces the business profit that is subject to self-employment taxes.

Of course, a taxpayer who lives in a rented house and otherwise qualifies for the office-at-home deductions may deduct a portion of the rent that would not otherwise be tax deductible.

The primary tax advantage comes from a deduction for an allocable portion of repairs, utility bills, and depreciation. Otherwise, these would not be deductible at all.

To arrive at the allocable portion, take the square footage of the space used for the business and divide that by the total square footage of the house. Multiply this fraction by your mortgage interest, property taxes, etc., for the amount to be deducted. How to determine the amount of allowable depreciation is too complex to discuss here, and you should discuss this with your accountant or tax advisor.

The total amount that can be deducted for an office or storage place in the home is limited. To determine the amount that can be deducted, take the total amount of money earned in the business and subtract the allocable portion of mortgage interest and property taxes, and the other deductions allocable to the business. The remainder is the maximum amount that you can deduct for the allocable portion of repairs, utilities, and depreciation. In other words, your total business deductions in this situation cannot be greater than your total business income minus all other business expenses. The home-office deduction, therefore, cannot be used to create a net loss. But disallowed losses can be carried forward and deducted in future years.

Besides the obvious complexity of the rules and the mathematics, there are several other factors that limit the benefit of taking a deduction for a studio or office in the home. One of these is the partial loss of the *nonrecognition of gain* (tax-deferred) treatment that is otherwise allowed when a taxpayer sells a principal residence. Ordinarily, when someone sells a principal residence for profit, the tax on the gain is deferred if the seller purchases another principal residence of at least the same value within two years. Most of the tax on this gain is never paid during the taxpayer's lifetime.

This deferral of gain, however, is not allowed to the extent that the house was used in the business. This means that the taxpayer must pay tax on the allocable portion of the gain from the sale, including tax on any recapture of accelerated depreciation taken in prior years.

For example, if you have been claiming 20 percent of your home as a business deduction, when you sell the home you will enjoy a tax deferral on only 80 percent of the profit. The other 20 percent will be subject to tax because that 20 percent represents the sale of a business asset.

In essence, for the price of a current deduction you may be converting what is essentially a nonrecognition, or tax-deferred, asset into a trade or business property.

However, there is one important exception that can work to your advantage. The IRS has ruled that *if you stop qualifying* for the office-at-home tax deduction for at least one year before you sell the house, you are entitled to the entire gain as *rollover*, no matter how many years you have been taking the deduction. (A rollover means you can reinvest the proceeds of the sale in another dwelling within the prescribed period and avoid paying taxes.)

The word *qualifying* in the IRS ruling has a very technical meaning. It does not only mean that you stop taking the business deduction for one year. It also means that you physically move the business out of your home so that it no longer qualifies as an office at home, whether or not you have taken it as a tax deduction. The same ruling applies to the one-time tax exemption of up to $125,000 on the sale of a home by persons over age fifty-five. If you plan to sell any time soon, check all this out with an accountant or tax advisor. A little planning might save you a great deal of money.

Another concern is that by deducting for an office in the home, the taxpayer in effect puts a red flag on the tax return. Obviously, when the tax return expressly asks whether expenses are being deducted for an office in the home, the question is not being asked for purely academic reasons. Although only the IRS knows how much the answer to this question affects someone's chances of being audited, there is no doubt that a "yes" answer does increase the likelihood of an audit.

Given this increased possibility of audit, it doesn't pay to deduct for an office in the home in doubtful situations. Taxpayers who lose the deduction must pay back taxes plus interest or fight in court. One unfortunate taxpayer not only lost the deduction on a technicality, but also lost the rollover treatment on the sale of his home.

If you believe that your office at home could qualify for the business deduction, you would be well advised to consult with a competent tax expert who can assist in calculating the deduction.

OTHER PROFESSIONAL EXPENSES

As mentioned earlier, deductible business expenses for a writer can include not only the work space, but all the ordinary and necessary expenditures involved in professional writing. Most of the expenses a writer incurs are classified as *current expenses*: items with a useful life of less than one year. For example, writing materials and supplies, postage, the cost of research books used for specific works, and telephone bills are all current expenses. These expenses are fully deductible in the year incurred.

There are some business expenses, however, that cannot be fully deducted in the year of purchase but must be depreciated. These kinds of costs are *capital expenditures*. For example, the cost of professional equipment such as a word processor or a typewriter, which have a useful life of more than one year, is a capital expenditure and cannot be fully deducted in the year of purchase. Instead, the taxpayer must depreciate, or allocate, the cost of the item over the estimated useful life of the asset. This is sometimes referred to as *capitalizing* the cost. Although the actual useful life of professional equipment will vary, fixed periods have been established in the Code over which depreciation may be deducted.

In some cases it may be difficult to decide whether an expense is a capital expenditure or a current expense. Repairs to machinery are one example. If you spend $200 servicing a word processor, this expense may or may not constitute a capital expenditure. The general test is whether the amount spent restoring the machine adds to the value, or substantially prolongs the useful life, of the machine.[8] Since the cost of replacing short-lived parts of a machine to keep it in efficient working condition does not substantially add to the useful life of a machine, such a cost would be a current cost and would be deductible. The cost of reconditioning a machine, on the other hand, significantly extends its useful life. Thus, such a cost is a capital expenditure and must be depreciated.

For many small businesses, an immediate deduction can be taken when equipment is purchased. Beginning in

1987, up to $10,000 of such purchases may be "expensed" each year, and need not be depreciated at all.

Commissions paid to agents, as well as fees paid to lawyers or accountants for business purposes, are generally deductible as current expenses. The same is true of salaries paid to typists, researchers, and others whose services are necessary for the writing business. If you need to hire help, it is a good idea to hire people on an individual-project basis as independent contractors rather than as regular employees. This avoids liability for social security, disability, and withholding-tax payments. When hiring, you should specify the job-by-job basis of the assignments, detail when each project is to be completed and, if possible, allow the person you are hiring to choose the place to do the work (since this might underscore the person's independence).

TRAVEL, ENTERTAINMENT, AND CONVENTIONS

Many writers travel abroad in order to gather information for whatever they are working on. Even more commonly, a writer might visit another city in the U.S. to conduct interviews and do research for an article or a book-length manuscript.

Although travel solely for education purposes is not deductible, there may be tax benefits available as the result of such trips if they are business-oriented. On a business trip, whether within the U.S. or abroad, ordinary and necessary expenses may be deductible if the travel is solely for business purposes. Transportation costs are fully deductible, except for "luxury water travel," as are costs of lodging while away from home on business. Beginning in 1987, only 80 percent of the costs of business meals, and meals consumed while on a business trip, are deductible.

If the trip is primarily for business, but part of the time is given to a personal vacation, you must indicate which expenses are for business and which for pleasure. This is *not* true in the case of foreign trips if one of the following exceptions applies:

You had no control over arranging the trip,

The trip outside of the U.S. was for a week or less,

You are not a managing executive or shareholder of the company that employed you.

If you are claiming one of these exceptions you should be careful to have supporting documentation. If you cannot take advantage of one of the exceptions, then you must allocate expenses for the trip abroad according to the percentage of the trip devoted to business versus vacation.

Whether inside or outside of the U.S., the definition of what constitutes "a business stay" can be very helpful to the taxpayer in determining a trip's deductibility. Travel days, including the day of departure and the day of return, count as a business day if business activities occurred on such days. If travel is outside the U.S., the same rules apply if the foreign trip is for more than seven days. *Any day which the taxpayer spends on business counts as a business day even if only a part of the day is spent on business.* A day in which business is canceled through no fault of the taxpayer counts as a business day. Saturdays, Sundays, and holidays count as business days even though no business is conducted, provided that business is conducted on the Friday before and the Monday after the weekend, or one day on either side of the holiday.

Entertainment expenses incurred for the purpose of developing an existing business are also deductible, in the amount of 80 percent of the actual cost. However, you must be especially careful about recording entertainment expenses. You should record in your logbook the amount, date, place, type of entertainment, business purpose, substance of the discussion, the participants in the discussion, and the business relationship of the parties who are being entertained. Keep receipts for any expenses over $25.

You should also keep in mind the new stipulation in the tax code which disallows deductibility for expenses which are "lavish or extravagant under the circumstances." No guidelines have yet been developed as to the definition of "lavish or extravagant," but you should be aware of the restriction nevertheless. If tickets to a sporting, cultural, or other event are purchased, only the face value of the ticket is allowed as a deduction. If a skybox or other luxury box seat is purchased or leased and is used for business entertaining, the maximum deduction now allowed is the cost of a non-luxury box seat.

The above rules cover business travel and entertainment expenses both inside and outside of the United States. The rules are more stringent for deducting expenses incurred while attending conventions and conferences outside the United States. Also, the IRS tends to review very carefully any deductions for attendance at business seminars that also involve a family vacation, whether inside the U.S. or abroad. In order to deduct the business expense, the taxpayer must be able to show, with documents, that the reason for attending the meeting was to promote production of income. Normally, for a spouse's expenses to be deductible, the spouse's presence must be required by the writer's employer. In the case of an independent writer who has organized into a partnership or small corporation, it is wise to make the spouse a partner, employee, or member of the board of the company. Often, seminars will offer special activities for husbands and wives that will provide documentation later on.

As a general rule, the business deductions are for conventions and seminars held in North America. The IRS is taking a closer look at cruise-ship seminars and is now requiring two statements to be attached to the tax return when such seminars are involved. The first statement substantiates the number of days on the ship, the number of hours spent each day on business, and the activities in the

program. The second statement must come from the
sponsor of the convention to verify the first information.
In addition, the ship must be registered in the U.S., and
all ports of call must be located in the U.S. or its posses-
sions. Again, the key for the taxpayer taking this sort of
deduction is careful documentation and substantiation.

Keeping a logbook or expense diary is probably the best
line of defense for the writer with respect to business expenses incurred while traveling. If you are on the road,
keep these things in mind:

(1) With respect to travel expenses:
   Keep proof of the costs,
   Record the time of departure,
   Record the number of days spent on business,
   List the places visited and the business purposes of
   your activities.
(2) With respect to the transportation costs:
   Keep copies of all receipts in excess of $25,
   If traveling by car, keep track of mileage, and
   Log all other expenses in your diary.
   Similarly, with meals, tips, and lodging, keep receipts
   for all items over $25 and make sure to record all less-
   expensive items in your logbook.

Writers may also take tax deductions for their attendance at writing workshops, seminars, retreats, and the
like, provided that they are careful to document the business nature of the trip. Accurate record-keeping is the
first line of defense for tax preparation.

Charitable Deductions

The law regarding charitable deductions by creative
people of their own work is not very advantageous. Individuals who donate items they have created may only deduct the cost of materials used to create those works. This
provision has had unfortunate effects on libraries and
museums, which, since the law's passage in 1969, have ex-

perienced enormous decreases in charitable contributions from authors, artists, and craftspeople. The Museum of Modern Art, for example, received fifty-two paintings and sculptures from artists from 1967 to 1969; between 1972 and 1975, only one work was donated.

The current tax law puts a further barrier in the way of charitable donations by requiring that a deduction may be taken only by those who itemize. The previous law allowed a charitable deduction whether the taxpayer took the standard deduction or itemized.

Although several modifications of the law have been proposed, Congress continues to resist change in the area of tax treatment regarding individuals' donations of their own work. However, some states have been more responsive. Oregon and Kansas now allow creators to deduct the fair market value of their creations donated to qualified charities, and California treats creative property as a capital asset.

GRANTS, PRIZES, AND AWARDS

Those writers who receive income from grants or fellowships should be aware that this income can be excluded from gross income and thus represents considerable tax savings. To qualify for this exclusion the grant must be for the purpose of furthering the writer's education and training. If the grant is given as compensation for services or is primarily for the benefit of the grant-giving organization, it cannot be excluded. Amounts received under a grant or fellowship that are specifically designated to cover related expenses for the purpose of the grant are no longer fully deductible.

For scholarships and fellowships granted after August 16, 1986, the above deductions are allowed only if the recipient is a degree candidate, and the amount of the exclusion from income is limited to the amounts used for tuition, fees, books, supplies and equipment. Amounts designated for room, board, and other incidental expenses are considered to be income. No exclusions from income are allowed for recipients who are not degree candidates.

The above rules apply to income from grants and fellowships. Unfortunately, the Tax Reform Act of 1986 also put tighter restrictions on money, goods, or services received as prizes or awards. Previously, the amounts received for certain awards were excluded from income in certain cases where the recipient was rewarded for past achievements, and he or she did not apply for the award.[10] Under the Tax Reform Act of 1986, any prizes or awards for charitable, scientific, or artistic achievements—including the Pulitzer Prize and the Nobel Prize—are included as income to the recipient, unless the prize is assigned to charity.

In conclusion, even though many writers do not consider themselves business persons, they may be taxed as such. Because many of the tax provisions designed to encourage the investment end of business are not available to writers, creative people need to concentrate on other methods of reducing taxes. The methods discussed here —income spreading and taking advantage of a variety of deductions—provide you with a starting point for reducing taxes. Be careful to avoid going beyond the realm of accepted tax planning. If a particular activity is questionable, you should consult with a competent CPA or tax advisor before embarking on it. In any case, consultation with competent tax professionals is always advisable to ensure maximum benefits.

3

What You Should Know about Contracts

In the normal course of business, writers enter into contracts with publishers, agents, other authors, or illustrators. The contractual terms may vary with the kind of service or product contracted for, but in every case the nature of legally binding agreements is the same.

In this chapter, I will describe the basic elements common to all contracts, be they personal-service agreements or agreements involving the sale of goods. The next chapter will deal specifically with author-publisher contracts and the various clauses that might be included in such contracts.

The word *contract* commonly brings to mind a long, complicated document replete with legal jargon designed to provide hours of work for lawyers. But this need not be the case. A simple, straightforward contract can be just as valid and enforceable as a complicated one.

A contract is a promise or set of promises, the performance of which the law recognizes as a duty, and for which the law gives a remedy in the event of nonperformance, or breach. These promises are *offers* and *acceptances*, and in order to be enforceable must be supported by *consideration*. Each of these terms has a specific legal definition.

An offer is defined as a demonstration of willingness by one party to enter into a bargain if a second party assents, the second one knowing that such assent is invited and would conclude the bargain. The party making the offer is the *offeror*, and the party to whom the offer is made is the *offeree*. An offer looks to the future and involves a definite commitment by the offeror to be bound if the offeree accepts the offer.

The various situations that can exist when a manuscript is submitted to a publisher illustrate some of the complications of sorting out the relationship of parties to a contract.

By far the most common situation in book publishing, so far as manuscript submission is concerned, is for a writer (or writer's agent) to submit a manuscript to a publisher. The submission is simply an invitation for the publisher to make an offer to purchase publication rights. No price is named.

A less routine, but by no means uncommon, kind of submission is the situation where an agent makes a submission to a publisher with a base price suggested. This is probably an offer.

A third situation is when an author tells a publisher that the author is planning to sell the rights to publish a manuscript to that publisher who offers the best terms. Again, the author is soliciting an offer from the publisher.

Offers should be distinguished from expressions of "present intentions," predictions, opinions, or preliminary negotiations. The statement of the author looking for whatever publisher will give the best terms does not involve any promise, commitment, or undertaking, but is only a statement of present intention. Likewise, when a publisher tells a writer that the writer has an excellent manuscript and that the author could probably receive up to $25,000 as an advance against royalties, no offer has occurred because the statement is merely one of prediction or opinion. This might be followed by preliminary negotiations, which include all of the various expressions of intent that flow between the parties prior to making a definite commitment. Thus, where a publisher expresses an interest in publishing the author's book and working out a deal, the publisher has expressed only a desire to reach an agreement, and has probably not yet made a binding offer.

Sometimes the distinction between an offer and a non-offer is unclear, so that whether a given statement is an offer or not will depend on whether a reasonable person would consider it to be an offer. This hypothetical reasonable person's understanding of a given statement will depend on its content as well as the circumstances in which it was made. The more definite and specific the statement, the more likely that it will be deemed an offer. For example, if a writer says to a book publisher, "I will sell you the right to publish my manuscript in return for your promise of a $5,000 advance and a 10 percent royalty," the author has probably made an offer, particularly if this statement has been preceded by preliminary negotiations. In this situation the reasonable person would be justified in believing that assent to the offer is requested and would conclude the bargain.

As a general rule, an offer can be revoked by the person who made it at any time before it is accepted. In two situations, however, offers are treated as irrevocable: option contracts and firm offers under the Uniform Commercial Code (UCC). The UCC is a body of commercial law which will be discussed later in this chapter.

The UCC declares an offer to be irrevocable if all of the four following conditions are met. First, the offer must be made by a merchant, defined as someone who regularly deals in the business or trade under discussion, or one who claims special knowledge or skill in that business or trade. The publisher will generally be considered a merchant, as will most of the business parties with whom the professional writer contracts. An experienced author can also be considered a merchant, but there is some question as to whether a neophyte writer would be. Section 2-104(1) of the UCC defines a merchant as follows:

"Merchant" means a person who deals in goods of the kind or otherwise by his occupation holds himself out as having knowledge or skill peculiar to the practices or goods involved in the transaction or to whom such knowledge or skill may be attributed by his employment of an agent or broker or other intermediary who by his occupation holds himself out as having such knowledge or skill.

Although at first glance the statute appears to apply to store owners selling goods from inventory, it can be interpreted to go further. Thus, an author who has written and published several books may well come under the occupation, knowledge, or skill description as being sufficiently experienced in the business aspects of writing to be considered a merchant. This is particularly true if the author engages a literary agent who does the actual negotiating. On the other hand, it is less likely that a neophyte writer would have the business knowledge or skill to be considered a merchant. As noted on page 54, the sale of rights in a manuscript, the norm in publishing agreements, is most commonly considered the sale of a service. Contractually agreeing to write a book is probably also a service, and thus article 2 of the UCC (which includes the definition quoted above) would probably not apply to the contract.

Second, the offer must be one involving the sale of goods. The UCC defines goods as including movable objects such as a manuscript, as opposed to a right, such as the right to publish a book, which is the subject of most author-publisher contracts. (For a more detailed analysis of how goods are defined, see "Written Contracts" later in this chapter.) Third, the offer must be in writing and signed by the person making the offer. Fourth, the written document must give some assurance that the offer will remain open for a stated time, or if no time is stated, for a reasonable time. If these four conditions are met, the offer will be irrevocable, but in no event for more than three months.

An *option contract* is one in which the offeror agrees not to revoke the offer for a given length of time, perhaps indefinitely. Unlike firm offers under the UCC, an option contract is deemed an irrevocable offer regardless of whether the offeror is a merchant or not, or whether the offer involves a sale of goods, so long as the option contract is paid for.

Author-publisher contracts often contain a first-option clause. Under this type of clause, the author agrees to submit his or her next manuscript, if and when it is produced, to the publisher. The publisher in turn is given first option to accept the manuscript and make an offer on it. If the manuscript is rejected, the author is free to have it published elsewhere, though the initial publisher usually retains the right to match any other publisher's offer. This type of offer is irrevocable for the time stated in the option clause. Significantly, there is no three-month limitation as in the case of a UCC firm offer, because, as will be discussed later, an unwritten manuscript is not within the UCC's definition of goods and is therefore not covered by that law.

ACCEPTANCE

An offer confers upon the person to whom it is made (the offeree) the power to create a legally binding relationship, if and when the offer is accepted.

The manner in which the offer may be accepted is subject to few constraints. As long as the acceptance is by a reasonable method of communication under the circumstances, it will generally be valid and therefore sufficient to bind the offering party to its terms. Fairness dictates that the offeree accept within a reasonable time and in a reasonable manner.

The question of whether acceptance was made within a reasonable time is basically determined by common sense. An author who waits for a year before responding to a publisher's offer has probably not accepted within a reasonable time, whereas an author who has responded within one month probably has. Whether or not a response has been made within a reasonable time may also be affected by informal standards within the book industry or by past dealings between the two parties. A response that is not made within the time limits established by the industry or the individual parties may not be considered to have taken place within a reasonable amount of time.

The question of whether an offer has been accepted in a reasonable manner is also determined by common sense. If, for example, the publisher submits an offer to the author by mail, a reasonable manner of communicating acceptance would include not only by mail, but also by telephone or any other personal communication.

In addition, an offer may be reasonably accepted either by promising to perform or by beginning performance as long as the acceptance is communicated to the other party in a reasonably prompt time and method. For example, a writer who is asked to ghostwrite a book for a celebrity could accept the offer (whether money has been discussed or not) by agreeing to do the work, or by actually starting to do it. If the offeree accepts by beginning performance, partial performance is interpreted as an implied promise to complete performance.

There is one important exception to the rule that an acceptance which is reasonable both in time and manner will be valid and enforceable. In every case the offeror is "master" of the offer. This means that if the offeror insists that acceptance be made within a given time or in a particular manner, the offeree must comply in order to make a binding contract. An acceptance which does not comply with the offeror's directions does not constitute a legally binding acceptance, even though it is in all other respects reasonable. If the celebrity specifically requires that the ghostwriter accept within five days by singing telegram, the ghostwriter must comply with that direction in order to make a valid acceptance.

DISTINGUISHING OFFEROR FROM OFFEREE

Because the offeree has the power to create a legally binding relationship by accepting the offer, it becomes important to know which party in a given transaction is the offeror. If you engage in a series of preliminary negotiations with another party and at some point one of you demonstrates a definite willingness to enter into a bargain, that party by that act becomes the offeror.

In other situations the reasoning is a bit different. Assume that a writer has developed several proposals for magazine articles and distributes a list of proposals and asking prices to various magazines, and that one or more magazines offers to buy from the writer's list. Between the writer and the magazine, which party is the offeror? The prevailing view in contract law is that catalogues, price lists, and the like are merely invitations to make offers. Thus, the writer was only inviting an offer; the magazine made the offer, so the writer would have the option of accepting or rejecting it. A minority of courts, however, have taken the position that catalogues and price lists are offers and thus it could be argued under this line of reasoning that the writer's proposal is an offer and that a magazine's responding order for an article constitutes an acceptance.

Another situation is an auction. Using a book publishing example, let us assume that an author's literary agent wishes to offer to a number of publishers at auction the opportunity to publish a manuscript. Generally, the author will be the offeree and the competing publishers will be the offerors since the auctioneer in a literary auction is merely inviting offers from the competing bidders.

Literary auctions are quite informal, though there are some generally accepted procedures. A literary auction can, as in the preceding example, be for the initial right to publish a book in either hard cover or paperback or both, or the auction can be for the right to reprint the book in hard cover or paperback. In the former situation, as noted above, the writer will make the ultimate decision, whereas in the latter case, the auction generally is conducted by a publisher and an author will rarely be permitted to retain the right to withhold consent to the sale. In some unusual situations, a writer may have so much market appeal that the original author-publisher contract will reserve to the writer the right of approval whenever any subsidiary rights are to be sold. Even in these situations, the contract will likely provide that such consent will not be unreasonably withheld. If the writer does retain the right to make final decisions, then he or she will be considered the offeree, since the publishers competing for the subsidiary rights will be considered to be making offers which will be transmitted to the writer by the publisher or agent conducting the auction.

At any time prior to the actual auction for either initial publication or subsidiary rights, any publisher may make a so-called "preemptive bid." This is a bid which is so favorable to the author or primary publisher because of the amount to be paid or other contract terms that it will preempt the auction. Once the auction has begun, a so-called "floor bid" is often made in which a publisher offers a stated set of floor terms and reserves the right to have the very last bid which must top that of the highest bidder by a stated amount (which is customarily set at the beginning of the auction). In this situation the writer or, in a subsidiary-rights auction, the initial publisher will still be considered the offeree, though the floor bidder has a privilege to top other offerors.

<h3 style="text-align:center">Consideration</h3>

A consideration is a legal term meaning something of value. A thing will have value if it involves either a benefit to the promisor or a detriment to the promisee.

An offer involves a promise, as, in most cases, does acceptance. These promises constitute a commitment that something will or will not happen in the future. The law interprets consideration broadly to include, among other things, an act of forbearance (e.g., waiver of a legal right to bring a lawsuit or to compete with a former employer), an alteration of a legal relationship, or the payment of money. Consequently, in the vast majority of agreements, a promise made by either party will be considered sufficient consideration to support a binding contract.

Not all promises, however, can be enforced by law. Assume, for example, that an unpublished author has an uncle who is a prestigious and highly successful author. Because the uncle is sympathetic to his nephew's plight, he promises that, as a favor, he will submit his nephew's manuscript to his own publisher and urge that it be published. A month later the uncle informs his nephew that his relationship with his publisher is no longer friendly and that he cannot help. Can the nephew legally enforce the uncle's promise? In this situation the promise is probably not enforceable because it was not supported by what the law calls consideration. It is clear that there was no bargained-for exchange between the nephew and his uncle. The nephew did not confer any benefit upon his uncle nor did he incur any detriment; hence, there was no consideration flowing to the uncle in return for his promise. And because the promise was not supported by consideration it cannot be enforced.

It should be emphasized that consideration is not necessarily equivalent to the fair market value of the promise received. If, in the hypothetical situation above, the nephew and uncle had agreed that the uncle would sell the publication rights for a nominal flat fee, say fifty dollars, the nephew could probably enforce his uncle's promise. There was a bargained-for exchange in which the nephew conferred a benefit to his uncle, and incurred a detriment to himself, in the amount of fifty dollars. The fact that fifty dollars may in no way reflect the fair market value of the publication rights is immaterial, provided the consideration was in fact bargained for.

Once the basic elements of offer, acceptance, and consideration have taken place, an enforceable contract has been made. This contract may be implied, oral, or written.

IMPLIED CONTRACTS

A contract may be *implied* by conduct. Suppose, for example, that a writer submits a manuscript for publication to a publisher who publishes the manuscript, but does not compensate the author for its use. Whether or not there was an implied contract depends upon the relationship between the author and the publisher. If the author can be said to have volunteered the manuscript with no expectation of payment, a contract would not have been implied. It is more likely, however, that circumstances would indicate the author was expecting to receive compensation, and so a promise by the publisher to pay would be deemed implied. The implied contract thus created is normally enforceable.

ORAL CONTRACTS

An oral contract is one on which the parties have verbally agreed but which is not recorded in writing. Theoretically, oral contracts are valid and enforceable. As a practical matter, though, oral contracts are often difficult to prove in court, since the main evidence is usually the conflicting testimony of the parties involved, and memories do fade. Even if an oral contract can be proven, it may not always be enforceable because there are some agreements which the law requires to be in writing.

WRITTEN CONTRACTS

The Statute of Frauds, a law designed to prevent fraud and perjury, provides that any contract which cannot be fully performed within one year must be in writing in order to be legally binding. This rule has been narrowly interpreted to mean that if a contract can conceivably be performed within one year of its making, it need not be in writing. Assume that a publisher and an author have entered into a multiple-book contract in which the author has agreed to complete five manuscripts. Assume further that the agreement requires that the author submit one manuscript per year for five years. In this hypothetical situation, the terms of the agreement make it impossible for the author to complete performance within one year. If, however, the author agrees to submit five manuscripts within a five-year period, it is possible that the author could submit all five manuscripts in the first year; therefore, the Statute of Frauds would not apply and the agreement need not be in writing to be enforceable. The fact that the author may not actually complete performance within one year is immaterial. So long as complete performance within one year is possible, the agreement may be oral.

The Statute of Frauds further provides that certain agreements relating to the sale of goods must be in writing to be enforceable. This provision was codified in the Uniform Sales Act and has now been incorporated into the Uniform Commercial Code. The UCC provides that a contract for the sale of goods costing over $500 is not enforceable unless it is in writing and is signed by the party against whom enforcement is sought. There is no such monetary restriction on service contracts, however. Regardless of the amount of payment, a contract for the sale of services which can be completed within one year need not be in writing.

DISTINGUISHING SALE OF GOODS FROM SALE OF SERVICES

Obviously, it is important to know whether a particular contract is regarded by the law as involving the sale of goods or the sale of services. The UCC defines goods as being all things that are movable at the time the contract is made, with the exception of the money (or investment securities or certain other types of documents) used as payment for the goods. This definition is sufficiently broad to enable most courts to find that the most basic materials a writer uses, such as paper and pens, as well as equipment such as typewriters and word processors, to be goods. Unfortunately, the distinction is not so clear in the case of agreements between an author and a publisher.

There are conflicting holdings concerning author-publisher agreements. At least one court has ruled that the subject of a publishing agreement, pamphlets, was movable and therefore met the UCC's definition of goods.[1] That court conceded that the publisher provided various services to the buyer, but it considered those services to be incidental to the production and sale of the goods, i.e., the pamphlets. This court might consider the author-publisher contract as a contract for the sale of goods, i.e., completed works. It cited a Pennsyvlania case in which a contract to take wedding pictures was considered a contract for the sale of goods.[2] This position is open to criticism since authors do not sell manuscripts, but rather sell rights to publish manuscripts.

Most courts have ruled that the author-publisher contract is primarily a service contract.[3] From this perspective, the publisher is deemed to be selling various services, such as editing, printing, and distribution, to the author in return for the author's service in creating the manuscript.

DETERMINING THE CONTRACT PRICE OF GOODS

Assuming for the moment that the various agreements entered into by the writer involve a sale of goods, a second matter to be determined is whether the price of the goods exceeds $500. In most cases, the answer will be clear—but not always.

A writer contracts to purchase several fine old fountain pens from an antique dealer. The price for the total purchase exceeds $500, but the price for the individual pens does not. Which price determines whether or not the statute applies?

A self-publisher sells books to a wholesaler. The list price exceeds $500, but the price after the wholesaler's discount is less than $500. Again, which price is used to determine whether the statute applies?

The UCC and the cases interpreting this law provide some guidelines for determining the contract price of goods. The statute provides that the definition of price is to be broadly interpreted to include a payment in money or some other thing of value. The definition of goods in the UCC may be sufficiently broad to include the pens but the problem of the sale of books to the wholesaler remains.

Obviously, a writer will not in every case be able to ascertain whether the price terms of a given contract exceed $500, any more than one can always be certain whether a given agreement involves the sale of goods or of services. Given the differences in interpretation by various courts, the best way to ensure that a contract will be enforceable is to put it in clear, unambiguous writing.

ACCEPTABLE FORMS FOR WRITTEN CONTRACTS

To comply with the Statute of Frauds, a written agreement does not have to be formal. Courts have upheld memoranda, letters, and telegrams as valid and enforceable writings so long as they contain the following information: the date of the agreement, identification of the parties involved, identification of the subject matter, the price or other consideration, and the signature of the party against whom enforcement is sought.

Most contracts contain considerably more information than the bare minimum necessary to comply with the Statute of Frauds, however. The typical contract will not only recite its basic terms, but may also include various covenants, conditions, and warranties.

Covenants and Conditions

A *covenant* is an absolute, unconditional promise to perform. Failure to perform a covenant is a breach of contract in and of itself. In an author-publisher contract, the author's promise to submit a manuscript is generally a covenant. Failure to submit a manuscript by the specified date will result in a breach of contract and will subject the author to liability unless the publisher has agreed to an extension.

A *condition*, on the other hand, is a fact or event whose occurrence creates—and whose failure to occur extinguishes—the duty to perform. Conditions can be either *precedent* to an agreement or *subsequent* to the agreement. A condition precedent is one which must occur before the agreement becomes effective or binding. A condition subsequent is a future event, the nonoccurrence of which may give one party the right to abandon his or her contractual promises. For example, in addition to being a covenant, the author's promise to submit a manuscript may be a condition precedent to the publisher's promise to pay and publish. In such a case, the publisher's promises to publish the author's manuscript and to pay the author are not enforceable until the author has in fact submitted a manuscript. But once the author submits a manuscript, a breach of these promises would make the publisher subject to liability. This would not be true in a situation in which the publisher has agreed to give the author an advance before the manuscript is completed. In this type of arrangement, the agreement to submit the manuscript might be seen as a condition subsequent, which, if not complied with, could result in a revocation of the author-publisher contract.

The variety of covenants and conditions that can be incorporated into author-publisher contracts will be described in the next chapter. Basically, the only limitations imposed by law upon the parties involved are that the covenants and conditions not be illegal or unconscionable. These limitations will be discussed later in this chapter.

Warranties

Warranties may apply to all forms of property, and they may be either *express* or *implied*. The Uniform Commercial Code defines both kinds of warranties in transactions involving goods.

An express warranty is defined as a promise or statement of fact the seller makes to the buyer about some quality or feature of the goods. A mere statement of opinion, called "puffing," will not create a warranty. If a publisher, in a sales talk to a bookseller, exclaims that the book is a potential best seller (a sure bet!), has the publisher warranted that the book will, in fact, become a best seller? Probably not. Here, the publisher is not making a statement of fact, but is merely stating an opinion, or puffing.

The distinction, however, may not always be so clear. In ambiguous situations, whether a given statement will be considered one of fact or mere puffing depends upon whether the statement becomes part of the basis of the bargain. Although the phrase, *basis of the bargain*, is hard to define precisely, it is reasonable to say that a given statement becomes part of the basis of the bargain if a contract to purchase is to a large extent induced by that statement. In the example of the enthusiastic publisher, the publisher's statements would probably not have been a determining factor in making the sale and were therefore not warranties but mere opinions.

An express warranty need not in every case be an oral or written statement. At times a warranty can be expressed through a sample product, a model, or a description. For example, if a stationery supplier provides a writer with sample computer paper, the stationery supplier has expressly warranted that all computer paper represented by the sample will be of the same kind and quality as the sample.

The UCC defines different types of implied warranties. The *implied warranty of merchantability* dictates that to fulfill a contract involving the sale of goods, the goods must be of fair and average quality. The *implied warranty of fitness* dictates that they must be fit for the ordinary use of such goods, and the *implied warranty of title* dictates that the seller have a valid title to the goods at the time of the sale. The implied warranty of merchantability, applied to a contract between an author/self-publisher and a printer, means that the books delivered must at the least be legibly printed and securely bound. This is not to say that each and every book in a given shipment must be flawless. The book-printing industry typically allows for a 10 percent margin of defective goods. The author/self-publisher could, therefore, receive a small percentage of defective books without the printer having violated the implied warranty of merchantability.

Periodically, publishers and authors have been sued for breach of an implied warranty because of the content of a book rather than its physical defects. In a litigated case in

Florida, a woman who had purchased a cookbook followed a recipe precisely and was poisoned by the concoction. She sued the publisher for breach of the implied warranty of merchantability.[4] The court ruled in favor of the defendant publisher, stating that the implied warranty of merchantability, when applied to books, is limited to their physical properties and does not extend to their intellectual contents. This rule has thus far been universally applied, although authors may some day be vulnerable to suits such as this. (A means by which an author can be insulated to some extent from this risk is incorporation, which is discussed in Chapter 1.)

The implied warranty of fitness for a particular purpose arises only in a narrow set of circumstances. If the seller knows or has reason to know of a particular purpose which the buyer of goods expects to make of the goods, and if the seller knows or has reason to know that the buyer is relying upon the seller's special skills and judgment to provide goods for that particular purpose, the law will find an implied warranty of fitness for a particular purpose in the seller's agreement.

Suppose, for example, a writer has just completed a manuscript and wants to self-publish it. Suppose further that the writer has never published anything before and wishes to have a very good-looking book. With this in mind, the writer approaches a bindery and states that this is to be a high-quality, long-lasting book and that it needs to be bound in a special way. A representative of the bindery agrees and the work is completed, but the books have been bound with ordinary binding. The question, then, is whether the bindery has violated the implied warranty of fitness for a particular purpose. Probably it has. The bindery knew that the goods were for a particular purpose, i.e., were to be of a specific quality and to last a long time. If the bindery also knew or should have known that the writer, as a neophyte, was relying on the bindery's special skill and knowledge, the implied warranty would be breached—even though the binding may have been adequate for the average book.

Under the implied warranty of title, the seller warrants that the title in the goods transferred is valid, that the transfer is not wrongful to some third party, and that the goods are free and clear of all liens and encumbrances except for those the buyer is aware of at the time of contracting. A lien is simply a claim or charge on property for payment of some debt, obligation, or duty. An encumbrance would be any right or interest held by a third party which tends to diminish the value of the goods sold. Thus, if a rare-book dealer purchases from a seller a first edition of *Bleak House* that the seller has stolen from a museum, the museum, as the lawful and true owner, could sue the book dealer for the return of the stolen book. The rare-book dealer could in turn sue the seller for breach of the implied warranty of title, since the seller lacked good title to the goods when they were sold.

Likewise—assuming the seller is a merchant normally dealing in the kind of goods sold—the seller by implication warrants that the goods transferred do not infringe any patent, trademark, copyright, or similar claim. But in this case, if the buyer is thereafter sued for an infringement, the buyer must give the merchant/seller notice of the suit and an opportunity to defend. Failure to give such notice constitutes a waiver of all rights under the warranty. If, after receipt of notice, the seller refuses to defend the suit, the buyer may sue for breach of the implied warranty against infringement, and the seller is liable for any expenses or losses incurred by the buyer in defending against the true owner's claims.

Disclaiming a Warranty

All warranties, express or implied, can be disclaimed. Express warranties can be disclaimed by words or conduct which negate the warranty, when it would be reasonable and fair to do so. Where a purported disclaimer directly contradicts an express warranty, however, the disclaimer is deemed unreasonable and is therefore ineffective.

To effectively disclaim the implied warranty of merchantability, it is generally necessary for the disclaimer to use the word *merchantability*. If the disclaimer is in writing, the word *merchantability* must be conspicuous. To effectively disclaim the implied warranty of fitness for a particular purpose the disclaimer need not contain any particular words, but it usually must be in writing and conspicuous. It should be noted, however, that both the implied warranty of merchantability and the implied warranty of fitness for a particular purpose can be disclaimed by the use of general expressions such as "with all faults" or "as is."

Thus, if a bookseller merely states that he or she is selling a book and indicates that it is not clear whether he or she has legal ownership of the book or the right to sell it, there is no implied warranty of title.

CAPACITY TO CONTRACT

Certain classes of people, for example minors, are deemed by law to lack capacity to contract. A person is legally a minor until the age of majority. This age varies from state to state, but in most cases is either eighteen or twenty-one. This is of particular relevance to writers since an author might wish to contract with a minor for an interview or use a minor as a model for an illustration. A contract entered into by a minor is not necessarily void, but generally such a contract is voidable. This means that the minor is free to rescind the contract until he or she reaches the age of majority, but that the other party is bound by the contract if and when the minor elects to enforce it. In some states a minor over eighteen must restore the consideration or its equivalent as a condition of rescission. Other states have a procedure for enabling minors to sign binding nonrescindable contracts. This generally requires the approval of a member of the judiciary. Such contracts are highly technical, and the writer who wishes to make one would be well advised to consult a lawyer.

ILLEGAL CONTRACTS

If either the consideration or the subject matter of the contract is illegal, the contract itself is illegal. This problem will not normally arise in publishing contracts, but it is possible that a writer could unwittingly become a party to an illegal contract. For example, the state of New York has enacted a statute, popularly known as the Son of Sam Law, that prohibits criminals from receiving economic compensation from the exploitation and commercialization of their crimes. Similar statutes have been enacted in numerous other states. As of mid-1986, states with Son of Sam laws include Alaska, Alabama, Arizona, Georgia, Idaho, Illinois, Kentucky, Massachusetts, Minnesota, Missouri, Nebraska, New Jersey, Oregon, South Carolina, Tennessee, Texas, and Washington. Federal law also contains such a provision. A publisher who contracts to pay a criminal royalties in return for the criminal's story would be violating the statute, and the contract would therefore be illegal. The same would probably be true of an agreement made by an author to write a criminal's story in exchange for some payment. It is not clear, however, whether someone could circumvent the statute by paying a criminal for other services. *Life* magazine paid $9,000 to Bernard Welch, alleged murderer of Michael Halberstam, for the exclusive rights to photographs from the Welch family album. It remains to be seen whether such conduct would fall within the scope of a Son of Sam type of statute.

A writer may also become a party to an illegal contract if the work to be published under that contract is found to be either obscene or libelous. (Obscenity is discussed in Chapter 8 and libel, in Chapter 9.)

The law generally treats an illegal contract as *void* rather than merely *voidable* — an important distinction. A voidable contract is valid until it is voided by the party possessing the right to rescind, whereas a void contract is not binding on either party, and neither party will be permitted to enjoy any fruits of the agreement. A void contract results when both parties are at fault or where the illegality involves a morally reprehensible crime. If, however, the illegality involves a crime which is *malum prohibitum* (i.e., an act which is wrong only because the law says that it is as, for example, illegal parking or not obtaining a necessary business license), one party may have some rights against the less innocent party. An author who anticipates entering into, or is already involved in, a contract of questionable legality would be well advised to consult a lawyer.

Unconscionability

The law generally gives the parties involved in a contract complete freedom to contract. Thus contractual terms which are unfair, unjust, or even ludicrous will generally be enforced if they are legal. But this freedom is not without limits; the parties are not free to make a contract which is unconscionable. *Unconscionability* is an elusive concept, but the courts have certain guidelines in ruling on it. A given contract is likely to be considered unconscionable if it is grossly unfair and the parties lack equal bargaining power. New authors are typically in a weaker bargaining position than publishers and are therefore more likely to win on an allegation of unconscionability. This is especially true where the author has simply signed the publisher's form contract. If the form contract is extremely one-sided in favor of the publisher, and if the author was given the choice of signing the contract unchanged or not contracting at all, the courts may find that the agreement was unconscionable. If that happens, the court may either treat the contract as void or strike the unconscionable clauses and enforce the remainder. It should be noted that unconscionability is generally used as a defense by the one who is sued for breach of contract, and that the defense is rarely successful, particularly where both parties are business people.

REMEDIES

The principle underlying all remedies for breach of contract is to satisfy the aggrieved party's expectations: that is, the courts will attempt to place the aggrieved party in the same position he or she would have enjoyed had the contract been fully performed. Courts and the legislatures have devised a number of remedies to provide aggrieved parties with the benefit of their bargains. Generally, this will take the form of monetary damages, but where monetary damages fail to restore the aggrieved party to the position the party would have enjoyed under the contract, the court may order *specific enforcement*. Specific enforcement means the breaching party is ordered to perform as he or she promised to do. This remedy is generally reserved for cases in which the contract involves unique goods. In publishing, a court might therefore specifically enforce an author-publisher contract by compelling the author to deliver the manuscript to the publisher, but only if the manuscript has been completed. A court would not be likely to compel an author to write a manuscript or complete an unfinished manuscript as a means of satisfying the aggrieved publisher. The Thirteenth Amendment of the Constitution prohibits one from being forced to perform labor against one's will. Thus, for breach of a personal-service contract for services to be performed in the future, monetary damages are generally awarded.

The question as to a publisher's obligation to publish a

work for which it has contracted, is more perplexing. This point was considered by New York's highest court in a 1974 case.[5] In that case, the publisher agreed to publish the author's book within 18 months of submission of the manuscript. Internal changes in the publishing company delayed publication, and the author sued for damages. Among the damages sought was an amount equal to the cost of having the book published by the author. The court ruled that to award such damages would confer on the author a greater advantage than he would have had if the publisher had actually published the work, and rejected that portion of the claim.

The court also rejected the claim for anticipated royalties as being too speculative to measure.

Although there have been no cases dealing directly with the subject, it seems unlikely that a court would order a publisher to specifically perform on a contract to publish a work. It is possible that a publisher who refuses to publish an author's work in breach of a contract may be liable to the author for monetary damages, but only if the amount is not too speculative.

The concepts discussed here are important to you as a writer because you need to have some grasp of the terminology and legal effects of contracts in general as a background to understanding the more complex specifics of contracts with book and magazine publishers, which follow.

4

Contracts with Book Publishers and Magazines

In the past, contracts between authors and book publishers were relatively cut and dried. In most cases the author would simply sign the publisher's form contract as it was written rather than bargain for more favorable terms. But in recent years the author's role, with the help of agents, has changed from one of acquiescence to one of aggressive negotiation. In order to protect their interests, writers as well as publishers may demand that certain contract clauses be deleted or included, and since the two parties today occupy more nearly equal bargaining positions, contract negotiations often involve a lively give and take in which the demands of both are at least partially met.

In this chapter we will consider the clauses typically included in an author-publisher contract and the demands that are likely to be made by the respective parties as to how these clauses should be written. Following that is a discussion of the variations appropriate for a freelance writer's contract with a magazine publisher.

ADVANCES

An advance against royalties is the first money received by an author and is, in effect, a payment of anticipated royalties before they are earned. The advance may be delivered to the author as a lump sum upon the occurrence of some event, such as the author's submission of a manuscript, or the advance may be paid in several installments. Thus, a portion of the advance could be paid when the parties sign the contract, another portion when the author delivers the manuscript, and the rest upon publication.

Advances may or may not be refundable to the publisher. If an advance is refundable, the author will have to return that portion which exceeds the royalties due from actual sales. For example, if the author received a $7,000 advance, but sales of the book warranted only $3,000 in royalties, the author would have to return the $4,000 that was not earned. In cases where the advance is refundable, it is important that both parties agree to a specific period within which the royalties are to be matched against the advance. A nonrefundable advance, sometimes called a guarantee, need not be returned by the author even if it is never earned. Most advances are nonrefundable.

For some authors the advance clause is the most important clause in the contract because it provides immediate cash. Some small publishers may not be in a position to provide an author with a large advance. They may nevertheless attract authors by offering them concessions in other areas of the contract—for example, a larger royalty rate or more subsidiary rights.

ROYALTIES

As soon as a book starts to sell, the publisher must begin paying royalties. If an advance has been given, royalties will be applied against the advance and no money paid until they exceed the amount of the advance. Royalties usually represent a given percentage of the publisher's *suggested retail price*. Publishers cannot dictate the price for which a store will sell a book; if the publisher suggests—and prints on the jacket—a price of $14.95 for a book on the state parks of Illinois, and a Springfield camping-equipment store decides to offer the book at $10.95 in order to attract customers, the publisher has no legal right to complain or take action because the book is being made to look less valuable. The reason for this rule is quite complex but generally involves the unenforceability of so-called "fair trade laws." Royalties may also be based on a percentage of the wholesale price or the publisher's net receipts. At first glance, it might appear that the author would prefer royalties based on retail price, but there appears to be a trend towards using net receipts, which will be discussed later in this chapter.

As a general rule, the royalty rate on hardbound books starts at 10 percent of the publisher's suggested retail price, but the rate may go as high as 20 percent. The author and publisher may adopt a sliding-scale agreement called an *escalation clause* whereby the author would receive, for example, 10 percent on the first 5,000 copies sold, 12.5 percent on the next 5,000, and 15 percent thereafter. Royalties are lower for paperbacks than they are for hardbound books and generally range from 6 percent to 12 percent.

The publisher will typically include a clause in the contract stating that no royalties will be paid on copies distributed for review or advertising or on copies furnished gratuitously to the author or as samples, or for copies destroyed by fire or water. Moreover, the publisher will normally stipulate that no royalties be paid on books which are returned from bookstores. Thus, if the royalty rate is 10 percent of the suggested retail price, 8,000 copies are sold, and 2,000 copies are returned, the author would only be entitled to royalties on 6,000 copies rather than on the full 8,000.

The publisher may also require that royalties on later printings be reduced if such reduction is necessary to keep the book in print. If sales of a given book decline, the costs of printing and distribution per book can increase since the print order will be lower and the unit price per book higher. If sales continue to decline, cost will at some point exceed sales and the publisher will probably sell the remaining books on hand for a greatly reduced price (known as remaindering the book) or let it go out of print. However, by decreasing royalties, the publisher may offset these increased publishing costs and thereby prolong the life of the book.

The publisher is likely to require that the royalty rate be reduced for copies sold at a substantial discount. Thus, a royalty of 10 percent might be reduced to 5 percent for copies sold to bulk purchasers at special discounts, or to wholesalers for specialized markets at larger-than-normal discounts. Similarly, the royalty rate might be reduced for all export, remainder, and premium sales. At times, the royalty-rate reduction may be determined by a particular formula. For example, the publisher might specify that the stated royalty will be reduced by one-quarter of the difference between a 50 percent discount and whatever discount is granted. A discount of 60 percent would, in this case, reduce the author's royalty rate by 2.5 percent. Of course, the author may demand that some limitations be placed on this type of clause to ensure that in every case some royalties, at least, will be forthcoming. The author might demand that the royalty rate will in no event be reduced by more than half.

A reduced-royalty clause was the subject of a lawsuit between the authors of *100 Best Companies to Work for in America* and Addison-Wesley Publishing Company in

1986.[1] The plaintiff-authors sued Addison-Wesley in U.S. District Court for breach of contract and fraud, claiming that they lost more than $100,000 as a result of the publisher's interpretation of a reduced-royalty clause.

The clause in question in the Addison-Wesley contract provided for a reduced-royalty rate (of 10 percent of the amount of the publisher's receipts) for copies or editions sold by the publisher at half the invoiced list price or less. Addison-Wesley had been applying the clause to regular sales to wholesalers (whenever a 50 percent or greater discount was given), as well as to special discount sales. The authors argued that the clause should be applied only to special sales outside regular trade channels, and not sales to wholesalers. The publisher asked the judge to dismiss the suit. Addison-Wesley maintained that because the contract gave the publisher sole discretion to sell the books at such prices and in such a manner as it found reasonble, the publisher had not breached the contract or committed fraud by calculating reduced royalties for discount sales to wholesalers.

U.S. District Court Judge Robert Peckam refused to dismiss the suit. Instead, he held that the publisher's conduct might have breached an implied duty of good faith, which is present in all contractual agreements. The court stated that "Defendant [Addison-Wesley] is expected to exercise its discretion [concerning sale of the books] in good faith, and set prices in a manner consistent with good faith and fair dealing." He went on to suggest that if the authors could prove that Addison-Wesley's application of the reduced-royalty clause to sales to wholesalers "contravenes the parties' intentions and industry custom," and that Addison-Wesley led the authors to believe the clause would apply only to special sales, the authors would have a claim for fraud. The case was settled before trial. Addison-Wesley paid the authors an additional sum of money of an undisclosed amount and released them from their obligations under a second contract; in addition, the authors dropped their counterclaims for breach of contract and defamation.

In light of the *Addison-Wesley* case, it would be a good idea for authors to negotiate to have reduced-royalty clauses deleted from their contracts entirely, or, if the publisher insists upon having them included, then the clause should be clarified to provide that the reduced royalties would not apply to books sold to the trade. The clause should be confined to the special situations argued for by the plaintiff in the *Addison-Wesley* case. It would also be worthwhile for an author to determine what a publisher's customary volume discounts are. Perhaps a provision could be added to limit the percentage of books sold in any period for which the author will receive a reduced royalty, 50 percent, for example. This would discourage publishers from taking undue advantage of the reduced-royalty clause when applied to volume discounts.

Royalties are customarily paid twice a year, usually accompanied by a royalty statement, which is an itemized account showing the number of copies printed, bound, sold, or given away by the publisher, the author's royalty rate, and, generally, the reserves for returns.

Authors have complained that royalty statements are often indecipherable or erroneous and that publishers have been known to understate sales so that they might pocket some of the royalties. Whether these complaints are justified or not, so many authors believe them that a writer would be well advised to include an *auditing clause* when working out a contract with a book publisher. This type of clause provides that the author may examine the publisher's books and records upon giving reasonable notice in advance. Bear in mind, though, that the cost of such examination may be quite high. I customarily urge my clients to gamble by providing that if any discrepancy exceeds 5 percent of the amount received by the writer, the publisher will pay all expenses attributable to the examination. If any discrepancy is less than 5 percent, the author will bear the cost.

The use of royalties based on publishers' net receipts (gross sales less returns), mentioned earlier, would eliminate some of the problems that affect author-publisher relationships. As commonly used by most university presses, textbook publishers, and smaller independent publishers, this method substitutes a single clause stating a flat royalty rate, commonly 15 to 20 percent, for the multitude of clauses specifying different royalty rates for different kinds of sales. This eliminates the potential for conflict shown in the Addison-Wesley case and provides the author with a simple, easily understood royalty statement. Its widespread acceptance will, however, require more sophisticated understanding by authors and agents of publishers' distribution systems and a willingness by publishers to provide enough information to compare the effective royalties based on suggested retail price.

An author who anticipates very high royalties may wish to include in the royalty clause a spread-forward provision that limits the total amount of royalties receivable in any given year to a stated amount, say $20,000. But the author should be aware of the drawbacks to this provision discussed in Chapter 2 under "Income in Installments and Deferred Payments." The excess will be spread forward to the following year or years, in which royalties are expected to have diminished. In this way the total tax burden is reduced because the author avoids being taxed in the higher income tax brackets. Generally, publishers use December 31 and June 30 as the dates for payment of royalties, which is a convenience for the author because it results in postponing the tax liability on the January payment for one year, since a check mailed on the 31st is not likely to be received until after January 1 and authors would not be taxed on their royalties until they are received. Tax strategies are further discussed in Chapter 2, "Keeping Taxes Low." Many contracts will state that royalties are payable on the date specified or as soon thereafter as is practicable. This is because the stated date may fall on a holiday and publishers are rarely willing to prepay. It is common for a royalty check to be received anywhere from fifteen to thirty days after the date specified in the author-publisher contract.

Format and Content of the Manuscript

In most author-publisher contracts the publisher has the right to require that the manuscript be in "satisfactory" condition—if typewritten, on 8½-by-11-inch paper, double-spaced, and reasonably "clean," with minimal strikeouts; if on disc, a laser or other letter-quality printer is preferable to a dot matrix. If much editing is needed, the author might be required to pay for retyping or rekeyboarding. As a practical matter, authors retain control over the style of the manuscript and its content, though publishers do control these factors to some extent. Unless the author is extremely valuable to the publisher, the publisher will generally have the last word with regard to all aspects of the work since the publisher can refuse to publish, relying on the "satisfactory manuscript" clause. The publisher may also require that the author provide a preface, notes, and index. In addition, the publisher usually has the exclusive right to determine the selling price of the published book and where and how it will be marketed.

In a few contracts, however, the author will demand some control over these matters. This may be the case, for example, with a very successful author, who might be in a position to demand approval of the book design or jacket design. But this is very much the exception. Another situation in which an author could demand control over matters of format would be in subsidy or copublishing agreements, in which the author agrees to finance all or some of the costs of publication. (See pages 126 to 129 for more on subsidy publishing and copublishing.) Moreover, the author, particularly one with a track record of books that sell well, may demand that the contract give him or her the final say in all questions relating to literary style, feeling that to grant the publisher this right might diminish the literary and artistic merits of the manuscript. If the book is technical or scholarly, the author may feel more qualified than the publisher to make decisions about style and content.

THE "SATISFACTORY MANUSCRIPT" CLAUSE

Typically, the author-publisher contract contains a clause in which the author promises to deliver a manuscript that is "satisfactory in form and content" or one that is "in all regards acceptable." Failure to produce a satisfactory manuscript may have several consequences. First, the publisher might decline to pay any further installments of the advance. Second, depending on the terms of the contract, either the author will have to repay whatever portion of the advance has already been received, or the author will have to make such repayment if the book is later sold to another publishing house.

Whenever a manuscript is rejected as unacceptable, the definition of the term *satisfactory* becomes crucial in determining the rights of the author and the publisher. Yet contracts almost never provide a standard for what is acceptable and what is not. The legal standard that has evolved is that the publisher's decision will generally be subjective rather than objective. In other words, the publisher involved must be personally satisfied. It is irrelevant that other publishers, or a hypothetical reasonable publisher, would find the manuscript in question to be satisfactory. The subjective satisfaction of the contracting publisher is controlling.

Given this subjective standard, the courts have been extremely reluctant to rule that a publisher has wrongfully rejected a manuscript. Generally, publishers are allowed to reject manuscripts when they have honest doubts as to quality, or when they decide it would be financially impractical to publish the manuscript. In the unlikely event that a court finds that a publisher has wrongfully rejected a manuscript which is in every respect acceptable or satisfactory, that rejection constitutes a breach of the publisher's duty to publish. Until very recently, the amount of damages the author could recover in this type of situation was limited. Typically, the author was allowed to retain the advance, but no other damages would be awarded because the courts felt that the extent of the author's loss was too speculative, i.e., there was no way for the court to determine how much the author would have realized from royalties and secondary benefits had the manuscript been published. Consequently, the publisher could reject perfectly acceptable manuscripts without fear of having to pay more than nominal damages.

A comparatively recent case, however, indicates that authors may be given better protection in the future. In this case the court held that if the publisher wrongfully rejects an author's manuscript the author will be entitled to damages equal to the amount the author would need to publish the manuscript himself. In this case, the court awarded the author damages of $11,000.[2]

Other recent cases from New York accord authors better protection by limiting publisher discretion to reject manuscripts in the first place. These cases involve a *duty to edit* on the part of the publisher.

The first duty-to-edit case was *Harcourt Brace Jovanovich, Inc.* v. *Goldwater*, a 1982 decision involving Senator Barry Goldwater.[3] In this case, the court found that Harcourt Brace had intentionally refrained from providing Goldwater with editorial help on his memoirs because the publisher did not approve of the ghostwriter Goldwater was using. Although Harcourt Brace never gave any indication, as sections of the book came in, that the work was unsatisfactory, it eventually rejected the finished manuscript as unacceptable. When Goldwater subsequently sold the book to another publisher, Harcourt sued for the $65,000 advance it had paid when the authors signed the contract.

The New York court held that the authors were not required to return the advance. The court stressed the need for communication between authors and publishers, particularly when specific faults are found. Significantly, the court found that an implied obligation to provide appropriate editorial work is part of these kinds of contracts. Because Harcourt Brace had given no editorial advice at all, it had violated its duty of good faith.

The newly discovered duty to edit was also significant in the 1984 decision in *Dell Publishing Co.* v. *Whedon*.[4] In *Dell*, author Julia Whedon entered into a contract based on a twelve-page outline of a novel. She received $8,000 of a $20,000 advance upon signing the contract, and a second installment of $6,000 two and a half years later upon submission of half of the manuscript. When she finally completed the manuscript after four years of effort, however, the editor informed her that "it just wasn't what we expected." Dell formally rejected the manuscript without providing any specific criticisms and demanded return of the $14,000.

As in *Goldwater*, the judge held that Whedon was not required to return the advance. The court emphasized Whedon's reliance on Dell's approval of the first half of the book, as evidenced by its payment of the second installment of the advance. The court found that Dell had breached its duties to Whedon by rejecting the book as unsatisfactory without giving "at the very least, a detailed explanation of the problems it saw in the manuscript, and an opportunity to revise it along those lines."[5]

Although *Goldwater* and *Dell* seem to indicate a limit on

publisher discretion based on a duty to edit, it is not yet clear exactly what this duty involves and when it arises. In *Doubleday & Co.* v. *Curtis*,[6] a federal appellate court, sitting in New York and applying New York State law, found that although there may be in some situations a minimal duty to edit, the duty does not extend to requiring skillful editing. In *Doubleday*, actor Tony Curtis's book, *Starstruck*, was rejected by the publisher as unacceptable. During the four years of intermittent work that Curtis put in on the manuscript, Doubleday had provided only one, generally encouraging, letter of comment. Nevertheless, the court refused to imply a duty on the part of Doubleday to perform adequate editorial services, since there was no express language in the contract requiring such service. The court indicated that such an implied duty would arise only in cases of a publisher's "wilful failure to respond to a request for editorial comment on a preliminary draft."[7] Curtis was therefore required to return the advance he had received.

Rather than depend on any implied duty to comment or edit, an author should discuss standards of acceptability with the publisher, and include criteria for judging the finished product in the contract. The Authors League of America, an advocacy organization for authors and dramatists, has advised that "a publishing contract should state, as objective conditions, the criteria a manuscript must satisfy—rather than allow acceptance or rejection to depend on the publisher's subjective judgment."[8] The League suggests a clause providing that the manuscript submitted must be, "in style and content, professionally competent and fit for publication." Another suggestion that has been made is to incorporate the proposal submitted by the author, along with language specifying that the manuscript will be deemed acceptable if it conforms basically to the proposal. The contract might also provide for arbitration—discussed later in this chapter—to determine whether the manuscript has been rightfully rejected.

Obviously it is important for authors to clarify what a satisfactory manuscript is. Of course, the publishing house is likely to approach this issue quite differently from the writer and be extremely reluctant to give up any of its traditional discretion to reject a finished product. Practically speaking, it is likely that only an author with a strong bargaining position or a good agent will be able to avoid the vague and troublesome satisfactory manuscript clause.

ALTERATIONS

The author generally agrees to pay the costs of making author's alterations or corrections on galley or page proofs that exceed a certain percentage of the typesetter's initial bill—for example, all the costs of these alterations which exceed 10 or 15 percent of the initial bill. This clause is designed to discourage authors from rewriting the book after it has been typeset. It is a good idea for writers to try to modify such a clause by requiring the publisher to absorb the cost of changes which are made for the purpose of updating material when a significant event has occurred. It is also important to make it clear that the author is not responsible for changes which merely correct the typesetters' errors.

PUBLICATION

The publication clause requires the publisher to publish the manuscript within a given time after accepting it. In addition, the clause specifies which party is to pay the publishing costs. If the contract calls for self- or copublishing, the author will pay all or some of these costs, but in most cases the publishing company agrees to publish the manuscript at its own expense. Finally, the author might be able to get the publisher to agree in this clause to produce a paperback version of the book as well as a hardcover edition, or vice versa.

REVISIONS

The revisions clause generally provides that if the publisher decides a revision of the book is desirable after it has been published, the author must be given first option to make such a revision. If the author is unable or unwilling to undertake the job, the publisher is free to contract with someone else to do it.

Where the author chooses to revise the book, the contract may provide that the royalty scheme for the revised edition will remain the same or revert to the base percentage—that is, the lowest percentage paid when royalties are determined on a sliding scale based on volume of sales. The contract often provides that the author's royalty rate is to revert to the base percentage if the revision involves a substantial resetting or new negatives—that is, the rates might revert if the revision required new negatives costing 50 percent or more of the typesetting and printing costs of the prior edition. To understand how this might work, assume that an author agrees to revise the first edition and that the revision costs exceed the stated 50 percent. Further, assume that royalty rates on the first edition were 10 percent for the first 5,000 copies sold and 15 percent thereafter, and that 7,000 copies of the first edition were sold. If the contract calls for the royalty rate to revert to the base percentage, the royalty on the revised edition will start at 10 percent even though the author was receiving 15 percent on the prior edition.

If someone other than the author undertakes and completes the revision, the publisher will compensate that party either with a flat fee or with royalties. The revision clause generally provides that the money paid to the reviser is to be deducted from any sums accruing to the original author so, in order to protect royalty interests, the author may demand that no revisions of the original edition be made until a certain period of time has elapsed, usually one to three years. In addition, the author may demand a phasing-out provision whereby the author's royalties may be reduced only by a stated percentage, and no more, upon each revision. Thus, the author's royalties might be reduced by one-fourth upon the first revision, one-half upon the second, three-fourths upon the third, and be eliminated upon the fourth.

COPYRIGHT

The copyright clause establishes which party, the author or the publisher, is to own the copyright. Each party would of course prefer to own the copyright because of the potential for economic gain and control over ungranted subsidiary rights. Where no owner is specified in the contract, the author is presumed by law to have retained the copyright. Prior to the Copyright Revision Act of 1976, which became effective January 1, 1978, the author was deemed to have transferred copyright ownership to the publisher unless it was expressly reserved. Since the new law became effective, the presumption is exactly the opposite; the author is deemed to have reserved the copyright unless the contract expressly transfers it.

The norm in trade-book contracts is for the author to retain the copyright, while publishers of scholarly books and academic texts usually ask that the copyright be assigned to them. This is justified because such works are frequently updated, and if the publisher retains the copyright, it can arrange for supplements or revisions even after the author is no longer able to update the work.

In trade-book contracts, the author will generally retain the copyright and grant the publisher a license to exercise certain of the rights included in the copyright—that is, the right to publish and sell the book and some of the subsidiary rights in it. Another approach is for the author to grant the publisher the copyright under the condition that the copyright revert to the author at some specified time or after some specified event (for example, when the book goes out of print). A copyright is divisible and the rights within it may be divided between the author and publisher. For example, the author may grant the publisher the right to publish and sell which, as noted above, is common in trade-book publishing.

The copyright clause usually requires the author to inform the publisher if any previously copyrighted material (whether by the author or someone else) has been incorporated into the manuscript. If it has, the author may be required to get written permission to use the material from the original publisher or the copyright owner, and to submit that written permission to the publisher. Often there will be a nominal fee for reproducing material from another book. As a general rule, the author pays the fee—that is, it is deducted from royalties—but this might be negotiable.

Whether the author or publisher retains copyright ownership, the publisher should be required to print the proper copyright notice on the completed book, register the copyright with the Copyright Office, and take any other actions necessary to protect the copyright. If the book is published internationally, the publisher may be required to comply with the rules of the various copyright treaties, for example, the Universal Copyright Convention, the Berne Convention, the Buenos Aires Convention, etc.

The author may want the appropriate clause in the contract to provide that if the publisher does not comply with these rules, the publication will be considered unauthorized.

If form publishing contracts are used, the writer should be certain that the copyright clauses in these contracts have been updated to comply with the Copyright Revision Act of 1976 (see Chapter 7).

Subsidiary Rights

The book publisher is apparently chiefly concerned with the rights to publish and sell a work. These rights are known as the *primary rights* and are always granted to the publisher, usually within a specified territory such as the United States, the Philippines, Canada, or the world. Ownership of *subsidiary rights*, however, is a source of considerable negotiation, as these may prove immensely valuable in some situations.

Subsidiary rights are defined as any conceivable rights of exploitation in markets not included in the primary grant of the right to publish and sell. For example, film rights would be subsidiary rights in a book-publishing contract, while book-publishing rights would be subsidiary rights in a film contract. Subsidiary rights in a publishing contract could include, in addition to film rights, book clubs, reprints—usually in paperback form—excerpts in magazines before or after book publication, newspaper syndication, records, foreign-language editions, abridgements and condensations, anthologies, dramatizations, and the rights to alternative forms of publishing, such as microfilm, microprint, and filmstrip. Subsidiary rights may be divided between the author and publisher in any number of ways. Of the major rights, however, particularly if the author has an agent, the author often retains motion-picture, television, dramatic, foreign and translation rights, with the book-club and paperback rights held by the publisher, and the income from the sale of these rights split fifty-fifty. Since the definition of subsidiary rights can vary from contract to contract, the author should scrutinize the definitions to make sure they are precise and not overly broad.

One of the subsidiary rights that is of concern in both book and magazine publishing is *serial rights*, the right to run parts of a book or article in serialized form in a magazine or newspaper. See the section later in this chapter, under "Contracts with Magazines," regarding the details and potential value of serial rights.

Recently, authors have been arguing for and winning a larger percentage of subsidiary rights and more control over the way subsidiary rights are exercised. For example, the author may demand that no license of subsidiary rights may be granted by the publisher without the author's consent. A publisher faced with a clause such as this may balance it with a provision in which it is agreed that the author's consent will not be unreasonably withheld. But the author may require that if the publisher does not dispose of the subsidiary rights within a stated time (for example, one year), all rights will revert to the author. Publishers are, of course, resisting this trend, because a substantial percent of their profits sometimes comes from the sale and exploitation of subsidiary rights rather than from sales to the trade.

Since subsidiary rights can mean money for authors as well as publishers, both parties should make clear in their contract which subsidiary rights belong to which party. Failure to do so may not only result in substantial financial losses, but may also cause the contract to be declared void for vagueness. To prevent this, a residual clause may be included in which one party is given all subsidiary rights not otherwise expressly granted. The residual clause recognizes that advances in technology are constantly broadening the uses of literary property, and states which party will receive the benefits of subsidiary rights in new technology. If a residual clause is not included, the party in whose name the book has been copyrighted will automatically receive all additional subsidiary rights.

The author should also be concerned with the method by which the subsidiary rights are exploited. After all, if a publisher makes a "sweetheart" deal with a movie producer in which rights are sold below usual terms, the author may suffer a financial loss.

WARRANTY AND INDEMNITY

The warranty and indemnity clause is to protect the publisher from claims or lawsuits brought by third parties. First, the author warrants that the work is in no way unlawful; that is, it is not libelous, obscene, an invasion of privacy, in violation of copyright, or the like. Second, the author agrees to indemnify, or reimburse, the publisher for any expenses incurred in defending any claim or lawsuit covered by the warranty. Occasionally, the warranty and indemnity clause gives the publisher the right to withhold all royalties accruing to an author if a claim or lawsuit has been filed.

The Authors League has suggested that the warranty and indemnity clause violates the author's freedom of speech. Because this clause is particularly repugnant to authors, you should attempt to have it deleted or modified, if possible. Several modifications are advisable. First, the author might agree to indemnify only when the claim or lawsuit has received a final judgment. (The term *final judgment* is ambiguous and could mean either a decision by the trial court or the result after all appeals are exhausted. You would prefer the latter interpretation and, if you are in a strong bargaining position, you should demand that the term *judgment* mean the final result after all rights of appeal have been exhausted.) Second, the author could refuse to indemnify claims or lawsuits caused by the publisher's changes or additions to the original manuscript. Third, the author may agree to indemnify the publisher if the lawsuit is settled prior to a final judgment, but only if such settlement is made with the author's consent. This gives the author the ability to control an overgenerous publisher during settlement negotiations. Fourth, the author might demand that indemnification will in no event exceed 50 percent of the damages. (In other words, the costs of the claim or lawsuit are to be divided equally between author and publisher.) And finally, where the clause allows the publisher to begin withholding royalties when a suit is filed, the author might demand that the amount of royalties withheld not exceed a reasonable estimate of the prospective damages.

Because it is unlikely that an author would write, or a publisher print, a manuscript knowing it to be in violation of libel, copyright, obscenity, or other laws, the issue becomes which party should assume the risks of an unforeseen claim or lawsuit. Perhaps the best solution is to limit the warranty and indemnity clause to the areas in which the author is more likely to have knowledge of the unlawful nature of the work or is otherwise more culpable. Thus, the author would warrant and indemnify against liability arising from copyright infringement, intentional invasion of privacy, and libel by extrinsic fact (that is, libel not necessarily apparent on reading the manuscript). On the other hand, the publisher might assume the risks of a claim or lawsuit arising from obscenity or libel per se (libel that is apparent on reading the manuscript), since the publisher is probably in a better position to know what the law regards as libelous or obscene. Libel and invasion of privacy are discussed in detail in Chapters 9 and 10.

COVENANTS NOT TO COMPETE

A covenant not to compete is an unconditional promise by one party not to compete with the other, usually in some specified market and over a specified period of time. The problems which give rise to a covenant not to compete can best be illustrated by two hypothetical situations.

First, suppose that a publisher contracts with author A to publish a book on electronics. Subsequently, the same publisher contracts with author B to publish another book on electronics which is in every respect similar to A's book, so that the publication of B's book substantially reduces the sales of A's. Can author A be protected from this type of competition?

Second, assume that an author's illustrated encyclopedia is published by publisher X, and that the same author subsequently contracts with publisher Y to produce another illustrated encyclopedia covering the same subjects as the first. Assuming there is no copyright infringement, can publisher X be protected from this type of competition?

Both of these examples are based on actual cases, but in neither case did the contract contain an express covenant not to compete. Rather, in the first case[9] the court addressed an express condition in A's contract that the publisher would use "best efforts" in promoting A's book, and found that the publisher's competing publication was so harmful to author A that it violated this covenant. In the second case,[10] the court maintained that the author's competing acts did not violate an implied covenant of fair dealing and good faith toward publisher X. The court recognized that the author's competition did result in economic harm to X, but was not willing to impose liability.

Significantly, the courts were not willing to find an implied covenant not to compete in either case. The question is raised, then, of how these cases would have been decided had either contract contained an express covenant not to compete. One suspects that liability would have been imposed in both situations.

When contracts do contain express covenants not to compete, most courts are generally willing to enforce the covenants, provided they are reasonable in time, place, and scope, with reasonableness being judged according to the facts of each case. For example, a typical clause may read:

(a) The Author shall not permit or arrange for the publication, distribution or sale in the Exclusive Territory otherwise than by the Publisher, of any work which will compete with the Work or diminish the value of any subsidiary or additional rights granted by this Agreement, except that the Author may grant licenses for the exploitation of any rights reserved to the Author under this Agreement.

Such a covenant would probably be enforced by most courts. Unfortunately, a publisher will rarely agree to delete this type of clause, though it might be willing to modify the clause. Even if the clause is ultimately declared invalid as overly broad, it is expensive to litigate such questions and the delay in having your work published could be seriously damaging. In some states, laws have been passed restricting or even invalidating covenants not to compete. You should check with your attorney regarding the enforceability of such a clause in your situation.

Time-Is-of-the-Essence Clauses

A time-is-of-the-essence clause is simply a clause in the contract explicitly stating that obligations must be performed in a timely manner—in other words, that time is a crucial factor of the contract. One form of such a clause would be a demand for prompt payment of royalties. These clauses can be unfair to the publisher if the penalty for failing to pay promptly is too severe.

In one instance, coauthors demanded that a time-is-of-the-essence clause relating to royalty payments be included in their author-publisher contract.[11] The clause stated:

Time of payment of royalties and of rendering an accounting by publisher to author is of the essence of this agreement. If any such payment is not timely made and if any such accounting is not timely rendered and if any such default shall continue for thirty days following written notification by author to publisher of such default, then at the option of author, all rights granted to publisher under this agreement shall automatically revert to author.

Obviously, this type of clause can cause substantial difficulties for a publisher experiencing cash-flow problems. It would not be unusual to miss a royalty payment or to be able to make only a partial payment on time, the consequence of which would be the reversion of all rights to the author. Generally, the courts do not favor time-is-of-the-essence clauses, particularly where such clauses call for a forfeiture of all rights under the contract. In the above example, some courts would hesitate to enforce the clause as written, but would instead award the author any actual damages occurring by reason of the late royalty payments. These courts would consider the reversion of all rights a harsh penalty which does not bear a rational relationship to the injury sustained by the writer due to late payment. Other courts might enforce the clause as written, pointing out that if the parties agreed to its inclusion, it is not for the court to rewrite the contract.

TERMINATION AND REVERSION

Either the author or the publisher may require that the contract terminate under certain stated circumstances. The author might demand termination if the publisher should fail to publish within a stated time or if the publisher should become bankrupt or insolvent. This would protect the author from having the contract or rights sold by a trustee in bankruptcy at auction to a publisher who might not be acceptable to the author. This clause may be unenforceable under the new bankruptcy code, although it is common to find it in form publishing contracts. On the other hand, the publisher might want a clause to provide that publication may be discontinued at any time if in the publisher's opinion the work would no longer be profitable.

Regardless of how the contract is terminated, the termination clause generally requires that the author be notified of such termination and given the option to purchase the offset negatives, unbound sheets, and any remaining copies of the book, usually at a certain percentage of their manufacturing costs. If the author does not exercise this option, the publisher may sell the remaining copies at any price to another party. If the remaining copies are sold by the publisher for a reduced price, the author may receive a reduced royalty, or none at all. Moreover, if the author does not purchase the negatives, sheets, etc., the contract may require the publisher to destroy them.

Most contracts provide that upon termination all rights held by the publisher revert to the author, except licenses already granted. The publisher, however, may want to qualify this clause to provide that the rights will not revert to the author if the author has an unearned advance against royalties or is otherwise indebted to the publisher.

The author-publisher contract may also provide that all rights will revert to the author if the work goes *out of print*. Because authors and publishers may not agree on when a work has gone out of print, the phrase should be clearly defined in the contract. The publisher will obviously prefer a narrow definition, whereas the author will prefer one that is broad. The author, for example, may demand that *out of print* be defined as that time when copies of the book are not available through normal trade channels, or when the number of copies printed and sold falls below a certain figure. The publisher, on the other hand, might want to look at the book in any of the following ways:

The work is out of print when marketing and distribution expenses fall below a stated figure. A definition of "out of print" which is based on marketing expenses, however, is quite unusual.

The work is not out of print so long as there is a contract outstanding for a new edition or a license has been granted to another party, even though no books are actually in print.

The publisher may also demand that the out-of-print clause not be effective until a stated number of years after the first publication, or that the work must be out of print for a stated time, such as six months, before the rights revert to the author.

If the publisher had subcontracted to a third party the exploitation of a particular right the publisher owned (a paperback reprint, for instance), thereby creating a license in the third party, the reversion rights of the author will usually be subject to the third party's license. In other words, even if the publisher's rights revert to the author, the third party will still have a valid license as granted by the publisher, providing the publisher was authorized to create the license in the first place. The author may get around this by demanding at the outset that any license granted by the publisher will be subject to the author's reversion rights. In this way the author ensures that all rights will revert. It is worth noting that few publishers will acquiesce to this demand.

Option Clause

The publisher may include a clause in the contract giving the publisher an option to publish the author's subsequent works to counterbalance the risks of publishing the first manuscript. The rationale is that if the publisher is willing to gamble on an unknown author, it is only fair that if the book proves to be successful, the publisher should have the right of first refusal on the author's later manuscripts. But the author may not want an option clause because it restricts flexibility. Consequently, the author may not consent to the clause, or may consent but make conditions. For example, the author may demand that the publisher accept or reject the subsequent works within thirty to sixty days after they have been submitted or that the publisher come to a decision on the basis of an outline and sample chapters, rather than a completed manuscript. Finally, the author may want the option restricted to the first subsequent manuscript so as to be free thereafter to contract with any other publisher.

If the author agrees to the option, the publisher will probably attempt to make the clause specific. Otherwise, if the option clause is vague about the advance and royalty rate to be paid for the subsequent manuscripts, courts may refuse to enforce it. For example, the typical option clause which entitles the publisher to publish subsequent works "on terms to be agreed upon" will probably be unenforceable. On the other hand, the option clause will probably be specific enough if it either fixes terms for the purchase of subsequent works, or provides a reasonable method for determining the terms or identifying the work. Even with an enforceable option clause for the author's next work, an author can intentionally submit inferior works to this publisher, thus satisfying the contractual obligation. In this way the author would be free to submit a later marketable work to any publisher he or she chooses.

It is not uncommon for publishers to have the option provision state that even if the publisher rejects the author's next work, it may nevertheless retain the right to match any offer the author obtains to publish the work on terms no less favorable than those tendered by any other publisher. In this situation the author may be inhibited to some extent since publishers contemplating publishing the work will have to offer better terms than the original publisher.

Multiple-Book Contracts

Publishers may attempt to hold successful authors by negotiating multiple-book contracts. These contracts differ from first-option contracts. A first-option contract grants the publisher the first right to publish any subsequent book by the author, but does not obligate the author ever to write again. A multiple-book contract, on the other hand, obligates the author to write two or more books for a given publisher. The problems that can arise from this kind of contract are substantial. What happens, for example, if the author fails to comply with the contract? The publisher may be able to sue for breach of contract. While the law will not require a person to perform a personal-service contract, such as writing a book, against one's will, damages may be awarded. In addition, the publisher may be able to obtain a court order prohibiting the author from writing for any other publisher. It should be noted that the amount of damages awarded the publisher would ordinarily be difficult to calculate in a case like this, since it would require speculation on the probable success of an unwritten book. For this reason, publishers will generally include a clause in the contract providing that the publisher can recover a specified amount in the event the author fails to perform this part of the multiple-book contract.

Author's Manuscript

In many contracts, the publisher will disclaim any responsibility for insuring the author's manuscript or illustrations and disclaim any liability that may arise from its loss or destruction. Moreover, the publisher may demand the right to destroy the author's manuscript after publication if it is not properly claimed within a given period of time. Or the publisher may require the author to retain a copy of the manuscript, illustrations, and any other materials submitted to the publisher.

The author may not agree to the inclusion of these provisions in the contract. Because the manuscript, illustrations, and related material will be of personal and possibly financial value, the author should demand that the publisher be held liable if the work is destroyed while in the publisher's control, or that the manuscript, page proofs, and other early stages of the book be returned within a stated time following publication.

The author should retain at least one complete copy of the manuscript so that the damages might be nominal; still, original illustrations, cover artwork and the like might be extremely valuable and thus damages for their loss might be substantial.

ARBITRATION

Arbitration is simply an arrangement for taking a dispute to some agreed-upon third party for resolution rather than going through the formalities and expense of courtroom litigation. The arbitration clause in a contract may provide that arbitration will be only the first step in resolving disputes, and that decisions may be appealed to a court for review. Alternatively, the contract may provide for binding arbitration, in which case the parties agree that the decision of the arbitrator shall be conclusive, and that the parties will not attempt to have this decision examined by a court.

The identity of the arbitrator is important, since a contractual provision selecting a friend of the publisher or of the author will likely predetermine the outcome of any controversy. For this reason, an independent nonpartisan arbitrator should be selected. It is common to state merely that the arbitrator shall be a member of the American Association of Arbitrators who is acceptable to both parties. If an arbitration panel is to be used, the contract may provide that both parties shall select an arbitrator to represent their interests and that the two arbitrators will pick a third member of the panel. Obviously, this latter method is more costly.

Although binding arbitration may save time and money, be aware that when a contract calls for binding arbitration, the resulting decision cannot be appealed and the process will not contain many of the procedural safeguards which are a part of the judicial process. On the other hand, an arbitration clause may prove beneficial to the writer dealing with a large publisher because it will decrease the publisher's negotiating leverage in the event a dispute arises. For example, if a disagreement arises and there is no arbitration clause, the large publisher's ability to absorb litigation costs may well be much greater than the individual author's. Thus, the publisher can take a harder line in negotiation. With an arbitration clause, the publisher cannot hold the economic threat of a lawsuit over the writer's head. Of course, this reasoning does not hold true when small publishers are involved. Thus, for writers contracting with small publishers, an arbitration clause will not reduce the publisher's leverage significantly. Nonetheless, it is generally desirable to resolve a conflict quickly so that the parties can fulfill their respective responsibilities. Binding arbitration may, therefore, be the best and most economical method of settling any disputes over the contract.

AUTHORSHIP CREDIT, FREE COPIES, AND AUTHOR PURCHASES

The author may demand that credit for authorship be published in a particular manner, and may dictate the relative size and location of the name not only of the author but of a coauthor, illustrator, or a subsequent reviser other than the author. In addition, most author-publisher contracts provide that the author is to receive a certain number of free or discounted copies. Occasionally, contracts will allow authors to buy any number of books for a discounted price, but publishers will usually be careful in setting the price so as to avoid having the author become a competitor. One means publishers have used to prevent this kind of competition is stating in the contract that free or discounted books are not to be sold by the author, or that if they are to be resold, the price must be no lower than that which the publisher is charging. In other cases, the publisher may see that the author is the best salesperson for the book, and encourage the author to buy books for resale.

AGENCY CLAUSE

If the author has an agent, the author-publisher contract will most likely provide that all payments that the publisher owes the author will be paid directly to the agent. (This clause is not in the standard contract, since not all writers have an agent.) If the agent is dishonest, a publisher may have to make a second payment or prove that the first payment was made. If the publisher states in the contract that payment to the agent discharges the publisher's obligation, then the author will suffer the consequences of choosing a dishonest agent. The solution is to deal with a well-established agency. Another method of protecting both author and publisher is for the publisher to make all payments by check, designating both author and agent as payee. In this situation both signatures are necessary to endorse the check.

BOILER-PLATE PROVISIONS

The author-publisher contract may include any or all of the following wrap-up provisions.

Merger. A merger clause will state that "the contract is intended to be the complete and final agreement of the parties." This statement is designed to prevent any outside deals from becoming part of the contract. It makes it clear that the written document embodies all prior understandings, negotiations, and promises. A clause such as this will probably prevent future misunderstandings. Another phrase likely to be found in a merger clause is, "No modification or waiver of the contract is valid or enforceable unless signed by the parties." This statement will protect both parties from an alleged oral change, which can be casually spoken and easily forgotten, and may protect the parties from a situation in which the publisher or author first adopts a casual posture concerning contract performance by the other, but later insists upon strict compliance with the contract. Some clauses may be more important than others and thus should demand strict compliance. Rather than force the parties to rank the quality or value of each contractual provision, this clause indicates that the parties may at any time demand strict compliance, notwithstanding the fact that they have not always done so.

Choice of Law. This clause determines which state's law will be applied when the parties live in different states. Each party will generally prefer to apply the party's own state's laws to interpret the contract. This is something the publisher is very unlikely to give up.

Attorneys' Fees. This clause will generally provide that if it becomes necessary to enforce the contract through legal means (by lawsuit or arbitration), the party who wins the case will be entitled to recover attorneys' fees in addition to any other monetary award. Be aware that some jurisdictions require that both the trial level and the appeal level be specified if the parties want attorneys' fees to be awarded following an appeal. The fact that the contract provides that the winning party will be entitled to recover attorneys' fees does not necessarily mean that that party will be reimbursed for the entire legal bill. The courts have traditionally held that the amount awarded will be "reasonable attorneys' fees" as determined by the court in which the lawsuit was tried, and it is not uncommon for a court to award an amount which is less than the actual bill. The clause may also provide that costs will be paid by the losing party. This means that any court costs or arbitration charges will be imposed on the losing party.

An attorneys'-fees-and-costs clause will discourage all concerned from breaching the contract, since both parties will realize that if they are found to be wrongdoers they may have to pay most of the prevailing party's expenses.

WAIVER OF BREACH

The contract might also contain a clause specifying, "a waiver of a breach of the contract shall not be deemed to waive any future breaches." This provision would allow a party to agree to less than strict compliance with the contract on one occasion, without giving up the right to strictly enforce the contract later on if performance becomes so shoddy as to affect the quality of the desired benefits from the contract.

The clauses discussed thus far are those typically included in a contract between a writer and a book publisher. These clauses are by no means the only ones that could be included, nor are variations on these clauses the only possibilities. Since the law generally recognizes that contracting parties enjoy an unfettered freedom of contract, the author-publisher contract can take almost any form, provided it is not unconscionable or illegal.

CONTRACTING WITH A MAGAZINE

When an author contracts with a magazine publisher rather than a book publisher, there will be certain variations on some of the contract clauses described above. There are three basic ways in which writers might deal with magazines. First, a writer may complete a story or article and then submit it. Second, the writer may submit an inquiry to ask for an assignment or establish interest before submitting a completed article or story. Third, the writer may be a staff writer with a magazine which employs the writer on a full- or part-time basis.

An important aspect of the staff writer's work is that the articles will likely be considered *works for hire*. As described in the copyright chapter, the work-for-hire doctrine provides that the magazine as employer, rather than the writer, owns the copyright in a work produced within the scope of employment. Freelance writers who are commissioned to write for a magazine on an agreed-upon subject may also come under this doctrine, if the idea originated with the magazine and the contract specifies that the article is a work for hire. The doctrine rarely applies to freelance writers who submit only completed articles or stories.

Many of the contract clauses generally found in book-publishing contracts will be in magazine contracts as well. For example, unless your work falls under the work-for-hire doctrine mentioned above, you own each of the separate rights that make up the copyright in your story or article, and the contract with the magazine should contain a copyright clause describing which of the rights you agree to transfer to the magazine. The contract may also contain a warranty and indemnity clause, an advance clause and a time-is-of-the-essence clause. However, magazine contracts generally do not contain royalty clauses, nor will the contract be likely to provide you with any rights to make alterations or revisions prior to publication. Following are some of the variations on general book-publishing contract clauses that are of particular concern when contracting with a magazine.

One-Time Publication Rights

As already pointed out, and as you will learn in the copyright chapter, when a freelance writer creates a work, he or she retains the copyright in that work. It is customary for freelance writers to sell one-time rights only for work published in magazines. Most often, magazine publishers will agree to this arrangement unless they own several magazines and want the work to appear in more than one. It is a good idea to specify exactly what is meant by one-time publication rights. For example, would you consider that one-time publication would allow republication in later reprints of the original magazine or in a collection of the magazine's work? What if the publisher wants to use your work in a series on a related subject in the future?

Another area that requires attention is the scope of the publication rights, both in regard to the length of time the magazine has in which to publish, and the geographical area within which the magazine will be distributed. You might wish to limit geographical publication to the United States and to the English language only. The right to publish your article in another language or in another country could prove valuable, especially if the article addresses a subject in the area of high technology, which could be of special interest to foreign publications.

SERIAL RIGHTS

Serial rights can be either *first serial rights* or *second serial rights*. First serial rights mean allowing parts or all of a work (be it an article, story, or book) to be published for the first time in a specific periodical, before it is published anywhere else. Magazines will sometimes want one-time publication rights to include first serial rights so that the magazine is guaranteed to be the first to break the story.

First serial rights (which apply more often to books than to magazine stories) can be extremely valuable. For example, in 1977 Gerald Ford contracted with Harper & Row for publication of his memoirs. The agreement gave Harper and Row the exclusive first serial right to license prepublication excerpts. Harper & Row sold *Time* magazine a license to prepublish excerpts of the book for $25,000, $12,500 in advance and $12,500 upon publication. However, before *Time* exercised its license, another magazine, *The Nation*, published an article containing several excerpts from Ford's as yet unpublished manuscript. *The Nation* had procured its material from an unauthorized source. Nevertheless, this publication, which prevented *Time* from being the first to publish the excerpts, provided grounds for *Time* to cancel its agreement with Harper & Row and refuse to pay the $12,500 still due under the contract.

As copyright owner, Harper & Row sued *The Nation* for copyright infringement. Harper & Row won in district court, but *The Nation* appealed, arguing that the use of the excerpt was a "fair use," protected by section 107 of the Copyright Act (for discussion of the fair use defense to copyright infringement, see Chapter 7). The United States Supreme Court decided the case in 1985,[12] holding that since *The Nation*'s unauthorized use was intended to usurp the commercially valuable right of first publication, the use was not a fair use.

Since the right of first publication is a valuable right, it is uncommon for a magazine to agree to simultaneous publication, which would allow two magazines to publish the work at the same time. Such permission may be granted, however, if noncompetitive magazines are involved, such as a Catholic magazine and a Presbyterian magazine, which are unlikely to have an overlapping readership.

Second serial rights give a magazine the right to reprint a story or part of a book after it has already been published elsewhere. Book publishers often arrange first or second serial rights for the books they publish. Customarily, in these situations the book publisher agrees to pay the author 50 percent of second serial profits.

TIME PERIOD FOR PUBLICATION

If possible, be sure your contract specifies a reasonable amount of time within which a magazine must exercise its publication rights. It is common for a writer to agree not to submit a work elsewhere for a certain period of time after it has appeared in a specific magazine. But if the magazine postpones publication of your work, you would be unable to reap further profit from it simply because of the magazine's delay.

REPUBLICATION OR ADAPTATION OF A WORK

Generally, you will want to reserve the right to authorize others to publish or adapt your work. Someone may wish to include your work in an anthology or use it in a television adaptation, which could be surprisingly valuable. While both of these situations may be beneficial, aside from any payment involved, if you reserve the right to authorize such uses, you will receive the full amount paid for those uses, rather than having to share it with a publisher.

But there may be situations in which authors can benefit by granting magazines the right to authorize other publications of their work, provided the magazine agrees to share in the proceeds. This is particularly true with major magazines such as *Esquire*, which help publicize an author's work and generally have excellent sales connections. In such cases, the magazine may act as an agent for the writer whose work it is authorized to sell.

KILL FEES

Kill-fee clauses commonly appear in contracts for commissioned works, where the magazine has agreed to publish a specified work upon its completion. The clause covers the situation in which the writer completes a piece, and the magazine decides not to publish it. The clause specifies a fee (they vary widely) which the magazine must pay the writer if the work is not published, generally a percentage of the price which would have been paid had the article been published.

OTHER CLAUSES

There are a few other clauses that may appear in a magazine contract. Many magazines insist upon a fact-checking clause, which requires the author to verify facts in the article. Such provisions generally require proof of verification. You should find out exactly what kind of documentation the magazine will require to satisfy this requirement. Since verification and documentation can be costly and time-consuming, if your contract contains such a provision you should be sure the compensation you receive for the article is sufficient to at least cover the fact-checking expenses.

A clause you might want to insert if you write fiction would be a clause reserving the right to develop the characters you have created. This is important if you plan later on to develop in some other medium or publication people you have invented for a short story or partly fictional article. This may also be important if your characters are copyrightable. The extent of copyright protection available for fictional characters is discussed in the copyright chapter.

Keep in mind when negotiating any contract with a publisher that as the copyright owner, you control all rights in your work. You should not grant any greater rights to a publisher than are necessary for the publisher's needs. Before you begin, you should identify which rights are most important to you and then make sure you either reserve them or receive appropriate compensation for their transfer. It is a good idea to include in the contract a clause such as "I reserve all rights in my work not otherwise expressly granted by this contract." In this way, you avoid unwitting transfers of more than you intended.

5

Finding a Publisher and Dealing with Agents

One of a writer's most difficult jobs is finding a book publisher. One step toward doing that successfully is being aware of the methods used by publishers to attract authors.

Publishers generally acquire manuscripts in one of two ways. They may start with an idea for a book and then find an author to write it, but probably more frequently they will select manuscripts and ideas from those that writers have submitted to them. The author may submit either a book proposal or an entire manuscript. A proposal, or *query*, usually consists of an outline or a table of contents and a sample chapter, but many publishers will accept as a book proposal any combination of work that demonstrates the author's ability as well as the sales potential of the completed book. A manuscript is basically the book in its completed form, subject, of course, to the inevitable editorial changes.

If you plan to submit a manuscript, or a portion of one, keep in mind that one of the first things a writer should do after completing a manuscript—besides breaking open a bottle of champagne, perhaps—is to get it to the nearest photocopying service. This can save untold anguish later on when something turns up missing, which does not happen often but is not without precedent. If you send an unsolicited manuscript to a book publisher, the publisher will usually keep conscientious track of it, but is not legally responsible if the manuscript is lost. If a publisher loses a manuscript that was requested, you probably could recover the costs of reproducing it if you had to replace it. But if that was the only copy of the manuscript, you would not be likely to recover damages sufficient to compensate you for rewriting the entire book. Having extra copies is a lot easier, quicker, and cheaper, not to mention more professional.

Authors are the lifeblood of the publishing industry. Every publishing company is constantly trying to attract new writers and works hard to keep the ones it already has.

In the distant past, publishers relied primarily on loyalty and contractual obligations to retain their previously published authors. Either the past relationship was fruitful and both parties enjoyed it, or the initial author-publisher contract granted the publisher first option to publish subsequent works by the author. In recent times this kind of loyalty has diminished considerably. Many authors are wary of contractual obligations and either refuse to grant a publisher future rights or agree to grant them only on condition that the publisher match any other offer. As a result of these developments, authors are beginning to submit their work to that publisher which they feel will make the best offer or do the best job of marketing their books. One reason for this change is that many authors see the publisher as a faceless corporate entity whose principal concern is making large profits without regard for the author's (or book's) well-being. Consequently, a smaller publishing house a long way from the large East Coast houses may be more attractive to an author than the larger companies. A small publisher may be more likely to respond quickly, to take a personal interest in the project, give it careful editorial and design attention, promote the book longer, and generally to regard publishing as a co-operative endeavor mutually beneficial to both author and publisher. Generally, however, only the large houses will pay large advances and have big advertising and promotional budgets.

Authors should look for publishers who have good reputations within the writing community. Equally important is the publisher's reputation for successful marketing and efficient distribution, both of which increase an author's royalties.

Trade journals for publishers and writers are a medium through which publishers attract the attention of potential authors. The Committee of Small Magazine Editors and Publishers (COSMEP) produces a regional newsletter that contains a "Manuscripts Wanted" section and a "Publishers Wanted" section. Comparable services are provided by other journals, such as *The Writer* and *Writer's Digest* magazine, both of which are published monthly. An author who has access to *Publishers Weekly*, which is known throughout the trade as *PW* and is the bible of the book-publishing business, can learn, over a period of time, what subjects are hot or, better, where there appear to be holes in a particular field. *PW* (which many libraries have) will also tell you which editors are moving from house to house, which is useful if you know that a certain editor is particularly interested in certain subjects.

Publishers occasionally sponsor contests to attract new talent. These may take the form of manuscript solicitations directed toward either a specific group of authors, such as experts on Central America, or a particular topic, such as women's issues. The winning writer may receive a cash award, but in most cases will be honored simply by being published. Contests of this nature are often beneficial in that they give writers some positive exposure as well as the chance to see their work in print.

Although large publishing houses pay minimal attention to unsolicited manuscripts or proposals, and many are now refusing to look at them, smaller companies usually give them more consideration. Either way—particularly with a large house—*try to find someone who knows someone who works for the publisher you are after*. A good contact at a larger house can give you prompt attention and save weeks (or months) of suspense. If, as an unpublished writer, you submit an unsolicited piece "over the transom," as it is known in the trade, you should always include a self-addressed envelope with sufficient return postage—otherwise it is not likely to be sent back by any publisher, large or small.

An author would be well advised to search out a publisher who has specialized in a particular subject and developed a good reputation in that field. An author who has completed a book on Alabama history, for example, will be better off dealing with a southern regional publisher than with a New York publishing house. Similarly, a mountain climber would have a better chance of getting a book on climbing published by the Sierra Club or Mountaineers Books than through a leading general publisher.

To find out which publishers specialize in which fields, do some library and bookstore research: check the shelves to see who has been publishing books in your field, or look in *The Literary Market Place*. The LMP, as it is known, is an annual directory covering much of the book-publishing business, published by R.R. Bowker and available in most public libraries. You will find in it a complete list of U.S. publishers, Canadian publishers, and foreign publishers with U.S. offices. Each publisher's special interests are listed along with its name and address. At the end of this listing are a couple of shorter, less time-consuming lists— one of publishers listed by state, one of publishers listed by specialization.

The Role of the Literary Agent

Many authors market their work through literary agents. Having a literary agent can save a lot of time and can provide valuable counsel in contract negotiations. But, for the writer who has never had a book published, finding an agent can be as time-consuming as going directly to the publisher oneself, and it often is less frustrating to simply make the publisher contact on one's own. This is a situation where connections can make a difference; if you know anyone who knows someone in a publishing house, use that connection; likewise, if you know anyone with an agent, use that connection to see if the agent will look at your work and consider representing you.

Agents may freelance or be employed by large literary agencies. In either case, they tend to be highly individualistic and idiosyncratic. A writer should be aware of an agent's particular skills, preferences, and tastes so that, when it comes to selecting one, the author will feel confident that his or her interests will be well represented.

Agents may occasionally seek out new writers, but in most cases they are inundated by manuscripts sent to them. If, upon reading a given manuscript, the agent believes it can be placed with a publisher, the agent may agree to represent the author and contract with the author for a commission on royalties. Generally the agent's commission is 10 percent of domestic sales and 20 percent of foreign sales, the additional 10 percent to be paid to a foreign agent, but it can be higher or lower depending upon the agent's skill or reputation and upon the services offered. If an author has never been published and the work does not appear to have a broad appeal, some agents will charge, in addition to the commission, a fee payable in advance for any representation. Fees may be charged by reputable agents for reading the manuscripts of unknown writers, while other fees may be charged by unscrupulous agents who require large fees for minimal services. Such unethical agents rely on the writer's lack of experience and inability to find a publisher to milk the writer of an unearned fee.

To find out which agents are reliable and where to find them, you can attend writers' conferences or look in *The Literary Market Place*. A list of agents can also be obtained by writing either the Independent Literary Agents Association, Box 5257, F.D.R. Station, New York, New York 10150, or the Society of Authors' Representatives, 40 East 49th Street, New York, New York 10016. Rosters of well-known agents are included in two annuals, *The Fiction Writer's Market* or *The Writer's Market* (both published by Writer's Digest Books).

Agents are extremely selective in choosing authors to represent since, in order to stay in business, they must be sure that a substantial number of the authors they select will not only be placed, but will be profitable as well. To turn out publishable manuscripts, agents sometimes work with authors and help edit the material before submitting it to a publisher.

Placing Manuscripts and Proposals

Once a manuscript or proposal is accepted by an agent there are a number of recognized procedures for placing it.

The Auction

A method which has become popular in the last fifteen to twenty years is the auction (discussed in more detail in Chapter 3 of this book), in which an agent will invite interested publishers to review a work, informing them that bidding will be opened on a particular day and run for a prescribed period. The participants must evaluate the possible worth of the book and determine their potential profit in order to make an intelligent bid. In addition, the bidders must try to outbid the competition while keeping their bids as low as practical—obviously not a process for amateurs. Auctions are generally reserved for potential best sellers, and since the bidding is invariably steep (some might say excessive), it would be unusual for a small publisher to bid at an auction. However, small publishers do become involved in auctions, since they occasionally auction off subsidiary rights to successful books they have already published—for example, paperback or movie rights.

Multiple Submissions

Another method of marketing is referred to as the *multiple submission*. In this method an agent submits the work to several publishers. Any publisher interested in publishing the work will begin negotiating an author-publisher contract. Several publishers may express interest, in which case the author's agent will attempt to obtain the best terms during the negotiations.

As a matter of good will, agents will notify publishers when they make multiple submissions. This way, if one publisher starts talking about a contract, the agents will not be in the embarrassing position of having to admit that they are really waiting to see what a second publisher offers before they can start talking business.

Informal Contacts

The most common method of placement is much more informal than either the auction or the multiple submission. The majority of manuscripts or proposals are placed with publishers through informal conferences, phone calls, or letters. Here, the agent's reputation is one of the most important factors. Successful agents enjoy a relationship of trust and understanding with a large number of publishers. The agent knows that success depends not only upon the quality of the author's work, but also upon the imagination, efficiency, productivity, and preferences of the publisher, and the agent will place the work accordingly. Some publishers are willing to accept proposals with little or no review, completely trusting the agent's judgment if the agent is either a well-respected one or has submitted proposals that made money in the past. Publishers will, obviously, scrutinize work submitted by neophyte literary agents much more carefully.

NEGOTIATING CONTRACTS

An agent performs a wide variety of services, but when acting as matchmaker between an author and a publisher, the agent must be sensitive to the needs of both parties. If those needs are in conflict, the agent will have to act as a negotiator. This intermediary role is never more important than in contractual matters.

If a publisher is interested in a work, the process of negotiating an author-publisher contract begins. The publisher generally offers the author a form or standard contract, but such a contract is rarely accepted in entirety. Rather, a series of offers and counteroffers will ensue until mutually satisfactory terms have been agreed upon, or until it becomes apparent that an agreement cannot be reached.

The agent's role in contract negotiations will normally be to attempt to get the best contract possible for the author without unduly antagonizing the publisher. Most publishers are glad to negotiate with an agent because agents familiar with the legal and trade terminology and practices tend to facilitate the process. Moreover, since agents are constantly involved in negotiations between various authors and publishers, they are usually in the best position to identify an acceptable contract, and can be trusted to moderate unreasonable or unrealistic demands made by either party.

Agents can also serve the important function of getting a publisher excited about a book. Convincing the publisher that a work is valuable can make a tremendous difference in how the publisher decides to market the book, how many copies are initially run, and, in the long run, how successfully the book sells. Morton L. Janklow, a well-known literary agent who is also a lawyer, tells the story of his role in the publication of a book called *I'm Dancing As Fast As I Can*.[1] He read the book, found it tremendously powerful, and agreed to step into the contract negotiations. The book had been placed with Harper & Row for a $7,000 advance, a relatively small amount; 35,000 copies were to be printed. Janklow asked for a delay in publication, and subsequently sold the movie rights for a very large amount by starting a bidding war between Jill Clayburgh, Barbra Streisand, Ellen Burstyn, and Jane Fonda. Harper & Row was convinced of the value of the book, eventually printed 150,000 copies of it, and sold them all.

The Law of Agency

Since the agent acts as an intermediary between the author and publisher, an important question arises: To whom is the agent responsible? In order to answer that question it is necessary to look at the *law of agency*. All agents, including literary agents, are said to be *fiduciaries*, or *trustees*. As such they owe a duty of loyalty, good faith, and obedience to the person they are representing, referred to in legal terminology as the *principal*. The technical definition of agency is a fiduciary relationship, whereby the principal consents to have an agent act on the principal's behalf, subject to the principal's control and the consent of the agent to accept this role.[2] Thus, the agency relationship is based on consent rather than contract, which means that agents need not be paid for their work, though they customarily are.

Agency may be express (created by a written or oral agreement) or implied (created by the words and conduct of the parties to the agency in light of the surrounding circumstances).

The Fiduciary Duty of an Agent

If, as in most instances, the literary agent has consented to act on behalf of the author rather than the publisher, the author is the principal to whom the agent owes a fiduciary duty. As a fiduciary, the agent must exercise the utmost good faith in dealing with the author, which means, among other things, that the agent cannot represent another party whose interests are in conflict with those of the author, except with the consent of both principals. Moreover, the literary agent may not disclose confidential information, make deals that are essentially self-serving, or receive any secret profit. Should an author's agent act in such a way as to interfere with the author's best interests, the agent may be liable for breach of the fiduciary duty.

The Principal's Duties to the Agent

The author, as principal, in turn owes certain duties to the agent. For example, a principal is generally obligated to provide the agent with an opportunity to perform the services for which the agent was hired; to indemnify, or compensate, the agent for economic losses incurred in rendering that service, if there was an agreement to this effect; and, if there is an oral or written contract, to compensate the agent for services rendered.

The author/principal also must not unreasonably interfere with the performance of the agent's work. Whether or not the principal will be considered to have unreasonably interfered may depend, in part, upon the nature of the agreement with the agent. If, for example, a literary agent is given an exclusive agency—i.e., the exclusive right to market the author's work—the author as principal cannot hire another agent for that purpose. To do so would be to unreasonably interfere with the original agent's ability to perform. But this type of exclusive relationship will not prevent the author from engaging in personal efforts to sell a work to publishers, since one cannot be an agent for oneself. However, if the author and agent agree to an exclusive contract under which the agent is given the exclusive right to sell the work, the author can neither hire another agent for that purpose nor personally undertake to sell it.[3]

Should the author breach the duty or duties owed to the agent, the agent may sue to be reimbursed for expenses, paid for services, or indemnified against losses.

LIABILITY FOR THE AGENT'S BREACH OF CONTRACT

Since an agent is appointed by the author/principal and is subject to the principal's control, the principal may be liable to third parties for certain acts of the agent. Thus, it is extremely important for authors who engage the services of agents to understand some of the liability principles involved. Liability will depend on several factors. The first concept to understand here is that liability will depend on whether an act done by the agent is legally classified as involving a contract or a tort. If the act involves a contract, liability will hinge on whether the act was authorized. If the act was a *tort*, i.e., an injurious or damaging act, but not one involving a breach of contract, liability will depend on whether the agent is legally classified as an employee or an independent contractor.

CONTRACT LIABILITY: TYPES OF AUTHORITY

The author as principal will be liable to third parties for the agent's breach of contract only if the agent was acting within the scope of the agent's authority. The law recognizes three different types of agency authority: actual, apparent, and inherent.

Actual authority is that which the author/principal intentionally confers upon the agent either by written or oral agreement. This authority may vary considerably. For example, the agreement might include a power of attorney that grants the agent absolute authority to contract on behalf of the author. This is not the norm, however. Generally, the author gives the literary agent the authority to negotiate contracts, but reserves the right to sign the contract after the negotiations have been completed. Sometimes the author may limit the agent's authority to negotiating in regard to specific works only, such as nonfiction or fiction, or certain rights only, such as primary rights or serial rights. The agent's authority may also be confined to a particular geographical area.

Actual authority need not always be express; sometimes it may be implied from circumstances. Implied actual authority is that which the principal intentionally or carelessly allows the agent to believe the agent possesses. If, for example, the agreement with the agent expressly limits the literary agent's authority to negotiation with New York publishers only, but that agent has customarily negotiated nationwide, then the agent probably does have implied actual authority to negotiate with any publisher in the country. In this example, the agent may also have apparent authority to act.

Apparent authority is authority the author/principal has not actually granted to the agent, but which the author indicates to a third party has been granted to the agent. Thus, if the author leads a particular publisher to believe that the agent is authorized to negotiate on the author's behalf, even if the publisher is outside the scope of the agency contract, the author will be responsible for the agent's negotiations with that particular publisher. It should be emphasized that apparent authority exists only in dealings with the third party to whom the agent's authority has been stated. A fourth party cannot allege the agent's apparent authority because of hearing about it from the third party.

Finally, an agent may have *inherent authority* to act. This type of authority encompasses all acts and responsibilities that are customarily permitted to an agent while carrying out an agreed-upon responsibility.

GENERAL AGENTS AND SPECIAL AGENTS

The scope of an agent's inherent authority depends upon whether a person is a *general* or a *special agent*. The distinction between these two types of agents is based on the agent's tenure, or status, especially in regard to the duration of the agent's relationship with the author. A general agent is authorized to act in a series of transactions involving continuous service, such as a general manager or purchasing agent. A special agent, on the other hand, is authorized to act in a single transaction only, or possibly in a short series of transactions not involving continuous service. The general agent is usually considered to have inherent authority to act on behalf of the principal in all matters connected with the job the agent has been hired to do. The special agent's inherent authority, on the other hand, is limited to specific acts dictated by the principal's instructions or necessarily implied from the act to be done.

If hired to market one manuscript and its subsidiary rights, the literary agent or special agent will not be considered to be continuously employed. The agent's inherent authority, therefore, will probably not extend beyond those acts which are actually or apparently authorized.

Should the literary agent be in the continuous employment of the author, and therefore a general agent, the inherent authority will encompass all acts customarily associated with literary agents. According to the Society of Authors' Representatives, a literary agent is customarily authorized to examine and negotiate contracts or contract modifications, and to advise the author of the advantages of accepting or rejecting such contracts. Since literary agents are generally not empowered to execute a contract—to actually complete the contract by signing it—in no event will an author be bound to a contract signed by the agent under the claim that the agent had inherent authority to execute it.

RATIFICATION OF UNAUTHORIZED ACTS

Ratification is an important concept in agency law. The term describes affirmation or confirmation by a principal of a prior, unauthorized act by an agent. By ratifying, the principal affirms the unauthorized act and is legally bound by it as if it had been initially authorized. Thus, although the author/principal will be liable for any of the agent's acts for which the agent has actual, apparent, or inherent authority, the principal will not be liable if the agent acts without authority *unless* the unauthorized act was once ratified.

Ratification may be express or implied from any act, words, or course of conduct which tends to show the principal's intent to ratify. Even silence may constitute ratification. If, for example, an author has full knowledge of a contract executed without authority by an agent, and accepts the benefits of the contract, the author may have ratified the act and therefore be bound to the contract.

Several conditions must be met before an unauthorized act is considered effectively ratified: (1) the act must be lawful (thus a crime can never be ratified); (2) the principal must have been in existence at the time of the act and at the time of ratification and, in addition, must have been legally competent at both times;* (3) the act may be rati-

---

* This wording is used because the definition thus covers business organizations as well as people yet unborn. For example, a newborn baby cannot ratify acts alleged to have been performed on behalf of the infant before birth. Similarly, a corporation cannot ratify acts performed by a promoter before the corporation was created.

fied only by the principal, which is to say the person upon whose behalf the unauthorized act was performed; and (4) the principal must have knowledge of all material facts. Another condition imposed by some courts is that the principal must ratify before the third party involved has withdrawn from the transaction, provided that the third party has informed either the agent or the principal of the intention to withdraw.[4]

The agent alone will be liable to the third party for breach of contract if the agent did not have authority (actual, apparent, or inherent) or the act was not ratified. Where the act was authorized or ratified, the agent, as well as the principal, may be liable depending upon whether the principal (and thus the agency relationship) was *disclosed*, *partially disclosed*, or *not disclosed*. If the agency relationship was fully disclosed, generally the principal alone will be a party to the contract, and is thus liable for its breach.

As a general rule, the agent will be liable as well if the principal was partially disclosed or undisclosed. The principal is partially disclosed if (1) the agent reveals that the agent is acting as an agent but does not say on whose behalf, or (2) the principal is named but there is no indication of an agency relationship. The principal is undisclosed where the agent does not name the principal or indicate the agency relationship, but instead appears to the third party to be acting alone. If both the agent and principal are liable for the same breach, the third party cannot sue them both but must elect to sue one or the other.

Liability for the Agent's Torts

The liability of a principal for an agent's torts (acts that are injurious or damaging, but not involving a breach of contract) is determined, in part, by the nature of the agent's employment; that is, by whether the agent is legally considered to be an independent contractor or a servant. The term *servant*, in the legal sense, applies not only to domestic help, but to an employee over whom an employer has more control than the employer has over an independent contractor. Thus, where the author has retained the right of control and approval over most or all of someone's activities and decisions, the law will probably regard that person as a servant, whether or not the author/principal actually exercises the right of control or approval. It is the right to exercise control, and not the actual exercising of it, that governs. It is highly unlikely that literary agents will be considered servants, though other helpers such as secretaries, research assistants, and the like will be.

If the person is a servant, the author will be liable for the servant's tortious acts only where those acts were within the servant's scope of employment—i.e., where the activities which led to the torts were part and parcel of the servant's occupation. If the servant is acting independently or is on a personal frolic, tortious acts are not within the scope of employment and the principal will therefore not be liable.

If the principal has retained only the right to control or approve the end result of the agent's activities, and leaves the means to the agent's discretion, the agent is probably an independent contractor. This is likely the characterization which would apply to a literary agent.

The author/principal will generally not be liable for the torts of an independent contractor, but there are exceptions. First, the principal will be liable for any tortious acts of the independent contractor that involve so-called *non-delegable duties*. These are duties which are so important to the public welfare that the principal has legal responsibility for their proper performance even if that performance is delegated to an independent contractor. For example, a writer will be liable for not procuring any required business licenses and may be subject to a fine even though the writer delegated responsibility for obtaining the licenses to an independent contractor who failed to do so. Similarly, a writer who writes a defamatory book will be liable even though a private detective had been hired to check out the accuracy of all facts. Second, the principal will be liable for acts of the independent contractor which are in and of themselves inherently dangerous or ultrahazardous, such as the use of explosives. Third, the principal will be liable if the principal did not exercise due care in hiring or retaining the independent contractor. For example, if the principal continues to employ a contractor known to be violent when angry, the principal may be liable to others hurt by the contractor. And fourth, the principal will be liable for deceit if the independent contractor makes authorized misrepresentations to a third party.

The independent contractor as well as the servant will, generally, be liable for their own tortious acts to third parties. This is the rule even when the servant is acting within the scope of employment. Where the principal is also liable for the tortious act of the agent (whether the agent is a servant or an independent contractor), both principal and agent are liable, and aggrieved third parties can sue them either together or separately. In other words, the third party does not have to choose between suing one party or the other, as would be the situation in the case of breach of contract.

TERMINATION OF AGENCY

The authority of the agent to act on behalf of the principal ceases with the termination of the relationship. By law, the relationship automatically terminates (1) upon the death or loss of capacity of either the agent or the principal, (2) when the goal of the agency becomes impossible to achieve, (3) once the purpose of the relationship has been fulfilled, or (4) when the time period for which the agency was created has elapsed.

The agency can generally be terminated voluntarily if the author/principal revokes, or if the agent renounces, the agency. With the exception discussed in the next paragraph, the parties are free to revoke or renounce at any time, regardless of whether the agency is governed by a contract, since the agency relationship is consensual. However, if a contract is involved, termination of the agency may result in liability for its breach. If, for example, the contract calls for the agency to last for five years, either party is free to terminate prior to that time, but not without incurring liability for damages.

The only exception to the rule of voluntary termination is an agency relationship that involves a power coupled with an interest. In this situation neither party may terminate prior to the expiration of the interest. A power coupled with an interest exists when the agent has a vested interest in the thing or property the agreement was created to deal with. For example, a literary agent might have a power coupled with an interest if the agent has contracted with the author for partial ownership of a work. The agent's power to negotiate or execute contracts for that work would thus be coupled with an interest—an ownership interest—and the agent's power would therefore be irrevocable. But when an agent is compensated simply for acting as an agent, as is the case when an agent receives a commission for negotiating an author-publisher contract, there is no power coupled with an interest, since the agent does not have an interest in the contract itself. A mere interest in the proceeds from the sale is not sufficient to make the power irrevocable. The concept of a power coupled with an interest is extremely complex, and a lawyer should be consulted if an irrevocable agency is desired or involved. It is not uncommon for a literary agent to have a provision in the author-publisher contract stating that the agent will continue to be paid under the contract even though the writer has terminated the relationship.

NOTICE TO THIRD PARTIES

When the agency is terminated, assuming the agent is a general agent, such as one who has been hired to represent the writer on an ongoing basis, the principal must actually give notice to third parties who have dealt with the agent, and "reasonable notice" to third parties who have knowledge of the agency but who have not actually dealt with the agent. Reasonable notice means reasonable efforts to notify these third parties, whether or not the efforts succeed and the third parties actually receive notice of the termination. The principal is not required to give notice to third parties who neither have dealt with the general agent nor know of the relationship. If the principal is required to give notice but fails to do so, the principal remains liable for the acts of the agent even though that agent's authority has in fact been terminated. The principal is not required to give notice of termination of a special agency, which is a situation where the agent has merely been hired for a single project or to accomplish a single goal. Third parties who deal with a special agent do so at their own risk.

SUGGESTED PRECAUTIONS

To protect against possible liability, an author should choose an experienced, legitimate agent and clearly delineate the scope of that agent's authority in a well-drafted agency agreement checked over by a lawyer familiar with publishing, since most established agencies have their own form contracts. Care should be taken to define the scope of the agent's authority to bind the author/principal.

Many lawyers act as literary agents on behalf of their clients, but the attorney who does this should take care. Attorneys' malpractice insurance policies generally provide that coverage is suspended for an insured who is engaged in business counseling as distinguished from the practice of law. Whether finding a publisher and negotiating an author-publisher contract would be considered business counseling is not clear, but it is likely that malpractice insurance companies would attempt to argue that it is.

6

Alternatives to Large Book-Publishing Houses

It is inevitable that many writers will be frustrated in their attempts to reach an audience simply because large trade publishers will not accept their manuscripts. Unfortunately, rejections by these publishers are usually based on profit considerations rather than merit. For most book publishers, staying in business means publishing only those works for which there is a likelihood of earning a profit in order to justify the investment necessary for publication, distribution, and promotion. A writer's work must be seen as commanding at least a large enough market to translate into the volume of sales necessary for the publisher to realize a fair return on its investment. In short, trade-book publishers cannot afford to take too many risks.

A writer, on the other hand, who has already put significant energy into completing a manuscript, will be less easily discouraged than a publisher by the risk of failing to make a profit on a book. Fortunately, for the resourceful writer whose work may not command a large commercial market, several alternatives exist. These include university presses, small presses, writers' cooperatives, vanity presses, self-publishing, copublishing, and subsidy publishing. University presses and small presses generally require the same submission process as large publishers. Be aware that some small publishers are not entirely profit-oriented, making them a particularly attractive alternative. Writers' cooperatives fund small-scale publishing efforts through dues paid by the members, and their criteria for publishing vary.

VANITY PRESSES

Vanity presses are a form of author-subsidized publication, with costs paid by the author to provide an automatic "profit" to the publisher, who will accept all submitted works, regardless of quality. Perhaps the biggest disadvantage to using vanity presses, aside from the expense, is the stigma attached to them. It is very rare that vanity-press works are reviewed. *Publishers Weekly* "Forecasts" and other major review media completely ignore them, and bookstores and libraries tend to view them with a healthy degree of cynicism. Nevertheless, for the writer who is not concerned with reviews or distribution of a book, but simply wants it to be competently printed and bound—as in the case of family memoirs, perhaps—a vanity publisher is not a bad way to go.

An advantage that is sometimes argued in regard to vanity publishing is that contracts may be individually tailored to an author's needs. Vanity presses operate somewhat like printers in that they will try to provide exactly what the author wants, at an agreed-upon fee. The writer can pick and choose among available services, which generally include design, proofreading, promotion, advertising, distribution, and bookkeeping. Some houses will provide editing services, but these services are almost always minimal and should never be relied upon to truly improve a work. Since vigorous editing often improves a book, the author should employ a competent freelance editor.

A seeming advantage in contracting with vanity presses is that the contracts often include generous royalty clauses or percentage returns on sales. Such promises are largely illusory, however, since sales are very rarely substantial. Less than 10 percent of authors get back their investment from sales after publication by a vanity press. One reason for low sales is the general lack of regard for vanity publishers throughout the industry. Another factor is that the presses need not worry about recouping expenses through sales, as the author has already covered the costs, and the press has made its profit, so sales motivation is low and vanity presses rarely have a distribution network.

Writers should approach advertisements by vanity houses with caution, since such ads are often misleading. Some courts have attempted to suppress these misleading advertisements and compel publishers to deliver all that is promised. In one case, a court found that a vanity press had committed fraud in using the word *publisher* in its advertisements because it had failed to undertake any of the distribution, marketing, or promotional functions of a normal publisher.[1] In another case, a vanity publisher was enjoined from advertising a 40 percent royalty rate because the use of the term *royalty* was misleading.[2] The court upheld a Federal Trade Commission order requiring vanity publishers to cease representing to the public, through use of the term *royalties* or in any other manner, that the publishing company would make payments to the author based on sale of the author's book without immediately disclosing that initial costs must be paid in whole or substantial part by the author.

A writer should always take special care in negotiating a contract with a vanity press. Because the press has no stake in eventual sales, the author is the only party interested in having the contract provide for *all* services necessary for distribution and sales. Gaps in the contract can lead to expensive litigation. Thus, key terms should al-

ways be defined. For example, if the contract provides
that the publisher will produce a complete first edition of
the book, the contract should state exactly what *first edition*
means. Vanity houses have been known to deliver unbound pages to an author because the contract did not
specifically call for the book to be bound. If the author
wishes to maintain some control over design, promotion,
or any other service, all details should be spelled out. An
author contracting with a vanity press will undoubtedly
benefit from legal advice. At the very least, the author
should not go into negotiation without a very clear picture
of what is expected.

SELF-PUBLICATION AND COPUBLICATION

Like vanity-press publication, self-publishing requires
the author to finance the costs of publishing, distribution,
and promotion. Unlike the vanity press, self-publishing
has a well-respected history. Such respectable writers as
Walt Whitman, Edgar Rice Burroughs, Beatrix Potter,
Virginia Woolf, and Stephen Crane are only a few examples of famous writers who at some point chose self-
publication as a means of reaching their audiences. Thus,
a writer who self-publishes generally runs less risk of incurring a stigma harmful to future career goals.

Copublishing is basically the same as self-publishing,
except that the author shares the costs of publication, and
the profits, with a copublisher. The copublisher may be
another author or a trade publisher who does not want to
take on the full risk of publishing the book. In copublishing as well as self-publishing, the author often retains significant control over production and promotion.

One important consideration for the self-publishing
writer is that his or her work will not be denied reviewers'
attention simply because it did not progress through the
editorial offices of a publishing house. For the writer who
is considering self-publishing but needs help in polishing

the manuscript, there are many good freelance editors throughout the United States. *The Literary Market Place* contains lengthy, although not exhaustive, listings of editorial services. If possible, look for someone whose experience is with books.

Once the work is ready for printing, the writer will contract with a printer to print, and a bindery to bind, a specified number of books. Many avenues exist for distribution and promotion, but costs can be high, especially where the writer has few marketing contacts. Most cities have consultants who will assist with making the necessary contacts and arrangements for printing, binding, and distribution. It is essential to check out the reputation of any consultant before contracting with one. One way to do this is to contact the local Better Business Bureau or state attorney general's office for consumer protection or any local publishing or writers' organizations. Clearly, a necessary prerequisite to the decision to self-publish is a *realistic* appraisal of total costs and the potential return. Anyone considering self-publishing should get bids from typesetters, printers, and binders once plans are definite as to what design and form the book will take and the audience it will be most likely to reach. Self-publication is essentially a small-business enterprise, but no matter how small the scope, generating and financing the enterprise will require a significant amount of energy and cash.

Since professional book publishers take years to learn their business, it is unrealistic to believe that a few inquiries here and there are all that are necessary to self-publish. If you are thinking of undertaking the publication of your own work, learn everything you can about how to do it. A library is the place to start (there are several good books on the subject). If you can find an experienced book publisher to serve as a consultant, learn everything you can from that person, and if there is a consultation fee involved, do not be stingy. The fee could save you thousands of dollars. Horror stories abound regarding self-publishers who believe that because they are competent writers, they can learn overnight how to attractively and economically design and manufacture a book and then distribute it to book stores throughout the country.

Certain types of books can be self-published more practically than others. The ideal book for self-publication is a nonfiction book (a how-to, for example) by an author who is an expert in the field. In these situations the expert/author will have direct access to an audience and be well equipped to promote the book in lectures or articles published in the field. Regional books, or books with a local focus on subjects such as travel or cooking, also have more accessible audiences. Promotion can be done on local radio or through local bookstores. In cases like these, if promotion costs can be kept down, lower shipping and order-fulfillment costs may even make self-publishing more profitable than going to a commercial publisher.

Poetry is a particularly logical candidate for self-publication simply because commercial publishers accept only very well-known poets, and even those are rarely a source of profit. Self-published poetry is not profitable either, but it may be the only way for a poet to see a number of his or her poems in print. Once the book is out, the poet should schedule readings, along with placing the book in local and regional book stores.

Anyone who self-publishes a work must exercise extra care to avoid legal problems. Thus an attorney specializing in publishing law should be consulted whenever a question arises so that precautionary steps can be taken. Defamation, privacy, and copyright issues can be difficult to evaluate. For example, a self-published writer should never hesitate to request copyright permission if use of another person's copyrighted work is contemplated, even if only a few phrases are involved or the use appears to be a fair use and thus legal. Gambling with the cost of litigation is never justified for the self-publisher, who cannot hope to absorb the costs of successfully defending a lawsuit. See the section on fair use in the next chapter for procedures for requesting permission to reprint copyrighted work.

Another legal consideration especially relevant to the self-publisher is the effect of incorporation. Incorporating an enterprise, no matter how small its scope, may well provide significant tax advantages and liability shields. For a detailed discussion of incorporation, see Chapter 1.

SUBSIDY PUBLICATION

One more option remains for the writer who cannot find a publisher: *subsidy publishing*. Again, it costs money, but not as much as some of the other possibilities. In this situation, the author contributes to the cost, but the publishing is done by a trade publishing house. The publishing house provides all the editing, design, typesetting, printing/binding, sales, and distribution that it would give to any other of its books. In addition, the publisher puts its own imprint on the book, giving it respectability in the eyes of the rest of the industry. What the author contributes and gets back will be negotiable. This is often a sensible route for the writer whose work is competent and worthwhile and that the publisher feels is worthy but would appeal to too small a market to be profitable for the publisher.

In sum, self-publication, copublication, or subsidy publication are often better options than vanity publishing. The author avoids any stigma and retains control. Self-publishing costs, if properly figured, will include the time and money spent promoting a book. Costs for the vanity press seldom will. For further information on self-publishing, a number of books have been published in the last few years that cover the subject thoroughly. *The Self-Publishing Manual: How to Write, Print & Sell Your Own Book,* by Dan Poynter (Para Publishing), is the most highly respected book on this subject. *How to Get Happily Published,* by Judith Appelbaum and Nancy Evans (hardcover, Harper & Row; paperback, New American Library), has an excellent annotated bibliography.

7

Copyright Law

Until the eighteenth century, written works were published without the protection of a copyright law. The first copyright law in England, the Statute of Anne, was passed in 1710. For existing works, authors were given the exclusive right of publication for twenty-one years. New works were protected for fourteen years, and the copyright could be renewed for another fourteen years if the author was still living. In order to get copyright protection under this law, the author had to register the title of the work with a designated register and deposit copies in certain libraries.

Copyright law in the United States has its foundations in the Constitution, which provides in Article I, section 8 that Congress shall have the power "to promote the progress of science and the useful arts, by securing for limited time to authors and inventors the exclusive right to their respective writings and discoveries." The first Congress exercised this power and enacted a copyright law. The legislation was periodically revised by later Congresses until after 1909.

The Copyright Act resulting from amendments passed

in 1909 remained in effect for more than half a century despite periodic complaints that it no longer reflected contemporary technology. At the time the 1909 Act was passed, the printing press was still the primary means of disseminating information. But new technology such as radio, television, videotape, computer software, and microfilm created the need for a revision that would provide specific statutory copyright protection for newer information systems.

The 1909 Act was finally substantially revised in 1976. The Copyright Revision Act of 1976 became effective on January 1, 1978, and covers works created or published on or after that date. The creation of copyright in all works published prior to January 1, 1978—the greater body of works now in print—is governed by the 1909 Act. Rights other than creation, such as duration of copyright, infringement penalties, and infringement remedies are governed by the new law. It is important to be aware of the basic differences in the two laws, and which law applies to a given work.

The 1976 Act was a product of compromise. Many of the clauses of the Act were drafted to appease competing special-interest groups. As a result, much of the language is ambiguous. In time these ambiguities will be clarified by the courts, but for now parts of modern copyright law resemble a guessing game.

Clearly, you as a writer need to know what protection you have under the present law, and all of the information in this chapter will be pertinent to you. Be aware, though, that if you are the author of a book, your publisher will take care of the details of copyright notice, deposit, and registration, so you need not concern yourself about dealing with the Copyright Office. Check your contract, of course, to make sure that the copyright is to be in your name.

FEDERAL PREEMPTION OF STATE COPYRIGHT LAW

One of the problems with the 1909 Act was that it was not the exclusive source of copyright law. Copyright protection or its equivalent was also provided by common law (i.e., that body of law developed by the courts independent of statutes) and various state laws. This caused considerable confusion since securing copyright protection or avoiding copyright infringement required careful examination of a variety of different laws.

The 1976 Act largely resolved this problem by preempting and nullifying all other copyright law—in other words, it is now the only legislation generally governing copyright protection. The Act does not, however, preempt the common law or the statutes of any state for copyright claims arising prior to January 1, 1978.

WHAT IS COPYRIGHT?

A copyright is actually a collection of five exclusive rights. First is the right to reproduce a work by any means. The scope of this right can be hard to define, especially when it involves photocopying, microform, videotape, and the like. Under the Copyright Act of 1976, someone may be permitted to reproduce protected works only if such reproduction involves either a fair or an exempted use as defined by the Act, which I will be explaining later in this chapter.

Second is the right to prepare derivative works based on the copyrighted work. A *derivative work* is one that transforms or adapts the subject matter of one or more pre-existing works. Derivative works of a book might include translations into other languages as well as adaptations into another medium, such as television or film.

Third is the right to distribute copies to the public for sale or lease. However, once an author sells a work, the right to control the further disposition of that work is, usually, ended. This rule, known as the *first-sale doctrine*, does not apply if the work is merely in the possession of someone else temporarily by virtue of bailment,* rental, lease, or loan.[1] In these instances the copyright owner retains the right to control the further sale or other disposition of the work. Moreover, the first-sale doctrine does not apply if the author or copyright owner has a contract with the purchaser restricting the purchaser's freedom to dispose of the work. In such a case, if the purchaser exceeds the restrictions, there may be liability. In this situation the copyright owner's remedy will be governed by contract law rather than copyright law.

Fourth is the right to perform the work publicly.

Fifth is the right to display the work publicly. Once the copyright owner has sold a copy of the work, however, the owner of the copy has the right to display that copy.

Who Owns the Copyright?

The general rule regarding ownership of copyright is that the *author*—the creator—of a work is the initial owner of the copyright in that work. Under the old law, when a work was sold, ownership of a common-law copyright was presumed to pass to the purchaser of that work unless the author explicitly provided otherwise in a written agreement. In other words, there was a presumption in the law that a sale included not only the work itself, but all rights in that work. However, merely granting a publisher the right to publish and sell the work (the right an author most commonly grants) would not be equivalent to an assignment of the copyright; the author would retain the copyright. The Copyright Act of 1976 reverses the pre-

---

* Bailment is the legal term for legal temporary possession of someone else's property; parking a car in a paid parking lot establishes a bailment; so does leaving a manuscript with a publisher who has requested it.

sumption that the sale of a work carries the copyright with it. Today, unless there is a written agreement that transfers the copyright to the publisher of a work, the author retains the copyright.

If the author of a work owns the copyright, the author also owns the exclusive rights. The authors of a *joint work* are co-owners of the copyright in the work.[2] A joint work is a work prepared by more than one author "with the intention that their contributions be merged into inseparable or interdependent parts of a unitary whole." Thus, whatever profit one coauthor makes from use of the work must be shared equally with the others unless they have a written agreement that states otherwise. If there is no intention to create a unitary, or indivisible, work, each author may own the copyright to that author's individual contribution. For example, one author may own the rights to the written text and another the rights in the illustrations.

Works considered to be *works for hire* are an important exception to the general rule that an author owns the copyright in a book he or she has written. If a book was written by an employee on the job, the law considers the book a work for hire, and the writer's employer will own the copyright. But the parties involved can avoid application of this rule if they write their contract carefully. If the employment contract itself provides, for example, that creating the copyrightable material in question is not part of the "scope of employment," the employee will likely be considered the owner of the copyright.

A work written on commission will be considered a work for hire only if the parties have signed a written agreement to that effect. This is also true if the work is specially ordered or commissioned as either a contribution to a collective work, a translation, a supplementary work (one that introduces, revises, comments upon or assists a work by another author), a compilation, an instructional text, answer material for a test, or an atlas. Thus, if there is no contractual agreement to the contrary, the author will own the copyright on these types of works.

A copyright owner may sell the entire copyright or any part of it, or may license any right within it. To accomplish this there must be a written document that describes the rights conveyed. The document must be signed by the copyright owner or the owner's duly authorized agent. A license authorizing a particular use of a work can be granted orally, but it will be revocable at the will of the copyright owner.

It is not uncommon for a writer to become the assignee or licensee of another person's copyright. This could happen, say, when a writer wishes to incorporate Ms. Smith's illustrations, photographs, recordings, writings, or other work into the writer's work; in this case the writer will often enter into a licensing agreement or assignment of ownership with Ms. Smith. Such an agreement is necessary to authorize use of the copyrighted work.

Both an assignment of ownership and a licensing agreement can, and should, be recorded with the Copyright Office. When the transaction is recorded, the rights of the assignee or licensee are protected in much the same way as the rights of an owner of real estate are protected by recording a deed. In a case of conflicting transfers of rights, if both transactions are recorded within one month of the execution, the person whose transaction was completed first will prevail. If the transactions are not recorded within a month, the one who records first will prevail. A nonexclusive license will prevail over any unrecorded transfer of ownership. Finally, before a transferee (either an assignee or licensee) can sue a third party for infringement, the document of transfer must be recorded. The cost to record a transfer is only ten dollars and is tax-deductible if it is a business expense. Considering the potential consequences of not recording a transfer of rights, the assignee or licensee is well advised to record.

One section of the 1976 Copyright Act pertains to the involuntary transfer of a copyright. This section, which states that such a transfer will be held invalid,[3] was included primarily because of problems arising from U.S. recognition of foreign copyrights. For example, if a country did not want a dissident author's works to be published, it could claim to be the copyright owner and thereby refuse to license foreign publication. Under the 1976 Act, the foreign government must produce a signed record of the transfer before its ownership will be recognized. Another situation covered in this section deals with a transfer that at first glance might appear to be involuntary but is not. This is the case where the courts transfer a copyright in a bankruptcy proceeding or in the foreclosure of a mortgage secured by the copyright. Such a transfer is considered voluntary rather than involuntary because the copyright owner freely chose to declare bankruptcy or to mortgage the copyright, even though the owner may not have chosen the consequences.

TERMINATION OF COPYRIGHT TRANSFERS AND LICENSES

It has not been unusual for a writer confronted with an unequal bargaining position vis-a-vis the publisher to transfer all rights in the copyright to the publisher for a pittance, only to see the work become valuable at a later date. The 1976 Copyright Act, in response to this injustice, provides that after a certain period has lapsed, the author, or certain other parties in special cases, may terminate the transfer of the copyright and reclaim the rights. Thus, the new Act grants the author a second chance to exploit his or her work after the original transfer of copyright. This right to terminate a transfer is called *termination interest*.

In most cases, the termination interest will belong to the author or authors. But if the author is no longer alive and is survived by a spouse but no children, the surviving spouse owns the termination interest. If the deceased author is not survived by a spouse, ownership of the interest belongs to any surviving children in equal shares. If the decedent is survived by both spouse and children, the interest is divided so that the spouse receives 50 percent and the children receive the remaining 50 percent in equal proportions.

Where the termination interest is owned by more than one party, be they joint authors or an author's survivors, a majority of the owners must agree to terminate. Under the new Act, the general rule is that termination may be effected at any time within a five-year period beginning at the end of the thirty-fifth year from the date on which the rights were transferred. If, however, the transfer included the right of publication, termination may go into effect at any time within a five-year period beginning at the end of thirty-five years from the date of publication, or forty years from the date of transfer, whichever is shorter.

The party wishing to terminate the transferred interest must serve an advance written notice on the transferee. This notice must state the intended termination date and must be served not less than two and no more than ten years prior to the stated termination date. A copy of the notice must be recorded in the Copyright Office before the effective date of termination.

WHAT CAN BE COPYRIGHTED?

The Constitution permits Congress to provide protection for a limited time to authors for their *writings*. Although there have been debates over what constitutes a writing, there has never been any doubt that this term includes printed works. Congress avoided use of the word *writings* in describing the scope of copyright protection. Instead it grants copyright protection to "original works of authorship fixed in any tangible medium of expression."

Legislative comments on this section of the Act suggest that Congress chose to use this wording rather than *writings* in order not to exhaust its full constitutional power to legislate in the copyright field.

The 1976 Act expressly exempts from copyright protection "any idea, procedure, process, system, method of operation, concept, principle, or discovery." In short, a copyright extends only to the *expression* of creations of the mind, not to the ideas themselves. Frequently there is no clear line of division between an idea and its expression, a problem which will be considered in greater detail in the "Infringement and Remedies" section of this chapter. For now, it is sufficient to note that a pure idea, such as a mathematical equation, cannot be copyrighted no matter how original or creative it is.

The law and the courts generally avoid using copyright law to arbitrate the public's taste. Thus, a work is not denied a copyright even if it makes no pretense to aesthetic or academic merit. The only requirements are that a work be original and show some creativity of authorship. Originality—as distinguished from uniqueness—requires that a book be written independently, but it need not be the only one of its kind. For example, a telephone book can be copyrighted, since it is original to the extent that its contents were not obtained from another telephone book. The requirements of authorship are met by the arrangement of names into alphabetical order and their placement in columns opposite their telephone numbers.[4] Note, however, that since the idea of telephone listings cannot be copyrighted, another phone book, virtually identical to the first, could be copyrighted simultaneously. The only requirement would be that the author of the second phone book acquire the names through independent research.

In the past, the Copyright Office occasionally denied protection to works considered immoral or obscene, even though it had no express authority for doing so. Today this practice has changed. The Copyright Office will not attempt to decide whether a work is obscene or not, and copyright registration will not be refused because of the questionable character of any work.[5]

The Copyright Office is empowered by the Copyright Act to draw up specific regulations defining the scope of copyright protection. One of these regulations states that "blank forms and similar works, designed to record rather than convey information, cannot be copyrighted." In this category would fall timecards, scorecards, address books, and the like. Even items like these, however, have been granted copyright protection for certain creative embellishments.[6]

Not everything in a copyrighted work is protected. For example, a title cannot be copyrighted, nor can slogans and mottos. Moreover, the Copyright Office has repeatedly refused to protect typefaces, no matter how original, reasoning that they, like slogans and titles, involve too little creativity or authorship to warrant protection.[7] However, some of these types of works can be protected under trademark law.

Whether a fictional character can be protected by copyright has caused the courts considerable difficulty. An early case involved Dashiell Hammett's great detective Sam Spade.[8] Hammett had licensed his copyright to the movie studio which was producing *The Maltese Falcon*. Later he granted a radio station a license to use Sam Spade in some radio mysteries. The court held that this did not violate the movie studio's rights since the license granted to the movie company did not include an exclusive right to the character of Sam Spade.

The current theory is that a character can be copyrighted only if the character is made sufficiently distinct, so a stock character is not protected. When the character is depicted in cartoons, it is sufficiently delineated. Superman and Mickey Mouse, for example, have both been successfully protected from being copied.[9 & 10]

Under the 1909 Act, most books and periodicals that qualified for copyright had to be published with the proper notice in order to get statutory protection. The 1976 Act dramatically changes the law in this respect. An author's works are now automatically copyrighted once they are "fixed in a tangible medium of expression"—typed, for instance. However, copyright can be lost if a work is later published without the proper notice, unless the "savings" clause from Section 405 of the Act applies. (The savings clause enables a writer to save a copyright in certain situations.) For further discussion of retrieving copyright protection after publication without notice, see "Deposit and Registration" later in this chapter. Works not fixed in tangible form, such as dramatic improvisations or unwritten speeches, are protectable, if at all, by common law or state statutes.

Once the copyright on a work has expired, or been lost, the work enters the public domain, where it can be exploited by anyone in any manner. An author can, however, get a copyright on a work derived from a work in the public domain if a distinguishable variation is created.[11] This means, for example, that the Latin text of Virgil's *Aeneid* cannot be copyrighted, but an original translation can be. As a result, no one would be able to copy the translation, whereas anyone can copy Virgil's original. The translation is thus a copyrightable derivative work of a pre-existing work. Other examples of copyrightable derivative works would include dramatizations, fictionalizations, film versions, abridgments, condensations, annotated editions, and any other work "recast, transformed, or adapted" from an original.

Compilations are also copyrightable, as long as the preexisting materials are gathered and arranged in a new or original form. Compilations such as magazines can be copyrightable as a whole even though individual contributions or articles are individually copyrighted.

DURATION OF COPYRIGHT

The Constitution permits Congress to grant copyright protection only "for limited times." The 1909 Copyright Act granted an author copyright protection for a twenty-eight-year period which could be renewed for only one additional twenty-eight-year period. Under the 1976 Act, copyright exists during the life of the author plus fifty years. There are no renewals for copyrights created under the 1976 Act. However, the 1976 Act does provide renewals for copyrights which were created under the 1909 Act and were not yet in their final renewal term when the 1976 Act became effective. For example, copyrights granted under the 1909 Act in their first twenty-eight-year term as of January 1, 1978, will continue for the remainder of the twenty-eight-year term and can be renewed for another forty-seven years. Copyrights granted under the 1909 Act and in their second twenty-eight-year term as of January 1, 1978, will automatically receive an extension of the number of years that would create a term of seventy-five years from the date copyright was first given. Applications for renewal must be made within one year before the first term ends. In all cases, copyright terms end on December 31 of the given year.

An author may assign the right to renew a copyright granted under the 1909 Act. In order for the renewal to be effective, the assignee must renew in the author's name. Since the assignee can act only in the name of the author, the assignment right becomes void after the author dies. In such cases the renewal right reverts to the author's legal survivors.

As previously noted, the employer who owns the copyright in a work done by an employee in the scope of employment is considered the author of the work and therefore owns the renewal right. However, if the employer should assign the renewal rights and then die before the renewal, the right does not revert to the employer's heirs. Since the 1909 statute did not distinguish between works by employees and works by independent contractors in works made for hire, there is some question as to whether the renewal rights on commissioned works revert to the author's heirs upon the author's death.

If the copyrighted work is a joint work, any of the authors may renew for the benefit of all. If the copyrights are owned separately, each author must renew individually. The copyright in a composite work, such as a dictionary, can be renewed by the owner of the copyright even if the owner was not an author.

For copyrights created under the 1976 Act, there is no renewal and thus no right to assign. If the work is created by one author, the work is copyrighted for the rest of the author's life plus fifty years. If the work was created jointly, the copyright expires fifty years after the last author dies. The Copyright Office has been keeping records of authors' deaths since the mid-1960s, but if the office does not have a record of an author's death, the author is assumed dead seventy-five years after the first publication date or a hundred years after creation, whichever occurs first. A composite work or a work for hire is copyrighted for seventy-five years after publication or a hundred years from creation, whichever expires first. The same applies to anonymous and pseudonymous works.

Works that were unpublished, but were fixed in a tangible medium prior to January 1, 1978 form their own special category for purposes of determining the duration of copyright protection. Since they are unpublished, they do not come under the 1909 Act. But since they were fixed in a tangible medium prior to January 1, 1978, they do not automatically come under the 1976 Act. Prior to the 1976 Act, these types of works were covered by state law, which protected them in perpetuity. The 1976 Act extends federal protection for these works for a limited amount of time: the author's life plus fifty years. The Act also provides that the earliest date when such a copyright can expire is December 31, 2002. If the work is published before that date, the term of copyright shall not expire before December 31, 2027, a twenty-five year extension. There are many unpublished works whose authors have been dead well over fifty years. For example, authors such as T.S. Eliot and Eugene O'Neill have left unpublished works which, in accordance with their wills, may not be published until some future date. The statute has not deprived these works of their potential value to their owners, since protection is automatically extended until December 31, 2002, but it does encourage owners of unpublished letters and manuscripts to publish these works before December 31, 2002, in order to obtain the twenty-five-year extension.

CREATION OF COPYRIGHT

As discussed earlier, all works are now automatically protected by the federal copyright law as soon as they are fixed in a tangible medium. There are no formal requirements of registration or deposit of copies. Unpublished works can be registered with the Copyright Office, and it is necessary that registration have taken place if an infringement suit is going to be filed. The prepublication registration can be made *after* the infringement, though, as long as the registration occurs before filing suit. One of the advantages to early registration is that after five years the facts contained in the registration are presumed to be true in an infringement case. This presumption, which will carry over even after the work is published, can greatly simplify the copyright owner's preparation for trial.

COPYRIGHT NOTICE

Works published under the 1909 Act had to contain the proper notice in order to be copyrighted. With few exceptions, any omission, misplacement, or imperfection in the notice on any copy of a work distributed by authority of the copyright owner placed the work forever in the public domain. Thus it was important for the copyright owner, when signing a contract, to make sure that granting a license to publish be conditioned on the publisher's inclusion of the proper copyright notice. That way, if the publisher made a mistake in the notice, the publication might be deemed unauthorized but the copyright would not be affected. The publisher could be liable to the copyright owner for the loss of copyright if it did occur.

Since notice is an inflexible requirement for works published before January 1, 1978, it is important to determine when publication occurred. Although the notice requirement is not as stringent for works published after that date, the publication date is still of some importance under the new law. For example, the duration of the copyright of a work for hire is measured from either creation or first publication. *Publication* in the context of copyright law is the distribution of copies of a work to the public by sale or other transfer of ownership, or by rental, lease, or loan.[12] A public performance or display of a work does not of itself constitute publication. Publication will not be deemed to have occurred, however, when the contents of a manuscript are communicated "to a definitely selected group and for a limited purpose, without the right of diffusion, reproduction, distribution or sale."[13] This is known as the *doctrine of limited publication*. Under the Copyright Act of 1909, when an author distributes copies of a manuscript to close friends or associates with the understanding that such copies are not to be further reproduced and distributed, the author has not published the manuscript,[14] nor would the distribution of an author's manuscript to trade journals, publishers, and the like for purposes of review and criticism constitute a publication.[15]

The Copyright Revision Act of 1976 makes no specific reference to this doctrine of limited publication. The statutory definition of publication does, however, require a "distribution of copies or phonorecords of a work to the public." The House Report explains that "the public" in this context refers to people who are under no explicit or implicit restrictions with respect to disclosure of the work's contents. This appears to suggest that the current Act is continuing the doctrine of limited publications.[16]

WORDING OF A COPYRIGHT NOTICE

A proper copyright notice on a written work has three elements. First there must be the word *copyright* (or any understandable abbreviation), followed by the letter c in a circle, ©. No variations are permitted. Second is the year of first publication (or, in the case of unpublished works governed by the 1909 Act, the year in which the copyright was registered). This date may be expressed in Arabic or Roman numerals or in words. Under the 1909 Act it was not clear when a derivative work—for example, a substantially revised textbook—was first published. To be safe, both dates, that of the original work and that of the revision, were usually given. The 1976 Act makes it clear that the date of the first publication of the revised work is sufficient. The year of the first publication can be omitted on certain works designated in the Act, but this category is extremely narrow. Since the date is necessary for some international protection, it should always be included. The third necessary element, following the date of publication, is the name of the copyright owner. If there are several, one name is sufficient. Usually the author's full name is used, but if the author is well known by a last name, the last name can be used alone or with initials. A business that owns a copyright may use its trade name if the name is legally recognized in its state of residence.

Copyright notice for this book would either be

Copyright © 1987 by Leonard DuBoff
or
Copr. © 1987 by Leonard DuBoff

The copyright owner may have to modify the copyright notice if international protection is desired. For example, under the Buenos Aires Convention (which includes most Central and South American countries as well as the United States), the statement *all rights reserved*, in either Spanish or English, must be included in the notice. If there is any possibility that the work will be sold in Central or South America, it would be advisable to include this statement. The Universal Copyright Convention (UCC) requires the use of the international copyright symbol, ©, accompanied by the name of the copyright owner and the year of first publication. If these requirements are met, any formalities required by the domestic law of a country are deemed to have been satisfied in all UCC signatory countries. The protection in the country where the work is sold will then be the same as whatever protection that country accords its own nationals. Most European nations have signed the UCC, as has the United States. However, UCC protection is available only for American works first published in the United States after the convention became effective, which was on September 16, 1955. Thus, works first published in the United States before that date are not entitled to UCC protection. Nevertheless, such works will have international protection under another agreement—the Berne Convention—if the works are simultaneously published in the U.S. and a Berne signatory country, even though the United States was not a party to that convention. This is one reason why many of the major publishers have offices in Paris. The closest country to the U.S. that participates in the Berne convention is Canada.

ERRORS IN A COPYRIGHT NOTICE

Failure to give notice or publishing an erroneous notice had very serious consequences under the old law. Under the 1909 Act, the copyright was lost if the wrong name appeared in the notice. If the author sold the copyright and recorded the sale, either the author's or the new owner's name could be used. But if the sale was not recorded with the Copyright Office, use of the subsequent owner's name in the notice destroyed the copyright.

Under the 1976 Act, a mistake in the name appearing in the notice is not fatal to the copyright. However, an infringer who is honestly misled by the incorrect name can use this as a defense to a suit for copyright infringement if the proper name was not on record with the Copyright Office. This is obviously another incentive for registering a sale or license of a copyright with the Copyright Office.

Under the 1909 Act, a mistake in the year of the first publication also could have serious consequences. If an earlier date was used, the copyright term would be measured from that year, thereby decreasing the duration of protection. If a later date was used, the copyright was forfeited and the work entered the public domain. But because of the harsh consequences of losing a copyright, a mistake of one year was not penalized.

Under the 1976 Act, using a later date will not be of any consequence when the duration of the copyright is determined by the author's life. When the duration of the copyright is determined by the date of first publication, as in the case of a composite work or work for hire, the later date will be used to measure how long the copyright will last. If an earlier year is used, the work is considered to have been published without notice, but this is not fatal to the copyright.

The 1909 Act contained complicated rules for the proper placement of the copyright notice within the work. Improper placement was one more error that was fatal to the copyright. Although the 1976 Act gives the Copyright Office the authority to regulate where the copyright should be placed, failure to comply with these regulations is not automatically fatal to the copyright.

On a published book, regulations specify that the copyright notice should go on the cover of the book, on the title page, or on the back of the title page. In fact, in the book-publishing industry the back of the title page is known as the copyright page, and that is where you will generally find the copyright information. On an unpublished work, when there has been an improper placement, the copyright owner must prove that such placement still gave reasonable notice to the public. The public is not expected to search high and low for a copyright notice. Should a court determine that the placement did not give reasonable notice, the work will be treated as if it were published without any notice. This does not, however, immediately cast the work into the public domain, as it would have under the 1909 Act.

Under the 1976 Act, if a work is published without notice, the copyright owner is still protected for five years. If during those five years the owner registers the copyright with the Copyright Office and makes a reasonable effort to place a notice on those copies published without notice and distributed within the United States, full copyright protection will be granted for the appropriate duration of the published work. If the notice has been omitted only from a relatively small number of copies, the owner need not register at all. However, risk of loss of copyright is not worth the gamble on how many copies constitute a "relatively small number." If there is any doubt, the author should register and attempt to get the omitted notice into copies that do not contain it.

A copyright owner is always forgiven for an omission of notice if the omission was in violation of a contract that made inclusion of the proper notice a condition of the right to publish. Also, if the notice is removed or obliterated by an unauthorized person, this will have no effect on the validity of the copyright.

Since the purpose of the notice is to inform members of the public that the copyright owner possesses the exclusive rights granted by the statute, it is logical that someone who infringes these rights should not be penalized if the error was made because of the absence of the notice. In some cases, the innocent infringer may be compelled to give up any profits made from the infringement. On the other hand, if the infringer has made a sizable investment for future production, the court may compel the copyright owner to grant a license to the infringer.

DEPOSIT AND REGISTRATION

While a copyright notice in a book or other written work tells readers who holds the copyright, so far the United States government has not been officially informed. Once the book has been published, *depositing the work* and *registering an application for copyright* must be taken care of. (Remember, if you are the author of a book, the publisher handles all of this.)

Depositing a work and registering an application are two different actions. Neither is a prerequisite for creating a federal copyright; as a general rule, copyright protection is automatic when an idea is "fixed in a tangible medium of expression," and, because of the copyright notice, copyright protection remains with the work after it is published or distributed to the public.

The obvious question, then, is why bother to deposit the

work and file the application? The reason is, should someone infringe on your copyright, you would have no remedy under the law unless the work had been deposited, and an application registered, prior to filing a lawsuit for infringement.

Under the *deposit section* of the new law, the owner of the copyright or the owner of the exclusive right of publication (usually a book publisher) must deposit in the Copyright Office, for the use of the Library of Congress, two copies of the "best edition" of the work within three months after the work has been published.[17] In the case of an unpublished work, or a collective work such as an anthology, only one copy need be deposited. The copies or copy should be sent to the Register of Copyrights, Library of Congress, Washington, D.C. 20559. This basic deposit requirement also applies to works published abroad when such works are either imported into the United States or become part of an American edition.

If the two copies are not deposited within the requisite three-month period, the Register of Copyrights may demand them. (The Register of Copyrights is not omniscient; the office would know that a particular book had been published because of other correspondence with a publisher. If you have self-published a book and never corresponded with the office, it is not likely that this demand will be made.) If the copies are not submitted within three months after demand, the person upon whom demand was made may be subject to a fine of up to $250 for each unsubmitted work. In addition, such person or persons may be required to pay the Library of Congress an amount equal to the retail cost of the work, or, if no retail cost has been established, the costs incurred by the library in acquiring the work, provided such costs are reasonable. Finally, a copyright proprietor who willfully and repeatedly refuses to comply with a demand may be liable for an additional fine of $2,500.

Depositing copies under the deposit section of the new law is not a condition of copyright protection, but in light of the penalty provisions, it would be foolish not to comply.

The *registration section* of the new act requires that the copyright proprietor complete an application form, obtained from the Register of Copyrights, Library of Congress, Washington, D.C. 20559, and pay a ten-dollar registration fee.[18] In addition, the proprietor must deposit two copies of the "best edition" of the work to be registered.

All of the above is very easy in view of two facts:

1. The form you should request, used for almost all written works, is Form TX. It is accompanied by brief, easy-to-follow instructions, and is itself brief and easy to understand. It is *not* an intimidating income-tax form. Anyone who can read this book can fill it out in ten or twenty minutes, unless the work being copyrighted is a complicated compilation.

2. Although depositing and registering are considered two separate actions, and can be done separately, if you send two copies of the "best edition"—or one copy in the case of an unpublished work or collection—to accompany your registration (i.e., Form TX), you will have completed the job. Various departments of the Library of Congress do know what the others are doing, and they will share your two copies.

In other words, to satisfy the government and assure yourself that your written work is protected, *you simply fill out the form and send it, along with the required number of copies of the work, to the Register of Copyrights.* That is it.

As mentioned earlier, a copyright can be lost if a work that once bore a copyright notice is subsequently published without that notice. For cases where that has happened, the new act contains a savings clause, which provides that registration within five years of any publication without a notice will regain copyright protection for the work if the copyright owner makes a good-faith effort to add the notice to all works distributed in the United States.[19] (One way someone might do this would be to have press-on stickers printed bearing the correct information, then sending them to stores that carry the work, with a request that the stores see that the stickers are put in.)

Although registration is not a condition to copyright protection, the 1976 Act specifies that the copyright owner cannot bring a lawsuit to enforce his or her copyright until the copyright has been registered. Additionally, if the copyright is registered after an infringement occurs, the owner's legal remedies will be limited. If the copyright was registered prior to the infringement, the owner may be entitled to more complete remedies, including attorneys' fees and statutory damages. No remedies shall be lost if registration is made within three months of publication. Thus, the owner of a copyright has a strong incentive to register the copyright at the earliest possible time, certainly within the three-month grace period.

COPYRIGHT INFRINGEMENT AND REMEDIES

A copyright infringement occurs any time an unauthorized person exercises any of the exclusive rights protected by a copyright. The fact that the infringing party did not intend to improperly use protected rights or did not know that the work was protected by copyright is relevant only with respect to the penalty. All actions for infringement of copyright must be brought in a federal court within three years of the date of the infringement. The copyright owner must prove that the work was copyrighted and registered, that the infringer had access to and used the copyrighted work, and that the infringer copied a substantial and material portion of the copyrighted work. In order to demonstrate the extent of the damage caused by the infringement, the copyright owner must also provide evidence that shows how widely the infringing copies were distributed.

The copyright owner must prove that the infringer had access to the protected work, because an independent creation of an identical work is not an infringement. Since maps are often identical to each other, cartographers frequently include a minor error in their work. If an identical map includes that error, it will be sufficient evidence of access. (In order to prove an infringement of the copyright in this book, typographical errors have also been intentionally included.) The likelihood that two literary works will be identical is so small that a jury might infer that one was copied from the other if they are identical. When the works are merely similar to each other, though, access becomes more difficult to prove.

Infringement can occur short of a verbatim copy of an entire work. Any unauthorized copying of a substantial portion of a work constitutes an infringement. The quality of the writing copied is considered as well as the quantity. If one sentence in a scientific work states a principle in a mundane way, another scientist using the same statement may not be an infringer. A short straightforward statement of fact cannot be protected. On the other hand, one line of poetry can be so highly creative that it would be protected.

The toughest infringement suits to prove are those in which a copyright owner claims that someone else's work is a derivation of a copyrighted work. In such cases the owner's language has not been copied, but the original writer claims that the infringer traced the pattern of the work while paraphrasing it. To prepare such a case, it must first be decided whether the similarity between the two works is due to similar abstract ideas or the expression of those ideas (remember, ideas are not protectable under the copyright law). In order to make this determination, the courts have used what is called an *abstractions test*.[20] In every work there can be found a great number of patterns, with the author's language being the least generalized pattern. A simple plot formula, like boy meets girl, boy marries girl, is the most generalized. At some point in this series of patterns, expression becomes so generalized that it gives way to ideas which cannot be protected. The court must decide what part of this series the allegedly infringing work falls into.

If the expression of ideas, rather than simply the ideas alone, is found to be similar, the court must decide whether the similarity is substantial. This is done in two steps. First, the court looks at the more general similarities of the writings, such as subject matter, setting, materials used, and the like. Expert testimony may be offered here. The second step involves a subjective judgment of the works' intrinsic similarity: Would a lay observer recognize that the alleged copy had been appropriated from the copyrighted work? No expert testimony is allowed in making this determination.

Even before the trial, the copyright owner may be able to obtain a preliminary court order against an infringer. The copyright owner can petition the court to seize all copies of the alleged infringing work and the negatives that produced them. To do this, the copyright owner must file a sworn statement that the work is an infringement and provide a substantial bond approved by the court. After the seizure, the alleged infringer has a chance to object to the amount or form of the bond.

After the trial, if the work is held to be an infringement, the court can order the destruction of all copies and negatives, and enjoin infringement. In addition, the copyright owner may be awarded damages. The copyright owner may request that the court grant, on the one hand, *actual damages*, or, on the other hand, *statutory damages* — a choice that can be made any time before the final judgment is recorded. Actual damages are either the amount of the financial injury sustained by the copyright owner or, as in most cases, the the equivalent of the profits made by the infringer. In proving profits, the copyright owner need only establish the gross revenues received for the illegal exploitation of the work. The infringer then must prove any deductible expenses.

The second option is statutory damages. The amount of statutory damages is decided by the court, within some statutory limits: no less than $250 and no more than $10,000. The maximum possible recovery is increased to $50,000 if the copyright owner proves that the infringer knew that an illegal act was being committed. The minimum possible recovery is reduced to $100 if the infringer proves ignorance of the fact that the work was copyrighted. The court has the option to award the prevailing party its costs and attorneys' fees. As previously noted, statutory damages and attorneys' fees may not be awarded in cases where the copyright was not registered prior to infringement, provided such infringement occurred more than three months after the copyrighted work was published.

The U.S. Justice Department can prosecute a copyright infringer. If the prosecutor proves beyond a reasonable doubt that the infringement was committed willfully and for commercial gain, the infringer can be fined up to $10,000 and sentenced to jail for up to one year. There is also a fine of up to $2,500 for fraudulently placing a false copyright notice on a work, for removing or obliterating a copyright notice, or for knowingly making a false statement in an application for a copyright.

FAIR USE

Not every copying of a protected work will constitute an infringement. There are two basic types of non-infringing use: *fair use* and *exempted use*.

The Copyright Act of 1976 recognizes that copies of a protected work "for purposes such as criticism, comment, news reporting, teaching (including multiple copies for classroom use), scholarship or research" can be considered fair use and therefore not an infringement. However, this list is not intended to be complete nor is it intended as a definition of fair use. Fair use, in fact, is not defined by the Act. Instead, the Act cites four factors to be considered in determining whether a particular use is or is not fair:

1. The purpose and character of the use, including whether it is for commercial use or for nonprofit educational purposes.
2. The nature of the copyrighted work.
3. The amount and substantiality of the portion used in relation to the copyrighted work as a whole.
4. The effect of the use upon the potential market for, or value of, the copyrighted work.

The Act does not rank these four factors, nor does it exclude other factors in determining the question of fair use. In effect, all that the Act does is leave the doctrine of fair use to be developed by the courts.

The first U.S. Supreme Court case to address the fair use doctrine under the Copyright Revision Act of 1976 was *Sony Corporation of America* v. *Universal Studios, Inc., et al.*, in 1985.[21] While the case does not deal with written work but with the home video recorder and its effect on copyrighted movies aired on TV, it is nevertheless an important step in defining the bounds of the fair use doctrine under the new law. Universal Studios sued Sony because Sony manufactures and sells home videotape recorders which are used to record copyrighted works shown on television. In a five-to-four decision, the Court stated that home video recording for noncommercial purposes is a fair use of copyrighted television programs.

The Supreme Court's analysis of fair use emphasized the economic consequences of home video recording to copyright owners. The Court looked to the first of the four factors listed in the 1976 Copyright Act as relevant to the fair use defense: "The purpose and character of the use." Consideration of this factor, reasoned the Court, requires a weighing of the commercial or nonprofit character of the activity. If the recorders had been used to make copies for commercial or profit-making purposes, the use would be unfair. But since video recording of television programs for private home use is a noncommercial, nonprofit activity, the court found that the use was a fair use.

The Court then considered "the effect of the use upon the potential market for or value of the copyrighted work," the fourth factor listed in the Act. Here, the Court found that although copying for noncommercial reasons may impair the copyright holder's ability to get the rewards Congress intended, to forbid a use that has no demonstrable effect upon the potential market, or upon the value of the work, would merely prohibit access to ideas without any benefit.

The rule that emerges from the Supreme Court's holding in *Sony* is that: A challenge to noncommercial use of a copyrighted work requires proof (1) that the use is harmful to the copyright owner or (2) that the use would adversely affect the potential market for the copyrighted work should the use become widespread. In *Sony*, the Court concluded that Universal Studios had failed to carry their burden of proof on the issue of actual or probable harm, and thus the recordings constituted fair use.

In *Sony*, the alleged copyright infringement was the unauthorized recording or copying of the movies by home viewers. Several other recent video cases involve a slightly different situation: the viewing of video movies by several members of the public in what is alleged to be an unauthorized public performance. At least one lower court has held that copyright is not infringed when guests at a resort are allowed to rent video discs and view them in their rooms.[22] The court rejected the copyright owners' argument that such viewing constituted unauthorized public performance of the movies and was thus an infringement of copyright. Two other courts have held that copyright is infringed when owners of video rental stores provide viewing rooms where members of the public can view the movies they have rented.[23] The courts found that because the viewing rooms were open to the public, showing video movies in the rooms amounted to unauthorized public performances of the movies and thus constituted copyright infringement. The primary issue in all of these cases was whether the uses constituted public performances, not whether the uses were fair. Nevertheless, like the *Sony* case, they illustrate the difficult copyright issue presented by the video industry. Clearly this area of the law is still developing, and any writer connected with the video market should consult with a lawyer to learn the extent of the writer's control over his or her work.

The United States Court of Appeals for the Second Circuit considered the extent of a writer's control over a copyrighted work in *Maxtone-Graham* v. *Burtchaell et al.*[24] Maxtone-Graham, author of a collection of interviews of women discussing abortion from a Pro-Choice prospective sued Burtchaell, a Catholic priest, for his unauthorized use of 4.3 percent of her material in his book, *Rachel Weeping*. The court, in upholding the summary judgment in favor of Burtchaell, stated

> Biographies, of course, are fundamentally personal histories and it is both reasonable and customary for biographers to refer to and utilize earlier works dealing with the subject of the work and occasionally to quote directly from such works.... This practice is permitted before the public benefit in encouraging the development of historical and biographical works and their public dis-

tribution.... Like the biography, the interview is an invaluable
source of material for social scientists and later use of verbatim
quotations within reason is both foreseeable and desirable.[25]

It would thus appear that copying a small portion of another's copyrighted work for comment, criticism or analysis will likely be considered fair use within the meaning of the statute.

Another area in which the fair use defense has been used successfully is in cases involving parody or burlesque. The courts have generally been sympathetic to the parodying of copyrighted works, often permitting incorporation of a substantial portion of a protected work. The test has traditionally been whether the amount copied exceeded that which was necessary to recall or conjure up in the mind of the viewers the work being parodied or burlesqued. In these cases the substantiality of the copy, and particularly the "conjuring up" test, may be more important than the factor of economic harm to the copyright proprietor.

One area in which the limits of fair use are hotly debated is the area of photocopying. The Copyright Act provides, remember, that "reproduction in copies ... for purposes such as criticism, comment, news reporting, teaching (including multiple copies for classroom use), scholarship or research" *can* be a fair use, which leaves many questions. Reproduction of what? A paragraph? A chapter? A work in print? Out of print? An entire work if it is short? A long work? How many copies? To help answer these questions, several interested organizations drafted a set of guidelines for classroom copying in nonprofit educational institutions. These guidelines are not a part of the Copyright Act but are printed in the Act's legislative history. Even though the writers of the guidelines defined the guide as "minimum standards of educational fair use," major educational groups have publicly expressed the fear that publishers would attempt to establish the guidelines as maximum standards beyond which there could be no fair use.

As the educators feared, the Association of American Publishers (AAP), in the late 1970s and early 1980s, sued several large businesses and corporations running photocopy shops near large universities. All of the defendants settled with AAP rather than face expensive litigation. The most significant AAP suit was settled in 1983 with New York University (NYU). The NYU suit directly involved the issue of what fair use means in the context of classroom copying.

NYU, like the corporate defendants, decided that litigation would be prohibitively expensive. As part of the settlement, NYU agreed to restrict faculty members' copying to the limits set out in the guidelines. The university promised that any photocopying not permitted under the guidelines would not be undertaken without seeking permission to copy from the copyright owner. In cases where permission is denied, the faculty member must refer the matter to the university's general counsel. If the general counsel does not OK the copying, the university will pay neither legal expenses nor the cost of any judgment rendered against a faculty member sued for infringement. Since the NYU settlement, the AAP has actively attempted to persuade other universities to adopt the same policy, using lawsuits as a threat.

The NYU settlement has been criticized on several grounds. First, the settlement effectively makes the guidelines a maximum rather than a minimum standard because any copying not covered by the guidelines must be approved by an attorney. Since the function of the university counsel is to avoid lawsuits, virtually all copying beyond the guidelines will be eliminated. The chilling effect on academic photocopying will inevitably affect the scope of classroom debate and learning.

A second complaint regarding the NYU settlement is

that seeking permission whenever copying is outside the guidelines involves considerable time and money. Only if the author has conveyed the copyright to the publisher will the publisher have the right to give permission. Otherwise, considerable research will be necessary in order to identify the copyright owner or the person who has the right to grant reprint permission. Of course, all of the costs involved in the research will be passed along in the fee charged for permission to copy. The NYU settlement mandates these added procedures and costs every time copying is outside the guidelines—even though the copying may be a fair use legally.

Third, the NYU settlement fails to consider the availability of the work copied—that is, whether it is in or out of print. Although photocopying of large sections of a work may be hard to justify when the work is easily available, greater latitude is logical where the work is out of print and available in no other reasonable way.

Finally, the NYU settlement may well lead to students doing the photocopying, since there is nothing in the agreement to prevent professors from simply placing the materials on reserve in the library for students to photocopy themselves. Neither the library nor the university can be held liable for such copying, and a suit by a publisher against an individual student is unlikely in view of the minimal damages and adverse publicity.

Certainly, not all universities will yield to AAP pressures and accept the restrictions on academic photocopying represented by the NYU settlement. When enough public colleges and universities band together and pool funds to defend a lawsuit for copyright infringement, we will likely see some of these vital copyright issues considered by the courts. In the meantime, rather than risk litigation costs, even individuals or universities that have not agreed to restrictions on copying should obtain written permission for any significant use of copyrighted material. Requests for permission can be addressed to the permissions department of the publisher. The rights requested should be carefully specified, as well as the date and the title of the original work. A copy of the material as it will appear in the new work should be enclosed. Fees for such permission can be nothing, or range from $50 to $100 or more. Do not proceed with use of the material until you have received a response. It may be that the publisher will be unable to grant permission because the author retained the copyright.

The question of fair use has also been litigated in the area of publication of personal letters. This question was raised in 1972 in *Meeropol* v. *Nizer*.[26] The defendant, Louis Nizer, had written a book about the trial of Julius and Ethel Rosenberg, who were convicted and executed in the early 1950s for conspiring to transmit to the Soviet Union information relating to the national defense of the United States. Doubleday & Company and Fawcett Publications published the book, which included, verbatim, twenty-eight letters written by the Rosenbergs. The Rosenberg children brought suit, alleging, among other things, that the use of the letters constituted copyright infringement.

The lower court held that, as a matter of law, the author's and publishers' use of the letters was a fair use, and thus no trial was necessary. The appellate court disagreed and found that the issue could not be so readily resolved. Conceding that "the mere fact that Nizer's book might be termed a popularized account of the Rosenberg trial lacking substantial scholarship and published for commercial gain, does not, standing alone, deprive Nizer or his publishers of the fair use defense,"[27] the court nevertheless maintained that the defendants' use might tend to diminish or prejudice the ability of the Rosenberg children to exploit the Rosenberg letters in the future. Thus, the court ruled that a trial should be held.

As all this demonstrates, it is not easy to define what sorts of uses are fair uses. Questions continue to be resolved on a case-by-case basis. Thus, an author should consult a lawyer where it appears that one of the author's works has been infringed or where the author intends to use someone else's copyrighted work. The lawyer can research what the courts have held in cases with similar facts.

EXEMPTED USES

In many instances the ambiguities of the fair use doctrine have been resolved by statutory exemptions. Exempted uses are those specifically permitted by statute in situations where the public interest in making a copy outweighs any harm to the copyright proprietor.

Perhaps the most significant of these exemptions is the library and archives exemption in Section 108 of the Act, which basically provides that libraries and archives may reproduce and distribute a single copy of a work provided that (1) such reproduction and distribution is not for the purpose of direct or indirect commercial gain; (2) the collections of the library or archives are available to the public or available to researchers affiliated with the library or archives as well as to others doing research in a specialized field; and (3) the reproduction and distribution of the work includes a copyright notice.

The exemption for libraries and archives is intended to cover only single copies of a work. It does not generally cover multiple reproductions of the same material, whether made on one occasion or over a period of time, and whether intended for use by one person or for separate use by the individual members of a group. Under interlibrary arrangements, various libraries may provide one another with works missing from their respective collections, unless these distribution arrangements substitute for a subscription or purchase of a given work.

This exemption in no way affects the applicability of fair use, nor does it apply where such copying is prohibited in contractual arrangements agreed to by the library or archives when it obtained the work.

The writer is well advised to consult a copyright lawyer to determine whether a desired use is either an exempted use or a fair use.

8

Censorship and Obscenity

The First Amendment of the United States Constitution
states in part, "Congress shall make no law . . . abridging
the freedom of speech, or of the press." First Amendment
absolutists insist that the words are all-encompassing and
that no law should ever be enacted that places any restriction whatsoever on the free exercise of speech or press.
Although a strict reading of the Constitution may support
this opinion, the judiciary has never fully upheld it and
has ruled that certain types of speech are not protected by
the First Amendment. Two theories have been used to
justify exceptions to First Amendment protection. The
first theory maintains that although certain expressions
do normally deserve First Amendment protection, such
protection will not be forthcoming if another right, either
public or private, outweighs the speaker's First Amendment rights. Examples of speech (which has been defined
as including the written word) that are not absolutely protected include defamatory remarks, remarks that advocate unlawful conduct, and remarks that invade someone's privacy. The second theory suggests that certain expressions do not constitute speech for purposes of First
Amendment protection because they are without serious

social value. Under this theory, courts often maintain that obscene works are not protected.

Prior Restraint

When the First Amendment was being written, the memory of the English licensing system, under which nothing could be published without prior approval, was still vivid in the minds of the framers of the Constitution. Some historians suggest that the First Amendment was written specifically to prevent such prior restraints. Today the First Amendment means more than freedom from prepublication censorship, but because of its potential for abuse, censorship before publication is still considered more serious than restrictions imposed after publication. The Supreme Court in *Near* v. *Minnesota* recognized that "liberty of the press . . . has meant, principally although not exclusively, immunity from previous restraints and censorship."[1]

Prior restraints impose an extreme burden upon the exercise of free speech since they limit open debate and the unfettered dissemination of knowledge. It is not surprising that the Supreme Court has almost universally found that it is unconstitutional to restrain speech prior to a determination of whether the speech is protected by the First Amendment.[2]

Prohibition of Political Speech

A prior-restraint lawsuit generally begins with a request, often by the government, for a court order prohibiting publication of information already in the media's possession. Where controversial political speech is involved, the government may argue that publication will cause substantial and irreparable harm to the United States. In *New York Times Co.* v. *United States*, for example, the government tried to stop the publication of the Pentagon Papers, which detailed U.S. involvement in Vietnam prior to 1968.[3] The government claimed that publication would prolong the war and embarrass the United States in the conduct of its diplomacy.

The Supreme Court found that the government's claim of potential injury to the U.S. was insufficient to justify prior restraint. The justices, although believing that publication would probably be harmful, were not persuaded that publication would "surely" cause the harm alleged. Justice Potter Stewart agreed and wrote a concurring opinion emphasizing that the government must show that disclosure "will surely result in direct, immediate, and irreparable damage to our nation or its people."[4]

In a later case, *United States* v. *The Progressive, Inc.*, the government used a similar argument: national security.[5] In the *Progressive* case, the government sought to prohibit publication of a magazine article which detailed a method for constructing a hydrogen bomb. The government's case was weak for a variety of reasons, not the least of which was the fact that the alleged secrets were not then classified and had in fact been published in books, journals, magazines, and the government's own reports. Any diligent reporter could have uncovered the same information. Perhaps realizing the impossibility of meeting the test of "direct, immediate, irreversible harm" laid out in the 1971 Pentagon Papers case, the government abandoned the suit, but not until after raising the chilling threat of prior restraint.[6]

PROHIBITION OF PRETRIAL PUBLICITY

Another kind of suppression of the free flow of information involves the restriction of pretrial publicity. Here the conflict is between the individual's right to a fair trial and the right of the press to its First Amendment guarantee of free speech. This conflict was addressed in *Nebraska Press Association* v. *Stuart*.[7]

The Nebraska Press Association appealed a court order

prohibiting the press from reporting on confessions and other information implicating an accused murderer after the murder of six family members had gained widespread public attention. The trial judge originally issued the order because he felt that pretrial publicity would make it difficult to select a jury that had not been exposed to prejudicial press coverage.

The Supreme Court nonetheless struck down the trial judge's order, finding that the impact of publicity on jurors was "speculative, dealing with factors unknown and unknowable."[8] The justices went on to suggest alternatives to restraining all publication, including changing the location of the trial, postponing the trial, asking in-depth questions of prospective jury members during the selection process to determine bias, explicitly instructing the jury to consider only evidence presented at trial, and isolating the jury.

This decision appears to go far in requiring that other methods of pretrial precautions be taken, and that an order restricting press coverage be used only as a last resort.

Prohibition of Commercial Speech

In other areas, however, the Court has been more tolerant of prior restraints. For example, the Court held in *Virginia State Board of Pharmacy* v. *Virginia Consumer Council* that prior restraints are sometimes permissible when purely commercial speech such as advertisements or other promotional material is involved.[9] In that case the Court considered the constitutionality of a Virginia statute which prohibited pharmacists from advertising prices of prescription drugs. The Court held that the statute was unconstitutional and thereby rejected the notion that commercial speech is never entitled to First Amendment protection. However, the Court distinguished commercial speech from ordinary speech in discussing the application of the First Amendment to it. The Court reasoned that since commercial statements are generally objective in content, whether they are true or false can be readily determined. Thus, the Court believed that there was little or no threat of prior restraints being arbitrarily imposed. In addition, the Court maintained that commercial speech lacks the urgency which often accompanies noncommercial speech, so that any delay caused by the restraint while its justification is being argued would be relatively harmless. Since many of the dangers associated with prior restraints (such as suppression of political dissent) were not deemed to be present, the Court ruled that prior restraints of commercial speech are not always unconstitutional.

PROHIBITION OF OBSCENE SPEECH

Prior restraints have also been upheld where the suppressed material was obscene, but the Supreme Court has imposed several procedural safeguards for this type of case. For example: (1) the accused must be given a prompt hearing; (2) the government agency making the accusation carries the burden of showing that the material is, in fact, obscene; (3) a valid final restraint can be issued only after a judicial proceeding; and (4) once the government agency has itself made a finding of obscenity, it must take action on its own behalf in a court of law to confirm its own finding.[10]

Prior restraints on commercial speech and alleged obscenity are less often condemned by the courts because the immediately topical nature of and public interest in the free flow of "political speech" are not characteristic of commercial or sexual expressions; therefore, the public interest is not compromised as much by publication delays of sexual expressions. As Justice John Harlan commented in *A Quantity of Books* v. *Kansas*, "sex is of constant but rarely particularly topical interest."[11]

The Scope of Permissible Prior Restraints

It should be emphasized that the major presumption the Court made in *Near* v. *Minnesota* is still applicable; the chief purpose of the First Amendment's freedom of the press provision was to prevent prior restraints on publication.[12] In *Near*, the Court listed only three situations which "might" justify prior restraint: (1) the need to prevent obstruction of a government's recruiting service, or to prevent publication of the sailing dates of transport ships or the number and location of troops; (2) failure to meet the requirements of decency, as in an obscene publication; and (3) the necessity of avoiding incitement to acts of violence and the overthrow by force of orderly government.[13] These three exceptions, along with the requirements that the government prove with certainty that particular speech is unprotected and is likely to cause irreparable harm, limit the scope of permissible prior restraint.

It is worth noting that the Supreme Court has held that a school could suspend a student because of a speech he made containing numerous sexual metaphors, despite the student's claim of First Amendment protection. The Court felt that the school's right to maintain an appropriate educational environment for children outweighed the student's right of free speech.[14]

Obscenity

Obscenity is perhaps the area where most of the censorship in this country has occurred.

A variety of laws are involved in regulating "obscene materials." Some state laws prohibit publication, distribution, public display or sales to minors of obscene material. Some city ordinances prohibit any commercial dealings in pornography whatsoever. Transporting obscene material across a state line or national border is forbidden by federal law, and it is a crime punishable by up to five years in jail to send obscene materials through the U.S. mail.

Since the private possession of obscene material is not unlawful, one who simply writes material which could be categorized as obscene has not thereby violated obscenity laws. Of course, if the writer self-publishes, liability can result. Otherwise, it is the publisher who is at risk of violating the law. However, the writer whose works involve especially graphic sexual descriptions may be foreclosed from publishing or distributing those works because a court has declared the work to be obscene. In addition, the writer whose work is declared obscene may face a lawsuit from his or her publisher, since many writer-publisher contracts contain a warranty or indemnity clause stating that nothing in the work is obscene. In the event that the writing is declared obscene, such a clause entitles the publisher to either sue the writer directly for breach of warranty, or bill the writer for any losses the publisher might have incurred in an obscenity suit. See the chapter on author-publisher contracts for more detailed discussion of these clauses.

One of the first major obscenity cases in the twentieth century was *Doubleday & Co.* v. *New York*.[15] At issue was Edmund Wilson's novel *Memoirs of Hectate County*. Because the novel contained two passages describing sexual intercourse, the novel's publisher, Doubleday & Co., was convicted in state court of violating a New York criminal obscenity law. The U.S. Supreme Court upheld the conviction. Significantly, neither the New York court nor the Supreme Court found the defendant's argument that the erotic passages were inextricably intertwined with the novel's literary merit to be persuasive.

A year after the Supreme Court affirmed the *Doubleday* decision, the case of *The Commonwealth* v. *Gordon* arose, in which several Philadelphia booksellers were charged with violating a Pennsylvania statute outlawing the sale of any "obscene, lascivious, filthy, indecent or disgusting book."[16] Several novels that today might be considered classics were involved in *Gordon*, including James Farrell's Studs Lonigan trilogy and *A World I Never Made*; William Faulkner's *Sanctuary* and *The Wild Palms*; Erskine Caldwell's *God's Little Acre*; and Harold Robbins's *Never Love a Stranger*.

The booksellers in the *Gordon* case were prosecuted in a state court that ruled that in order to determine whether a work is obscene, the work must be considered as a whole and some consideration must be given to its artistic merit. Moreover, the court commented that a link between the sale of the allegedly obscene books and actual criminal behavior resulting from exposure to the work must be found. Finding no such connection, and evidently finding some artistic merit, the court acquitted the booksellers.

Defining Obscenity

The fact that these two cases, *Doubleday* and *Gordon*, could be decided within such a short time of one another and yet reach such different results points directly to the core problem of obscenity: that of developing a practical definition. It has been the task of the Supreme Court, as the ultimate interpreter of the Constitution, to devise a definition that is specific and at the same time flexible. It must be specific if it is to provide useful guidance to authors and publishers, and it must be flexible to accommodate changes in social mores and ethics. *Gordon* makes it clear that what may be obscene today may not be considered obscene in the future.

As the Court has attempted to formulate a definition which accomplishes these two objectives, the law of obscenity has undergone rapid changes.

The Roth Definition

In *Roth* v. *United States* a New York publisher and distributor of books, photographs, and magazines was convicted in the 1950s of violating a federal obscenity statute by mailing obscene circulars and advertising an obscene book.[17] He appealed to the U.S. Supreme Court, claiming that his conduct was protected by the First Amendment. The Court rejected this argument and affirmed the conviction, but in the course of its opinion it did away with the standard which had been applied to obscenity cases since 1868, the ancient test devised by a British court in *Regina* v. *Hicklin*.[18]

The *Regina* court had held that a publication which condemned certain practices of Roman Catholic priests in the confessional was obscene. There, the test for obscenity was "whether the tendency of the matter charged as obscenity is to deprave and corrupt those whose minds are open to such immoral influences and into whose hands a publication of this sort may fall." Because this test dictated that the material be judged according to the effect of an isolated excerpt upon persons of delicate sensibilities, it subjected to threat of censorship any adult treatment of sex, among other things, and endangered the right to publish and distribute many highly acclaimed literary works. In recognition of these problems the Court, in considering *Roth*, set forth a new standard: a work would be considered obscene if "to the average person, applying contemporary community standards, the dominant theme of the material taken as a whole appeals to prurient interest."[19]

It was hoped that *Roth* would stabilize the law of obscenity, but confusion remained nonetheless. In *Jacobellis* v. *Ohio*, the Supreme Court reversed a conviction for violation of an Ohio statute which prohibited the possession and exhibition of obscene films.[20] The Supreme Court held that the lower court had erroneously construed the phrase "contemporary community standards" to mean local rather than national standards. The Court thought that allowing local standards to govern would have the effect of denying some areas of the country access to materials that were acceptable in those areas, simply because publishers and distributors would be reluctant to risk prosecution under the laws of more conservative states where the same materials would be unacceptable. By applying a national standard to the case, the Court maintained that the film was not obscene. The question remains, however, of how to define the national standard. In *Roth*, it seems to have been found in the personal tastes and predilections of the majority of the justices, particularly in light of Justice Stewart's statement on the nature of obscenity: "I know it when I see it."

The Memoirs Definition

When the attorney general of Massachusetts requested a court order declaring the book *Fanny Hill* obscene, the Massachusetts courts ruled in his favor. On appeal, the Supreme Court in *Memoirs* v. *Massachusetts* reversed the Massachusetts courts, holding that the mere risk that a work might be exploited by advertisers because of its treatment of sexual matters is not sufficient to make it obscene.[21] Instead, the Court held in a plurality opinion that the prosecution must establish three separate elements to prove obscenity:

(a) the dominant theme of the material taken as a whole appeals to a prurient interest in sex; (b) the material is patently offensive because it affronts contemporary community standards relating to the description or representation of sexual matters; and (c) the material is utterly without redeeming social value.[22]

However, even this three-part test has not brought clarity to the law of obscenity. In 1972, six years after the *Memoirs* decision, the Supreme Court was again confronted with a state court's overly broad definition of obscenity. The case was *Kois* v. *Wisconsin*.[23]

In *Kois*, the Wisconsin state court convicted the pub-

lisher of an underground newspaper of two counts of violating a state obscenity statute which prohibited the dissemination of "lewd, obscene, or indecent written matter,
pictures, sound recording, or film." The first count was
for publication of an article that reported the arrest of one
of the newspaper's photographers on a charge of possession of obscene material. Two relatively small pictures,
showing a nude couple embracing in a sitting position, accompanied the article. The second count was for distributing a newspaper containing a poem entitled "Sex Poem,"
which was a frank, play-by-play account of the author's
recollection of sexual intercourse.

The Supreme Court reversed the obscenity conviction,
finding that, for the first count, the pictures were ra-
tionally related to an article that was clearly entitled to
First Amendment protection. As for the second count, the
poem had "some of the earmarks of an attempt at serious
art."[24]

The Miller Definition

The Supreme Court tried again to provide a workable
definition in its 1973 *Miller* v. *California* decision.[25]

In reviewing *Roth* and *Memoirs*, the Court concluded
that one thing had been categorically settled: "Obscene
material is unprotected by the First Amendment."[26] But
because any limitation on an absolute freedom of expression could lead to undesirable and dangerous censorship,
it was deemed essential that state obscenity laws be limited
in scope and properly applied. These concerns are mani-
fest in the *Miller* obscenity test, which substantially modified the *Roth-Memoirs* test. The *Miller* test is:

(a) whether "the average person, applying contemporary community standards" would find that the work, taken as a whole,
appeals to the prurient interest, (b) whether the work depicts or
describes in a patently offensive way, sexual conduct specifically
defined by the applicable state law, and (c) whether the work,

taken as a whole, lacks serious literary, artistic, political, or scientific values.[27]

Thus, the *Roth-Memoirs* requirement that prosecutors prove that the challenged material is "utterly without social value" was replaced by a new standard which merely required the absence of "serious social value." Moreover, the Court upheld the right of a state to apply a local, rather than a national, standard in enforcing its obscenity laws.

The intent of *Miller* was to provide much clearer guidelines for protected speech, both to state legislatures enacting statutes and to prosecutors enforcing that legislation. *Miller* required that state statutes be more specific, so the states attempted to define the *Miller* test for their own communities. However, instead of clarifying the law, the hodgepodge of legislation spurred by *Miller* has only contributed to the vagueness, increased breadth, and chilling effect of obscenity legislation. Inconsistencies in the laws require the writer to be aware of local statutes and ordinances in each area where distribution of a given publication is planned.

DEFINING "COMMUNITY STANDARDS"

One of the greatest difficulties courts have had in applying the *Miller* test has involved defining "community" for the purposes of ascertaining moral standards. The Supreme Court said in 1974 that *Miller*'s effect "is to permit the juror in an obscenity case to draw on his own knowledge of the community from which he comes in deciding what conclusion an 'average person' would reach in a given case."[28] The Court, however, does not require that the juror be instructed as to how large the relevant community is geographically. Instructions which direct the jury to apply "community standards" without specifying the boundaries of that community are acceptable.[29] In reaffirming the idea that jurors are to draw on their own knowledge, the Court has emphasized that community standards are not to be defined legislatively.[30]

A juror is to draw on personal knowledge of the community, but not on personal standards of what is good or bad. Therefore, the defense must try to demonstrate the popular attitude toward certain forms of sexual expression. Magazines and books readily available in grocery stores and magazine stands may be said to reflect community standards. Firms that specialize in conducting community surveys could be helpful in defending an obscenity charge and ought to be consulted if the need arises.

A serious problem caused by differences in community standards has been a tendency on the part of prosecutors to try to bring their cases in locations where a jury might be more likely to decide against the defendant. It is only natural for prosecutors to bring suit in whatever locations they believe offer the best opportunity for a conviction. This troubling new development is demonstrated in *Blucher* v. *The United States*, a case concerning an Oregon resident who was tried and convicted in Wyoming.[31] His only contact with Wyoming was when he mailed allegedly obscene materials which had been solicited by Wyoming postal authorities. These officials apparently wanted to try the case in Wyoming, probably believing that Wyoming would have more restrictive community standards than Oregon. The U.S. Supreme Court dismissed the judgment against the distributor, though without issuing an opinion stating its reasons. Perhaps this ruling will discourage choices of location based solely on the expected political and religious makeup of the jury.

Defining "Patently Offensive"

The Supreme Court in *Miller* provided some guidance as to the meaning of "patently offensive," indicating that the phrase refers to "hard-core" materials which, among other things, include "patently offensive representations or descriptions of ultimate sexual acts, normal or perverted, actual or simulated," and "patently offensive representations or descriptions of masturbation, excretory functions, and lewd exhibitions of the genitals."[32] These examples indicate that materials less than "patently offensive" may well be entitled to First Amendment protection, and thus serve as a limitation on the states' power to arbitrarily define obscenity.

In *Jenkins* v. *Georgia*, the Supreme Court applied this standard to the Academy Award-winning film *Carnal Knowledge*.[33] A Georgia court had convicted the defendant after a jury determined that the film was obscene. Although the Court recognized that the issue of obscenity was primarily a question of fact to be determined by the jury, it was not willing to grant the jury unlimited license in making that determination. Because the Court decided that the film was not sufficiently hard-core to be considered patently offensive, it reversed the jury's decision and the resulting conviction.

DEFINING THE "PRURIENT INTEREST" OF THE "AVERAGE PERSON"

According to the ruling in *Miller*, to be judged obscene, a work must appeal to the "prurient interest" of the "average person." *Prurient interest* is an elusive concept, but that did not stop the Supreme Court from attempting to define it in *Roth* as that which "beckons to a shameful, morbid, degrading, unhealthy, or unwholesome interest in sex."[34] Some states have attempted to write their own definition of prurient interest into their obscenity statutes. One such attempt that was challenged as overly broad led to yet another Supreme Court decision on obscenity in *Brockett* v. *Spokane Arcades, Inc.*[35]

The statute challenged in *Brockett* defined obscene matter as that appealing to the prurient interest, which was further defined as "that which incites lasciviousness or lust." The Supreme Court held that by including lust in its definition of prurient, the statute extended to material which merely stimulated normal sexual responses. Thus, the statute was overly broad and unconstitutional. The Court indicated that material said to appeal to prurient interests is to be judged by its impact on the normal person, not by its effect on those who are easily influenced or unusually sensitive. Thus, a jury is not to consider the effect the material in question would have on children or adolescents under eighteen.[36] These statements by the Court raise the possibility of a defense argument that if a work obviously appeals to a bizarre or deviant sexual appetite, acquittal is required because the "average person" is not affected. A widely recognized exception to the "average person" standard has been established by the Court, however, where it can be shown that a given book, magazine, or film was designed for and distributed to a well-defined deviant group.[37]

The issue of whether material appeals primarily to the prurient interest may be influenced by the manner in which it is advertised. Evidence of an advertising practice known legally as "pandering" may contribute to the likelihood that a work will be declared obscene. Pandering occurs when materials are marketed by emphasizing their sexually provocative nature.

The relevance of pandering was first determined by the Supreme Court in 1966, in *Ginzburg* v. *U.S.*[38] In *Ginzburg*, the Supreme Court reviewed a conviction under a federal obscenity statute for distribution of several publications containing erotic materials which, because they were of some value to psychiatrists and other professionals, were not in and of themselves obscene. However, since the defendants had portrayed the materials as salacious and lewd in their marketing, and had indiscriminately distributed those works to the general public, the trial court had found the materials to be obscene. The Supreme Court affirmed, stating that evidence of pandering is relevant to the question of obscenity.

The Supreme Court again upheld the relevance of pandering in *Hamling* v. *United States*.[39] In that case, the Court made it clear that where the obscenity question is a close one, evidence of pandering may be considered. Such evidence is but one factor in determining whether a work is obscene, however, and does not replace the *Miller* test.

THEMATIC OBSCENITY

Thematic obscenity refers to supposedly obscene material that is more or less the central theme of a work, and thus is relevant to the ideas the work intends to express. Such material is not completely beyond the states' reach if it is in fact obscene. At the same time, the Supreme Court is extremely suspicious of state obscenity statutes that appear to prohibit sexually explicit materials which convey certain ideas, rather than sexually explicit (and patently offensive) materials in and of themselves.

The Supreme Court addressed thematic obscenity in *Kingsley International Pictures Corp.* v. *Regents of New York University*.[40] In this case, the Court reviewed a New York statute which forbade licenses for the exhibition of motion pictures that portrayed "acts of sexual immorality ... as desirable, acceptable, or as a proper pattern of behavior."[41] Application of the statute had resulted in denial of a license for *Lady Chatterley's Lover*, a film that portrayed an adulterous relationship.

The Court found that the New York statute went beyond regulating the depiction of patently offensive sexual acts and, in effect, prevented the expression of an idea—namely, that an adulterous relationship could under some circumstances be condoned. Since the right to express ideas is expressly protected by the First Amendment, and since the statute denied that right, the statute was deemed unconstitutional.

Another attempt to suppress thematic obscenity was overturned by the Court in 1962 in *Manual Enterprises* v. *Day*.[42] This time the Court held that a magazine for homosexuals was not obscene. Obscenity, it said, requires proof of two elements: (1) patent offensiveness and (2) appeal to prurient interest. Since pictures in the magazine under attack were found to be no more objectionable than the pictures of female nudes that society tolerates in other magazines, they could not be prohibited simply because they conveyed the idea of homosexuality.

CHILD PORNOGRAPHY LEGISLATION

Attempts to regulate pornography have also been made by legislators enacting child pornography laws. This legislation is designed to curb sexual abuse of children by making it unlawful to use children in explicit sexual performances or pornographic pictures. The Supreme Court has been relatively supportive of state efforts to outlaw pornography dealing with children. In the 1982 case of *New York* v. *Ferber*, the Court held that a state may ban the distribution of materials showing children engaged in sexual conduct even though the material is not legally obscene.[43] Since state child-pornography laws vary widely, the writer who plans to use any illustrations, even cartoons, of children in sexual circumstances would be well advised to consult with a lawyer.

INFORMAL CENSORSHIP

There is the possibility that government funding could be distributed in such a way as to constitute informal censorship. The problem is illustrated by the case of *Advocates for the Arts* v. *Thompson*.[44] In that case the plaintiff,

Granite Publications, was to receive a grant from the New Hampshire Commission on the Arts, which was funded largely by the National Endowment for the Arts. The commission withdrew its pledge of funding upon discovering that a poem previously published by Granite was, in the commission's opinion, obscene. Granite sued, alleging that its First Amendment rights had been violated. The federal court ruled in favor of the arts commission.

Although the court was not willing to rule that the poem was obscene under the *Miller* test, neither was it willing to intrude upon the discretion of the arts commission to determine which projects would or would not receive government funds. As long as it could be argued that the commission's selections were based on the issue of artistic or literary merit, the First Amendment was not violated. The Court did intimate that the commission might not have exercised the best judgment with respect to the poem. Nevertheless, the Court refused to place itself in a position of being the final arbiter of questions of literary merit. Moreover, the Court refused to require the commission to draw up narrow standards and guidelines by which artistic merit could be judged, since these qualities are by their very nature subjective.

The Court concluded that refusal of the government to provide funds for the arts will not normally constitute censorship, since such refusal does not prohibit the publication of a given work, although inability to publish may be the practical result. Writers may therefore find that their creations are unacceptable to publishers who are concerned about this informal type of censorship. This is not to say that government funding agencies are completely immune from attack on the basis of constitutional rights. The court in *Thompson* did suggest that, should an agency develop a "pattern of discrimination impinging upon the basic First Amendment rights to free and full

debate on matters of public interest," an argument concerning the writer's constitutional rights might have
merit.[45]

Once a work has received some form of government
funding, the recission of the government sponsorship
may be a First Amendment violation. Thus in *American
Council for the Blind* v. *The Librarian of Congress*[46] it was
held that Congress's refusal to continue funding for the
purpose of putting into Braille and recording *Playboy*
magazine infringed the constitutional rights of the
plaintiff, the American Council for the Blind.

Predicting Liability

As I have indicated here, whether or not a publication is
likely to be deemed obscene under the *Miller* test is extremely difficult to predict. Courts have experienced numerous problems in applying the *Miller* test, and there is
no indication that these problems are likely to be resolved
in the near future.

Perhaps the most significant barrier to predictability in
obscenity cases is that obscenity is a factual question to be
determined by a jury. Presumably, juries are composed of
reasonable persons, but it has long been recognized that
reasonable persons may disagree. Consequently it is not
particularly surprising that different juries have come up
with different results in obscenity cases involving essentially the same facts and issues.

Censorship in the United States is far from a fading issue or a shrinking problem for the writer. In fact, passage
and enforcement of even more restrictive obscenity laws
may be on the horizon. This scenario is recommended to
the American people in the report of the United States Attorney General's Commission on Pornography, released
July 9, 1986.

The eleven-member "Meese Commission," appointed
in May of 1985 and stacked unabashedly with anti-vice

prosecutors and activists, reviewed social research and conducted over 300 hours of emotional hearings which one critic has referred to as a "show trial in which pornography was found guilty."[47]

The commission wrestled unsuccessfully with the problem of defining pornography, and in the end was unable to articulate any category of sexual imagery which it would consider harmless, ultimately overturning the findings of the 1970 report of the President's Commission on Pornography which had concluded there was no evidence that sexually explicit material caused antisocial behavior.

The Meese Commission not only recommended passage of new state obscenity laws, but also endorsed citizen action groups and provided instructions for canvassing local bookstores, organizing demonstrations and boycotts, and other grassroots censorship-oriented activities.

How, then, is the writer to predict whether a particular jury might reasonably find a writing to be obscene? You probably cannot make this prediction, at least not without the assistance of a lawyer familiar with the relevant decisions. By analyzing the various obscenity cases in which the defendant was convicted and contrasting them with those in which the defendant was acquitted, and by staying on top of any new obscenity laws which may be enacted in the future, an attorney should be able to provide a fairly accurate prediction as to whether the work in question will or will not be considered obscene. Fortunately, written material is much less often found to be obscene than graphic material such as pictures and films.

The next two chapters will cover the laws against defamation and libel, and invasion of privacy, two distinct legal areas that present the writer with problems similar to those discussed in this chapter.

9

Defamation and Libel

In the year 400 B.C., the Greek philosopher Socrates was convicted of teaching atheism to the children of Athens and was sentenced to death. Of the four hundred jurors, all but two voted for conviction. In his defense, Socrates claimed that most of the charges were based on lies and that his reputation had been unjustly attacked for years. For example, he argued, in *The Clouds*, a play by Aristophanes that was performed before the entire population of Athens, the bumbling teacher of philosophy was named Socrates. However, in Athens free speech was an absolute right, and Socrates had no protection against statements which today would be considered defamatory.

Despite the First Amendment guarantee that freedom of speech will not be abridged, in contemporary America that freedom is limited. Defamatory statements, among other kinds of speech, are not absolutely protected—and are in fact prohibited by law in all fifty states.

A statement will generally be considered defamatory if it tends to subject a person to hatred, contempt, or ridicule or if it results in injury to that person's reputation while in office, in business, or at work.

A defamatory statement may be written or oral. If it is

written, it is *libel*; if it is oral, it is *slander*. For the most part the same laws and principles govern all defamatory statements, but since a writer's liability involves words that appear in print, we will focus here on libel. As a writer, you must be cautious about any written descriptions that might be considered defamatory. If the work is published—and as you will see, "published" has a very broad meaning in the context of libel—you, as the writer, could be sued along with the publisher, under the libel statutes.

It is not always easy to determine whether a written work is defamatory. An important fact to keep in mind is that groups of people, corporations, and partnerships can sue under libel statutes, as well as individuals. In order to give you some idea of the scope of libelous writings, let us take a closer look at what kinds of writings the courts have found to be libelous. Then we will look at who can sue a writer for libel, and various defenses a writer can use against different plaintiffs.

ACTIONABLE LIBEL

Actionable libel is libel that would furnish legal grounds for a lawsuit. In order for a piece of writing to be actionable libel, it must, in legal terminology, *convey a defamatory meaning* about an identifiable person or persons, and must have been published. A writing might not convey a defamatory meaning if the potentially defamatory adjectives are used simply for effect, or as a generic insult.

For example, if an author writes, "X is a bastard," a judge would no doubt rule that the statement is *capable* of defamatory meaning. Nevertheless, the statement will not convey a defamatory meaning unless the jury finds that, given the context of the statement, a third party could interpret the writing to mean that X was born out of wedlock. If not, the statement is merely a strong, but generic, insult.

Courts have traditionally put libelous expressions into two categories: *libel per se* and *libel per quod*. In libel per se the defamatory meaning is apparent from the statement itself. In libel per quod, the defamatory meaning is conveyed only in conjunction with other statements. In libel per quod, the writing may be susceptible to more than one reasonable interpretation but as long as any one of the interpretations is defamatory, the statement will constitute libel.

LIBEL PER SE

One example of libel per se is an accusation of criminal or morally reprehensible acts. An accusation of criminal conduct is libelous per se even though it is not explicitly stated; if the writer has stated facts that describe a crime or has cast suspicion by innuendo, that is sufficient for libel per se. On the other hand, it is never libel per se to accuse someone of exercising a legal right—even though some members of the public may not approve of it. For example, it is not libel per se to say that a man killed someone in self-defense, that he brought a divorce suit against his wife, or that he invoked the Fifth Amendment forty times. Although these statements may cast suspicion, they cannot be libelous per se because they merely report the exercise of a legal right.

A statement that describes deviant sexual conduct or unchastity, particularly by a woman, is libelous per se. Moreover, to state that someone has a loathsome or contagious disease such as syphilis, tuberculosis, or AIDS, is libelous per se.

When the statement involves politics, the determination of libel per se is more difficult. Today, courts generally agree that a statement that a person belongs to a particular political group will be libel per se only if that group advocates the use of violence as a means of achieving politi-

cal ends. Thus, to say that someone belongs to the Ku
Klux Klan would probably be libel per se. But to say that
someone is a racist would probably not be, since racism is
not necessarily intertwined with the use of violence. In
some instances, though, a statement concerning someone's political affiliation may constitute libel per se even
though the political group involved does not advocate violence. For example, to state that someone is a communist
may be libel per se because communist affiliation is generally injurious to a person's reputation within significant
portions of society today.

It is usually deemed libel per se to impute to a professional person a breach of professional ethics, general unfitness or inefficiency. For example, it may be libel per se
to say that a person's business is bankrupt, because the
statement implies a general unfitness to do business. However, to say that the business person did not pay a certain
debt is not libel per se, because everyone has a legal right
to contest a debt. Similarly, it may be libel per se to say that
a doctor is a butcher, because it implies general incom-
petence. But it is not libel per se to say that the doctor
made a mistake, so long as it does not imply general in-
competence. Everyone makes mistakes.

There is a gray area concerning statements about certain business practices which may not be illegal but which
nonetheless could give a business bad publicity. To say
someone is cutting prices would not be libel per se, but to
say someone is cutting prices to drive a competitor out of
business would be.

It is impossible to describe every phrase or statement
that could constitute libel per se, since any statement can
be libel per se if it is likely to produce a reprehensible
opinion of someone in the minds of a large number of
reasonable people. Remember, the rule of thumb is that a
statement is libelous per se when the defamatory meaning
is clear from the statement itself.

LIBEL PER QUOD

In libel per quod, since the defamatory meaning of a statement is conveyed only in conjunction with other statements, the plaintiff who sues for libel must introduce the context of the statement and demonstrate to the court how the writing as a whole results in a defamatory innuendo. For example, the statement "X burned down his barn" is not enough. Although it may be peculiar to burn down one's own barn, such an act would not normally subject someone to hatred, ridicule, or contempt. A plaintiff contending that such a statement is libelous would have to show that it was accompanied by other information; for example, a statement that the barn was heavily insured. Then the whole passage might well constitute libel per quod, since one implication of these statements taken together (i.e., the innuendo) could be that X is trying to defraud an insurance company.

PROOF OF DAMAGE

The distinction between libel per se and libel per quod is important primarily because it determines whether the plaintiff has to prove damage. Where there is libel per se, damage to reputation will be presumed and the plaintiff need not prove it. If, however, the charge is libel per quod, damage normally must be proved, although there are some exceptions to this general rule. If the innuendo in the libel per quod falls within one of four categories, damage will be presumed as in libel per se. The four categories are innuendos that (1) adversely reflect upon someone's ability to conduct business, trade or profession, (2) impute unchastity to an unmarried woman, (3) accuse someone of committing a crime of moral turpitude,* or (4)

---

* A crime of moral turpitude is something that is immoral in itself, irrespective of the fact that it is punished by law. Examples are rape and murder.

accuse someone of having a loathsome disease such as leprosy or a venereal disease.

PUBLICATION

As mentioned earlier, a writing must be published in order to constitute actionable libel. The legal meaning of *publication* in the libel context is very broad. Once a statement or written work is communicated to a third person who understands it, the statement, in the eyes of the law, has been published. Thus, if you show a letter to someone other than the person the letter is addressed to, you have published the contents of the letter once that third person reads it.

Generally, the person who is defamed can bring a separate lawsuit for each repetition of the defamatory remark. However, when the remark is contained in a book, magazine, or newspaper, a majority of courts have adopted what is known as the *single-publication rule*. Under this rule, a person cannot make each copy of the book grounds for a separate suit. Rather, the number of copies is taken into account only for purposes of determining the extent of damages.

WHO CAN SUE FOR LIBEL?

In order for someone to sue for libel, the written work at issue must identify that person or entity. This is easy to prove, of course, when the plaintiff is identified by name in the work, but if a plaintiff is not identified by name, the plaintiff can prove that he or she was nonetheless "identified" by showing that a third party could reasonably infer that the statement was "of and concerning" the plaintiff. Thus, it does no good to change names in a story if anyone could recognize the character under another name.

The opposite situation is more troublesome. This is the situation where the writer of a piece of fiction uses a name because the writer likes the sound of it, and by chance that name is the same as that of a living person. If readers might reasonably think that the story refers to the living person, and if the work conveys a defamatory meaning, the writer may be liable even though there was no intention to defame. Fortunately, the courts will find such unintentional libel only where the fictional character and the plaintiff have a comparable geographic location, vocation, age, physical features or some combination of these. These reasonable requirements make it improbable that a fiction writer could unintentionally defame someone.

The courts have uniformly held that corporations and partnerships can sue for libel just as an individual can. Although there has been disagreement among the states as to whether not-for-profit corporations should be protected, the trend seems to be to allow nonprofit corporations to sue when they are injured in their ability to collect or distribute funds. For example, in *New York Society for the Suppression of Vice* v. *MacFadden Publications*, the defendant newspaper had published articles charging the president of a nonprofit institution with crimes and highly improper and reprehensible conduct.[1] The court held that the institution had the right to sue for libel since benevolent, religious, and similar corporations have interests connected with income and property which should have the same protection and rights as corporations engaged in business for profit. The plaintiff corporation depended entirely on contributions for its support, and the court held that the number and amount of those contributions would be directly affected by the publication of false and malicious articles accusing the corporation of engaging in illegal and reprehensible conduct in the management of its affairs.

If a defamatory statement is made about an identified group of people, the possibility of each member of that group having a good cause of action will depend on the size of the group and whether the statement defames all or only a part of the group.

Where the group is composed of more than one hundred members, the individuals generally do not have a good cause of action. If, for example, someone publishes the statement "all writers are thieves," an individual writer could not prevail in a defamation suit, since it can hardly be said that the one writer's reputation was damaged as a result of the statement. On the other hand, if that same statement was directed to all writers within a particular small town, individual writers could probably prevail, since they would be more likely to be subject to contempt, hatred, or ridicule as a result of the defamatory statement.

The individual members of a group might not prevail if the allegedly defamatory statement referred only to a portion of the group. If, for example, someone states that "some members" of a particular trade group "are communists," the individual members probably cannot prevail in a defamation suit, since the statement is not all-inclusive, and since those included are not named. Again, the size of the group could affect the court's ruling. If the partially defamed group is small, it would be more likely that the reputation of each member had been damaged, even though the statement was not all-inclusive.

A writer confronted with the question of whether or not to publish a work that identifies a person, group, or entity should make a two-step analysis. First, does the piece defame a reputation? If the answer is no, then it may be safely published (assuming no other form of liability such as copyright infringement or invasion of privacy is involved). If the answer is yes, the second step is to determine whether there is a valid defense.

DEFENSES TO LIBEL

Even if a plaintiff proves defamation, publication, and damages (where damages must be proved), the writer may nevertheless prevail in a lawsuit if he or she is able to establish a valid defense.

Truth

Truth is an absolute defense to a charge of defamation, although it may not protect against other charges such as invasion of privacy. It is not necessary for a potentially defamatory statement to be correct in every respect in order to be considered true. As long as the statement is true in all essential particulars, the defense will be acceptable. For example, the statement "X robbed Bank A" would be considered true, and therefore not actionable, even though X in fact robbed Bank B. The essential fact is that X was convicted of robbing a bank, so it is irrelevant which bank was robbed.

Opinion

A second possible defense is that the supposedly defamatory statement was one of opinion rather than fact. The rationale for this defense is that one's opinion can never be false, and therefore cannot be defamatory. Of course, the line between a statement of fact and an opinion is often hard to draw, particularly in the area of literary or artistic criticism.

Not surprisingly, art, literary, and drama critics have frequently been accused of libel after they have published particularly scathing reviews. When criticizing the work of artists, the critic is free to use rhetorical hyperbole as long as the statements do not reflect on the character of the artist. For example, in the early '70s Gore Vidal sued William F. Buckley, Jr., for calling Vidal's book, *Myra Breckenridge*, pornography.[2] The court held that, in context, this statement did not assail Vidal's character by actually suggesting that he himself was a pornographer. Thus the statement was not defamatory.

An example of criticism that did assail character is a famous case from the 1890s, in which the American artist James Whistler won a defamation suit against John Ruskin, the English art critic. In his assessment of Whistler's

"Nocturne in Brown and Gold," Ruskin wrote: "I have seen, and heard, much of Cockney impudence before now, but never expected to hear a coxcomb ask 200 guineas for flinging a pot of paint in the public's face."[3] On the surface, this statement was an expression of opinion of the painting's worth. At the same time it implied facts about Whistler's motives, suggesting that he was defrauding the public by charging money for something that was not even art. The court found these implied facts to be defamatory since they described Whistler as unfit professionally.

Consent

Someone accused of defamation may also raise the defense of consent. It is not libelous to print material about a person who has consented to its publication. In this situation, the extent of the material that may be legally published is governed by the terms and context of the consent. For example, someone may consent to a one-time publication of a story by a newspaper. If the paper runs the story again, the paper may be liable.

An interesting case that turned on what constitutes consent concerned a student humor magazine that had run a piece for Mother's Day consisting of four pictures.[4] One picture was totally black. Under it was the caption, "Father Loves Mother." Another picture showed a little girl with the caption, "Daughter Loves Mother (And wants to be one too!)." A third picture showed a boy whose arm was tattooed with a heart enclosing the word "Mother," labeled "Sailor Boy Loves Mother," and the final picture showed a face partly covered by a hood, labeled "Midwife Loves Mother." The picture of the little girl happened to be a photograph of the daughter of a local Methodist minister, a Mr. Langford, and it was rumored that he was about to sue the school newspaper for libel. Langford maintained that the pictures and captions made innuendos about the unchastity of his daughter, his wife, and himself. Another student newspaper sent two reporters to interview the minister, and he gladly consented to the interview. When the minister filed suit, the newspaper that had conducted the interview published an article which truthfully set out the facts of the suit and contained material from the interview. It also republished the allegedly libelous material. The minister then sued the second paper, but he lost because the court found that he had consented to republication of the material. This case illustrates that consent may be obtained indirectly, without the subject's knowing exactly the extent of the consent.

Reports of Official Proceedings

Another defense to what would otherwise be considered defamation is that the written statement was made in a report of official proceedings or a public meeting. As long as the context is a "fair and accurate" account of those proceedings, there can be no liability, even if what the statement reported is both defamatory and false. The requirement that the publication be fair and accurate means that whatever was written must be a balanced and unbiased account. For example, a writer may not quote only one side of an argument made in court if there was also a rebuttal to that argument. The account need not be an exact quote, and it is permissible to include some background material to put the report into proper perspective. However, a writer must be careful not to include extraneous information such as editorial comments (which are themselves defamatory), because these will not be protected by the Report of Official Proceedings defense.

Journalists and lawyers learned long ago that it is not always clear what constitutes an official proceeding or public meeting. Court proceedings from arrest to conviction are definitely official proceedings. On the other hand, comments made outside of court are not. A newsletter

sent by a legislator to constituents does not generally constitute an official proceeding, whereas a political convention probably does.

Reply

Another defense to an accusation of libel is that of
reply. If someone is defamed, that person is privileged to
reply, even if the first writer is defamed in the process.
This privilege is limited to the extent that the reply may
not exceed the provocation. For example, if A calls B a
communist, B has a right to reply that A is a liar or that A
is a right-wing extremist, because either of these comments bears some relation to the original comment. If,
later on, A sues B for libel because of the statement about
A being a right-wing extremist, B can simply show that the
statement was in response to the accusation made by A:
the reply defense. But if B made the mistake of responding to A by calling A a thief—a statement that bears no relation to A's accusation—B cannot have recourse to the
reply defense.

Statute of Limitations

Another possible defense is the statute of limitations.
Basically, statutes of limitations limit the time period
within which an injured party can sue. The reason for
these time limits is the difficulty of resolving old claims
once the evidence becomes stale and the witnesses forget
or disappear.

In the case of libel, the injured party must generally sue
within one or two years from the date of first publication,
although in some states the period is longer. If suit is
brought after this time has elapsed, the statute of limitations will bar the suit.

The period of time allowed by statutes of limitations for
libel begins when a statement is first published. Since publication means the act of communicating the matter at is-

sue to one or more persons, the first publication of a book, magazine, or newspaper is deemed to occur when the publisher releases the finished product for sale. A second edition is generally not considered a separate publication for calculating time elapsed under the statute of limitations, at least where the single-publication rule (page 191) is followed.

Absence of Actual Malice

The defense most frequently used in recent libel suits was created by the United State Supreme Court in 1964 in *The New York Times Co.* v. *Sullivan*.[5] The case against *The Times* concerned an advertisement it published which contained some inaccuracies and supposedly defamed L.B. Sullivan, the police chief of Montgomery, Alabama. The Supreme Court held that *The New York Times* was not guilty of libel, citing a

> profound national commitment to the principle that debate on public issues should be uninhibited, robust, and wide-open, and that it may well include vehement, caustic, and sometimes unpleasantly sharp attacks on government and public officials.[6]

Thus the Court found that the First Amendment provides some protection to writings which criticize public officials for anything they do that is in any way relevant to their official conduct.

By virtue of the First Amendment protection, or privilege, when a public official sues for defamation the official must prove with "convincing clarity" that the defendant published the statement with "actual malice." Actual malice is defined as knowledge of the falsity, or a reckless disregard for the truth or falsity, of the statements published. Reckless disregard is further defined as serious doubts about the truth of the statement. Conflicts often arise in suits against newspapers when a public official is the plaintiff and tries to find the source of a paper's information in order to show reckless disregard of the truth, while the newspaper tries to protect its source.

The *Sullivan* case placed a greater burden of proof upon public officials in defamation suits. Prior to *Sullivan*, a preponderance of the evidence was simply proof of defamation, but now the courts require "convincing clarity," which is somewhere between the "preponderance of the evidence" required in most civil suits and the "proof beyond a reasonable doubt" required in criminal cases.

For the writer, the result of *Sullivan* was the public-official privilege—the privilege to examine public officials with considerable scrutiny.

The standards resulting from *Sullivan* were applied in 1984 in the highly publicized case of *Sharon* v. *Time Inc.*, which arose after the massacre of Palestinian refugees by Lebanese Phalangists in retaliation for the assassination of Lebanon's President Gemayel.[7] At the time, Lebanon was occupied by Israeli forces and Ariel Sharon was Israel's defense minister. *Time* magazine published a story alleging that Sharon had secretly discussed the possibility of such a retaliatory attack with Gemayel's family, who remained politically powerful. Sharon sued *Time*, which steadfastly refused to retract the allegations.

The jury held that *Time*'s article was false, and that Sharon was defamed by it. But the jury also found that *Time* did not possess actual malice, which meant that the magazine did not have to pay any damages. Both sides claimed victory. Sharon declared himself vindicated of the allegations, while *Time* pointed to the fact that it did not have to pay damages to Sharon. Most commentators, however, agreed that *Time* suffered great damage to its journalistic reputation.

Ariel Sharon went on to file a second lawsuit for libel against *Time* in Israel. According to a legal treaty between the United States and Israel, judgments of Israeli courts are recognized in America and vice versa. The Tel Aviv district court judge ruled that he would accept the American jury's ruling that *Time* had defamed Sharon and printed false material about him. Significantly, it is not necessary to prove malice in a libel suit under Israeli law; it is necessary only to show that a story is false and defamatory. Consequently, *Time*'s Israeli lawyer was reported as stating that the magazine had little chance of winning in the Israeli court.

In January of 1986, while the Tel Aviv judge was in the process of deciding the case, the parties announced an out-of-court settlement. In return for Ariel Sharon's dropping his libel action, *Time* stated to the Tel Aviv court that the reference to Sharon's supposed conversation in Beirut was "erroneous." In addition, *Time* agreed to pay part of the Israeli minister's legal fees. The *Time* statement appeared to acknowledge more culpability than had previously been admitted. The difference in the outcomes in the two cases illustrates the importance of requiring a plaintiff to prove actual malice in a libel suit. To some extent, this requirement in American law results in broader protection for the press than exists in other countries.

The American jury's verdict in *Sharon* may have spurred a settlement in another much-publicized case being tried at the same time, *Westmoreland* v. *CBS*.[8] In *Westmoreland*, the former commander of American troops in Vietnam challenged allegations of wrong-doing on his part made by CBS in a documentary about the war.

It has been speculated that the parties in *Westmoreland* realized that a verdict similar to that in *Sharon* would be damaging to both of them. Settlement of the case allowed both sides to claim victory without the necessity of submitting the issues to the jury.

The depth of criticism required for a finding of libel under the public-official privilege created in *Sharon* varies from case to case. The most intimate aspects of private life are fair game when one is discussing a candidate's qualifications for political office or an elected official. On the other hand, when discussing civil servants such as police and firefighters, only comments directly related to their function as civil servants are similarly privileged.

The Supreme Court has defined public officials as those "who have, or appear to the public to have, substantial responsibility for or control over the conduct of governmental affairs."[9] This category has been held to include all civil servants from police officers to secretaries. Recently, the Court has begun applying the public-official exception to public figures as well—but it has experienced a good deal of difficulty in determining who should be considered a public figure.

A Public Figure

In 1971, in the Supreme Court's first attempt to define a public figure, it was agreed that a person is a public figure if he or she is involved in a "newsworthy" event.[10] This definition was rejected three years later in *Gertz* v. *Robert Welch, Inc.*[11] Elmer Gertz, a well-known attorney in Chicago, represented the family of a child who had been killed by the police. The family was suing the police for wrongful death. *American Opinion*, a publication of the John Birch Society, published an article stating that Gertz was involved in a communist conspiracy to undermine the police. It was alleged that Gertz was a member of several communist groups.

When Gertz sued the paper's owner, Robert Welch, for defamation, the paper argued that Gertz was a public figure and thus was required to prove that the article had been published with actual malice. The Court held that Gertz was not a public figure and that he therefore did not need to prove actual malice. However, the Court did find that the First Amendment required Gertz at least to prove the paper had been negligent in making its false assertions. "Negligence," in this context, means that the paper failed to exercise ordinary and reasonable care in its investigation of the truth of what it printed. If by the exercise of reasonable care the paper could not have discovered that the story was false, then the paper would not have been liable for defamation. In addition to negligence, the Court required the plaintiff to prove some actual injury, monetary or emotional, and restricted his damages to compensation for such actual injury.

At present the Court recognizes two ways in which a person may become a public figure. The first is to "occupy positions of such persuasive power and influence that they are deemed public figures for all purposes."[12] This category includes those who are frequently in the news but are not public officials, such as Henry Kissinger, Bob Dylan, and Walter Cronkite. The fact that they are deemed public figures "for all purposes" means that the scope of privileged comment about them is virtually without limit.

The second way of becoming a public figure is to "thrust [oneself] to the forefront of particular public controversies in order to influence the resolution of the issues involved."[13] This category has two requirements. First, there must be a public controversy. The Court in *Time, Inc.* v. *Firestone* held that not every newsworthy event is a public controversy.[14] Nor is an event a public controversy merely because there may be different opinions as to the propriety of an act.

The *Firestone* case is a good example of how narrowly the Court applies the term "public controversy." *Time* magazine accidentally published a story stating that Mr. Firestone was divorced from Mrs. Firestone because of "extreme cruelty and adultery." In fact, the divorce was granted because the judge found that neither party to the divorce displayed "the least susceptibility to domestication," a novel ground for divorce under Florida law. *Time* went astray because the judge himself had once commented that there was enough testimony of extramarital adventures on both sides "to make Dr. Freud's hair curl." In its defense against Mrs. Firestone's suit for libel, *Time* insisted that Mrs. Firestone was a public figure. As evidence of this, it showed that the divorce had been covered in nearly every major newspaper and that Mrs. Firestone herself had held periodic press conferences during the trial. But the Court refused to equate a *cause celebre* with a public controversy. As a result, Mrs. Firestone was required to prove only that *Time* had been negligent in its reading of the Court's opinion and that there was actual injury.

The second requirement in this public-figure category is that the person has voluntarily thrust himself or herself into the controversy in order to influence the issues. This requirement would be met if someone's actions were calculated to draw attention to that person or to arouse public sentiment, but not if the person were merely arrested or convicted. A student who makes a speech during a peace demonstration, say, is considered a public figure only with respect to the subject of the demonstration. In matters that have nothing to do with the political controversy, the courts would probably regard the speaker as a private individual.

To reiterate, the Supreme Court will require only public officials and public figures to prove actual malice in a defamation suit. Yet even private persons may have to prove negligence if they sue a newspaper for libel which occurred in a piece relating to a matter of public concern. Although the Supreme Court held that the plaintiffs in *Gertz* and *Firestone* did not have the heavy burden of proof of public figures, they still had to prove negligence in their suits for libel. This is a more difficult burden of proof than that carried by the average person who has been defamed in regard to some private, unnewsworthy matter. You may remember from the earlier discussion of actionable libel that, generally, the everyday, private person who sues for libel does not need to prove actual malice or any other state of mind. All he or she need demonstrate to the court is that a writing identifying him or her conveyed a defamatory meaning and was published.

The Supreme Court recently increased the burden of proof for private plaintiffs suing newspapers writing about matters of public concern. In *Philadelphia Newspapers, Inc.* v. *Hepps*, a 1986 case, a businessman operating a franchise in Philadelphia sued the *Philadelphia Inquirer* for publication of several articles asserting that the plaintiff had links to organized crime and had used these links to influence local government.[15] The Court held that in such a case the plaintiff, not the defendant, will bear the burden of proof on the issue of the truth or falsity of the statement. The Court found that the Constitution requires that the burden be so shifted in order to ensure that true speech on matters of public concern not be stifled.

Hepps and *Gertz* together seem to indicate that a private person suing a newspaper writing on a matter of public concern will have to prove both that there was negligence on the part of the defendant, and that the information published was in fact false. How does one determine whether the information involved is of public concern? The distinction may hinge on whether or not the defendant represents the media. The Supreme Court dealt with the media-nonmedia distinction in *Dun & Bradstreet Inc.* v. *Greenmoss Builders, Inc.*[16] *Greenmoss Builders* involved a company which was the subject of a credit report that turned out to be false and grossly inaccurate regarding the financial condition of the plaintiff company. The report was sent to five subscribers of the reporting service. Subsequently, the company sued, maintaining that it was libelled by the report. Dun & Bradstreet maintained that the report was protected by the First Amendment, and that the plaintiff would have to prove falsity and negligence. The Court, by a five to four vote, held that since the credit report was not a "matter of public concern," it was not entitled to protection by the First Amendment. Thus, plaintiff had only to prove defamation and publication.

Greenmoss Builders leaves troubling questions unanswered, because the Court did not specifically define what speech is not of "public concern." Lacking such a definition, even writers who deal in news reporting and analysis need to be extremely careful about the subjects of their reports.

A question that has often been raised by legal scholars, but has as yet not received an answer from the courts, is whether a person who at one time was a public figure or involved in a matter of public concern can ever effectively return to private life. It is probably better to remain on the safe side and treat anyone who has been out of the limelight for more than five years as a private person.

Despite the tremendous burden of proof placed upon public officials and public figures, they are still able to win in many defamation suits. For example, Barry Goldwater was successful in his suit against Ralph Ginzburg,[17] who had published an article which stated that Goldwater was psychotic and therefore unfit to be president. Goldwater proved that material in the article was intentionally distorted. In a later case, actress Carol Burnett won a libel suit against the *National Enquirer*.[18] The article said that Burnett had been drunk and boisterous in a Washington restaurant when in fact her behavior had been beyond reproach. Burnett was able to show that the article was published with reckless disregard for the truth or falsity of the facts and thus satisfied the malice requirement.

PROTECTION AGAINST DEFAMATION SUITS

Since the law on libel is complicated, and subject to continual modification by the Supreme Court, any potentially

libelous work should be submitted to a lawyer before publication is considered. Remember, everyone directly involved in the publication of a libelous writing can be held
liable. Publishers usually protect themselves with a clause
in the writer's contract stating that the author guarantees
not to have libeled anyone and accepts responsibility for
covering costs if the publisher is sued. The risks involved
in agreeing to such a clause are obvious.

Although an article, feature story or book can sometimes be reworked to exclude any unverified facts or to
modify any fictional characters resembling living persons,
such alterations could be seen as destroying the integrity
of a work. Disclaimers, such as "All circumstances in this
novel are imaginary and none of the characters exist in
real life," will not protect the author if readers actually
and reasonably understand otherwise. Written consent
forms can protect the writer if persons discussed in a non-
fictional work are willing to sign them, agreeing not to sue
for libel. For the author who faces risk of libel and cannot
alter the work, the only solution may be purchasing insurance coverage. In fact, several publishers now include
writers in their policies. Some risk remains in the amount
of the deductible, but the economic impact of a libel lawsuit thus can be drastically reduced.

10

The Right of Privacy

The right to be protected from a wrongful invasion of privacy, largely taken for granted today, is a relatively new legal concept. In fact, the right of privacy was not suggested as a legal principle until 1890, when arguments for developing the right appeared in a *Harvard Law Review* article written by the late Justice Louis Brandeis and his law partner, Samuel Warren.[1] This article, written largely because of excessive media attention given to the social affairs of Warren's wife, maintained that the media were persistently "overstepping in every direction the obvious bounds of propriety and of decency" in violation of the individual's right "to be let alone."[2]

From this rather modest beginning the concept of a right to privacy began to take hold. In many of the early privacy cases the *Harvard Law Review* article was cited as justification for upholding privacy claims, although courts also found their own justifications. For example, in 1905 a Georgia court suggested that the right of privacy is rooted in natural law.[3] In the words of the court: "The right of privacy has its foundations in the instincts of nature. It is recognized intuitively, consciousness being the witness that can be called to establish its existence."[4] Other courts

have upheld right-of-privacy laws on constitutional
grounds, both state and federal, arguing that although
there is no express recognition of a right to privacy in the
U.S. Constitution, it can nevertheless be inferred from the
combined language of the First, Fourth, Fifth, Ninth, and
Fourteenth Amendments.

Although the right of privacy is now generally recognized, the precise nature of the right varies from state to
state. Some states, such as New York, Oklahoma, Utah,
Virginia, and California, have enacted right-of-privacy
statutes.[5] Others simply recognize the right as a matter of
common law. Others—Texas, Nebraska, Rhode Island,
and Wisconsin—expressly refuse to recognize a right of
privacy,[6] while still others have not yet taken a position.
Because the right of privacy is not consistent throughout
the states, you should keep in mind that the situations discussed in this chapter might be handled differently in the
state where you live. The cases here should not be relied
upon to determine a writer's rights and liabilities. They
are included simply to illustrate some of the legal developments in the area of privacy rights so that you can avoid
obvious traps, identify problems as they arise, and know
when to consult a lawyer.

Some of the confusion surrounding the right of privacy
can be resolved by dividing the right of privacy into four
separate categories: (1) intrusion upon another's seclusion, (2) public disclosure of private facts, (3) portrayal of
another in a false light, and (4) commercial appropriation
of another's name or likeness. These categories represent
the four different types of civil invasion of privacy currently recognized by the courts. Privacy rights may also
arise in the context of criminal prosecution; thus, in a recent Supreme Court case, Georgia's sodomy statute was
challenged as unconstitutional as an invasion of privacy of
the two consenting adults. The United States Supreme
Court declared that the statute was not an unconstitu-

tional invasion of the defendants' privacy, stating that there is extended no "fundamental right to homosexuals to engage in acts of consensual sodomy."[7]

Intrusion upon Another's Seclusion

At issue in intrusion upon another's seclusion is the extent to which an author intrudes upon someone's right of privacy for purposes of writing political, personal, or biographical works. An intrusion upon another's seclusion will be wrongful if three elements are present. First, there must be an actual intrusion of some sort. Second, the intrusion must be of a type that would be offensive to a reasonable person; courts will not consider the particular sensibilities of the plaintiff. Third, the intruder must have entered that which is considered someone's private domain. Thus, for example, it is generally not unlawful to take pictures of a person in a public place or disclose facts the person discussed publicly. It is likely, however, that an intrusion will be wrongful if someone goes on someone else's land without permission or opens someone else's private desk and reads materials found there. Publication is not a necessary element in a case for intrusion since the intrusion itself is the invasion of privacy.

The nature of a wrongful intrusion upon another's seclusion is well illustrated by two cases: *Dieteman* v. *Time, Inc.*[8] and *Galella* v. *Onassis*.[9] In *Dieteman*, the plaintiff claimed to be a healer. Investigators for *Life* magazine sought to prove that he was in fact a charlatan. In the process of checking out his claim, the reporters entered Dieteman's house under false pretenses, and while in his house they surreptitiously took pictures and recorded conversations. This information was then written up in an expose appearing in *Life*. The court held that the plaintiff's right of privacy had indeed been violated, since there was no question that his seclusion was invaded unreasonably.

An even more obvious intrusion is illustrated by *Galella* v. *Onassis*. Robert Galella is a freelance photographer specializing in photographs of celebrities, and the persistence and manner in which he performs his job are unparalleled. For a number of years Jacqueline Onassis, Caroline Kennedy, John Kennedy, Jr., and other members of the Kennedy family were among his favorite subjects. Onassis and the others were constantly confronted by Galella, who used highly offensive photography techniques, in parks and churches, at funeral services, theatres, schools and elsewhere. One of his practices was to shock or surprise his subjects in order to photograph them in a state of distress. While taking these photographs, he would sometimes utter offensive or snide comments. After hearing a wealth of evidence regarding this type of behavior, the court, in a fairly scathing opinion, held that Galella had wrongfully intruded upon the seclusion of his subjects. Finding monetary damages to be an inadequate remedy, the court issued a permanent injunction that prohibited Galella from getting within a certain distance of Onassis and the others.

In both *Dieteman* and *Galella* the defendants maintained that any attempt to restrain their efforts to get information or photographs was constitutionally suspect, since it would infringe upon their First Amendment freedoms. These arguments are not particularly persuasive. Courts have universally attempted to *balance* rights in intrusion cases: The right of the press to obtain information is balanced against the equal right of the individual to enjoy privacy and seclusion. Thus, the courts have refused to construe the First Amendment as a license to steal, trespass, harass, or engage in any other conduct that would clearly be wrongful or offensive.[10]

This balancing approach is apparent in *Galella*. The court found that the intrusions were so pervasive and offensive that it did not matter that many of the acts occurred while Onassis and the others were in public rather than private places such as their home. Their right to privacy had been significantly infringed. Furthermore, the products of Galella's efforts were trivial, being nothing more than fodder for gossip magazines. Thus, the harmful effect of suppressing his First Amendment freedoms was found to be slight or nonexistent. Significantly, the court did not forbid further photographs, but merely regulated the manner in which they could be taken.

Note that neither writers nor publishers risk liability for intrusion unless they themselves, or their agents, are directly involved in an intrusion, as the case of *Dodd* v. *Pearson* makes clear.[11] In *Dodd*, certain documents of a rather sensitive nature belonging to Senator Thomas Dodd of Connecticut had been surreptitiously removed, copied, and replaced by members of Dodd's staff in clear violation of his privacy rights. These documents were given to newspaper columnists Drew Pearson and Jack Anderson, who subsequently wrote and published a series of articles about them. Although Pearson and Anderson knew how the documents had been obtained, they themselves had played no role in the intrusion. Since the essence of the cause of action for intrusion is the intrusion itself, not subsequent publication, Pearson and Anderson were not held liable. They could have been liable only if they themselves had been the intruders or if they had hired agents, such as members of Dodd's staff, to take the documents.

Exposure to liability for wrongful intrusion thus generally arises during the fact-gathering process, not during the actual writing of a piece. For the dedicated journalist, the possibility of an intrusion suit should always be weighed against the natural tendency to aggressively pursue the facts, but even reporters on important assignments have no right to harass, trespass, use electronic surveillance, or enter a private domain.

PUBLIC DISCLOSURE OF PRIVATE FACTS

The public disclosure of private facts was the aspect of the right of privacy that first prompted Warren and Brandeis to publish their article in the *Harvard Law Review*. Plaintiffs are less likely to win in these circumstances, however, because the First Amendment protection that modern courts apply to "newsworthy information" makes it unlikely that writers dealing in matters of public interest will incur liability for public disclosure. Where the information disclosed is true, the First Amendment freedoms afforded to the press almost invariably outweigh an individual's right of privacy. Only in very limited circumstances will the balance be shifted in favor of the individual.

In order to bring a case for this kind of invasion of privacy, the plaintiff must prove that private facts about him or her were publicly disclosed and that the disclosure would be objectionable to a person of ordinary sensibilities.

The first question, then, is whether the information disclosed involves private facts. This is basically a matter of common sense; anything that one keeps to oneself and would obviously not wish to be made public is probably a private fact. Thus, private debts, criminal records, certain diseases, psychological problems, and the like usually involve private facts.

There is some seemingly private information which courts will treat as public. For example, information contained in a public record is never considered to be private. This principle was firmly established by the Supreme Court in the mid-'70s in *Cox Broadcasting Corp.* v. *Cohn*.[12] At issue was the constitutionality of a Georgia statute which made it a misdemeanor to publicly disclose the identity of a rape victim. In violation of this statute, someone at the broadcasting company made known the name of a rape victim, based upon information gleaned from a court indictment. The plaintiff, the father of the deceased victim, sued the broadcaster for publicly disclosing private facts, arguing that the statute converted the information into private facts. The highest Georgia court ruled in favor of Cohn, but when the case reached the Supreme Court, the decision was reversed. In a sweeping opinion, the Court declared that no one could be liable for truthfully disclosing information contained in an official court record, or, by implication, any other public record. Such disclosures enjoy an "absolute privilege" and are treated as public facts, regardless of how personal the information may be. An absolute privilege also exists for public disclosure of private facts made in the context of judicial, legislative, or executive proceedings.

The second requirement a plaintiff must meet in a case for public disclosure is proving that the public disclosure of private facts would be offensive to a reasonable person of ordinary sensibilities. Although a recluse may place a very high premium on absolute privacy, the law does not give such special rights. If a disclosure is minimal and therefore not offensive to the sensibilities of reasonable persons, the recluse will have no cause of action even though, from a recluse's personal perspective, the disclosure may seem egregious.

As mentioned in the preceding chapter, disclosures of newsworthy information are generally protected by the First Amendment. As long as such disclosure is truthful, the disclosure is privileged, and an individual's right to privacy will outweigh First Amendment freedoms only when the disclosure is outrageous in the extreme. This privilege regarding newsworthy information significantly insulates media writers from liability for invasion of privacy.

Generally, truthful disclosures pertaining to public figures or public officials are considered newsworthy, at least to the extent that the disclosure bears some reasonable relationship to the public role. If, however, the disclosure is highly personal, such as sexual habits, and has no bearing upon the individual's public role, the disclosure may not be privileged and thus may be actionable. This is particularly true where the individual does not enjoy a great deal of fame or notoriety. A presidential candidate or a mass murderer, for example, could expect considerably greater intrusions into and disclosure of his or her private affairs than a minor public official or a one-time traffic offender. Similarly, private persons who are involuntarily thrust into the public light will receive more protection than those persons who seek fame and notoriety.

A person no longer in the public eye may or may not be considered newsworthy. Generally, the newsworthiness of persons who once were public officials or public figures tends to decrease with the passage of time. To the extent that these people become less newsworthy, their right to privacy becomes stronger. Some people, of course, remain newsworthy even though they have long since left the public eye.

Such was the case in *Sidis* v. *F-R Publishing Corp.*[13] The defendant, publisher of *The New Yorker* magazine, published an article about the plaintiff's life. As a child, Sidis had shown a remarkable gift for mathematics and other intellectual pursuits, for which he had received considerable media attention. In his adult life, however, he had done little or nothing to develop his potential. He lived in relative squalor, had a series of menial jobs, and became excessively preoccupied with privacy. Sidis sued the magazine, alleging among other things that its article contained public disclosure of private facts. The court described the *The New Yorker* article as "merciless in its dissection of intimate details,"[14] so it can hardly be said that the court condoned the disclosures. Nevertheless, the court felt compelled to rule in favor of the magazine, since it deemed Sidis's present condition to be newsworthy. The court reasoned that "the misfortunes and frailties of neighbors and 'public figures' are subjects of considerable interest and discussion to the rest of the population. And when such are the mores of the community it would be unwise . . . to bar their expression . . . "[15]

The *Sidis* court did confirm, however, that the privilege to disclose newsworthy information was not without limits. Some disclosures may be so intimate and unwarranted as to "outrage the community's notions of decency."[16] Thus, the privilege has been tempered by a test that considers community mores: If the disclosure would shock the conscience of a reasonable person, the privilege is lost.

The community mores test articulated in *Sidis*, along with similar reasoning elsewhere, may weaken the disclosure privilege even in cases where the matter disclosed bears a direct relationship to the cause or source of the plaintiff's notoriety. *Melvin* v. *Reid*, decided in 1931, illustrates the point.[17] The plaintiff in this case was a former prostitute who had been charged with murder but was acquitted after a rather sensational trial. Thereafter, she led a conventional life; she married and made new friends who were unaware of her sordid past. Some years after the trial the defendants made a movie of the plaintiff's early life in which she was identified by her maiden name. The plaintiff sued, alleging public disclosure of private facts, and the court ruled in her favor. The court conceded that the events that initially brought the plaintiff into the public eye remained newsworthy, but stated that to identify her by name constituted a "willful and wanton disregard of the charity which should actuate us in our social intercourse."[18] In other words, the court applied a community mores test. The moviemakers' disclosure was deemed so outrageous that it could not be considered newsworthy and the disclosure privilege therefore did not apply.

The case of *Briscoe* v. *Reader's Digest Association, Inc.* provides an interesting contrast.[19] In this 1971 case, the defendant had published an article in *Reader's Digest* about truck hijacking. The article related a hijack attempt involving the plaintiff, Briscoe, who was identified by name. During the years between the hijack attempt and the defendant's disclosure, Briscoe had led an exemplary life. He sued for public disclosure of private facts, alleging that as a result of the article he had been shunned and abandoned by his daughter and friends, who previously had not known of the incident.

Although the facts of *Briscoe* were very similar to those of *Melvin*, and although the issue of outrageous disclosure was raised, the information in the *Briscoe* case was considered newsworthy and thus privileged. That this disclosure was considered newsworthy, whereas the disclosure in the *Melvin* case was not, might best be explained by the fact that the *Melvin* disclosure intruded upon the sex life of the plaintiff, revealing that she had once been a prostitute. It would appear that a disclosure is most likely to be considered unconscionable, and thus not newsworthy, if it relates to someone's sexuality, which is perhaps the most private aspect of anyone's life.

It should be observed that the social mores or outrageous disclosure test applies only where the plaintiff is in some way newsworthy. A public disclosure involving an ordinary person who is not newsworthy will be actionable if it is merely offensive to the sensibilities of reasonable persons. So, the question is really one of degree.

One final question that has been the subject of litigation in this area is whether an excerpt taken from a publication and used in an advertisement is privileged to the same extent as it is in the original publication. Although the answer is not altogether clear, it appears to depend on whether the advertisement is used to promote the work from which the excerpt was taken or to promote something else.

In *Friedan* v. *Friedan*,[20] the defendant, Betty Friedan, the noted feminist, wrote and published an account of her early domestic life. She included several photographs of those early years, one of which was a family portrait of the defendant, her former husband, and their child. This picture was selected for use in a television commercial promoting the defendant's publication. Carl Friedan, the defendant's former husband, sued her, alleging that the original publication, as well as the advertisements, constituted an invasion of his privacy as a public disclosure of private facts.

The court easily disposed of Carl Friedan's case. Since Betty Friedan was a noted feminist, her life was a matter of public interest. By virtue of being her former spouse, the plaintiff also became newsworthy, despite the fact that he had persistently sought to avoid publicity. Because he was deemed newsworthy, the public disclosure about his past private life was privileged. As to the commercial, the court held that where an advertisement is used to promote the publication from which the excerpt was taken, the advertisement will enjoy the same protection as the original publication. Since the defendant's biographical account was permissible, the television commercial was also permissible.

The case of *Rinaldi* v. *Village Voice, Inc.*[21] involved a slightly different situation. The plaintiff was a prominent judge. *The Village Voice* published an article critical of his performance on the bench. There was no question as to whether the article was permissible, since the plaintiff was clearly newsworthy and the disclosure pertained to his public role. At issue was the question of whether *The Village Voice* could incorporate excerpts from that article into an advertisement for itself. The court held that the advertisement was not permissible since the excerpts were used for the purpose of increasing subscriptions for subsequent issues of the newspaper. *The Village Voice* was held liable for public disclosure of private facts. Had the advertisement been used to promote the particular issue from which the excerpts were taken, it would, presumably, have been permissible under the reasoning applied in *Friedan*.

Where excerpts are used for purposes other than advertising, such as the circulation of galley proofs of forthcoming books to newspapers and magazines for review, the excerpts are more likely to enjoy the same privilege as information published in complete form. In *Estate of Hemingway* v. *Random House, Inc.*,[22] Ernest Hemingway's widow brought an action against the writer and publisher of the book *Papa Hemingway*. The author had drawn largely on his own recollections of conversations with Ernest Hemingway, and included two chapters on the famous novelist's illness and death. The court found that Hemingway was clearly a public figure and rejected the widow's argument that the description of her feelings and conduct during the time of her husband's mental illness was so intimate and unwarranted as to constitute outrageous disclosure. The court also rejected her claim that even if disclosures in the book were protected by the First Amendment, circulation of galley proofs to book reviewers of sixteen journals and newspapers amounted to unlawful use of private facts for advertising purposes. In holding that circulation of proofs to reviewers is not generally advertisement, the court stated:

> A publisher, in circulating a book for review, risks unfavorable comment as well as praise; he places the work in the arena of debate. The same reasons which support the author's freedom to write and publish books require a similar freedom for their circulation, before publication, for comment by reviewers.[23]

In summary, a public disclosure of private facts will support a lawsuit if the effect of the disclosure would be objectionable to persons of ordinary sensibilities, unless the disclosure is newsworthy. Whether a disclosure is or is not newsworthy will depend upon the social value of the facts disclosed, the extent to which the plaintiff voluntarily assumed public fame or notoriety, and the extent to which the disclosure related to the plaintiff's public role. Finally, even a disclosure relating to newsworthy persons may be actionable if it would outrage reasonable persons.

PORTRAYAL OF ANOTHER IN A FALSE LIGHT

Portrayal of another in a false light has been actionable as an invasion of privacy for some time. *Lord Byron* v. *Johnston*, decided in 1816, was probably the first case to address the issue.[24] In this case, the poet Lord Byron successfully enjoined the publication under his name of a rather bad poem which he did not in fact write. Byron was extremely protective of his reputation and apparently felt that the inferior piece would harm his image as an artist. Although the courts have handled similar cases over the years, the theory of false light as a separate and distinct cause of action has developed only recently.

To bring a suit for false light, a plaintiff must prove that the defendant publicly portrayed the plaintiff in a false light and that the portrayal would be offensive to reasonable people. In cases involving the media, the plaintiff must also prove that the portrayal was done with malice.

Thus, false-light cases often involve works that falsely ascribe to the plaintiff particular conduct or action. *Leverton* v. *Curtis Publishing Co.* was one such case.[25] A young girl who had been struck by an automobile was photographed while a bystander lifted her to her feet, and that photograph appeared in a local newspaper the following day. Nearly two years later the *Saturday Evening Post* published an article entitled "They Ask to Be Killed," the gist of which was that most pedestrian injuries are the result of carelessness on the part of the pedestrian. The photograph of the plaintiff was used to illustrate the story. The plaintiff sued the *Post* for invasion of privacy, alleging among other things that the *Post* had portrayed her in a false light. The court ruled in her favor because the rational inference from the use of the photograph in the article was that the plaintiff had been injured because of her carelessness, when in fact she had been completely without fault in the accident. Thus, the *Post*'s portrayal of the accident victim as having engaged in careless conduct was essentially false.

A frequent cause of false-light cases involves publications that attribute to someone views or opinions that the person does not actually hold or statements that the person did not make. For example, in *Cantrell* v. *Forest City Publishing Co.* a newspaper published an article concerning the destitute condition of a family that had been the victim of a natural disaster.[26] Among other things, the article contained excerpts from an interview with the mother of the family. In fact, there had never been such an interview. The newspaper was held liable for portraying the family in a false light by attributing to the mother statements that she never made.

Biographies may also be the subject of false-light suits. The factual biography, especially one concerning a newsworthy figure, is rarely actionable. But a biography that is fictionalized may well constitute a false-light invasion of privacy. Generally, courts will not impose liability if the publication merely contains insignificant distortions or errors. In such cases it is believed that the First Amendment guarantee of a free press outweighs the possible harm done to the individual falsely portrayed. In *Carlisle* v. *Fawcett Publications, Inc.*, for example, the court refused to impose liability for minor inaccuracies.[27] The defendant published an article concerning the life of the actress Janet Leigh. The article discussed one of Leigh's early romances and a subsequent marriage. The article was inaccurate, however, with respect to the plaintiff's age at the time of this romance as well as at the time of the marriage.

Although these mistakes tended to portray the plaintiff in a false light, the court nevertheless ruled that the article did not constitute an invasion of privacy.

Carlisle involves one extreme; the errors in that case were of little or no consequence. At the other extreme is the case of *Spahn* v. *Julian Messner, Inc.* in which the defendant published a biography of Warren Spahn, a renowned baseball player.[28] Unlike the biographical article in *Carlisle*, this biography was replete with fictionalized events, dramatizations, distorted chronologies, and fictionalized dialogues. Although the biography tended to glorify Spahn, it nevertheless placed him in a false, albeit radiant, light. As a result, the defendant was held liable for invasion of privacy.

Between these two extremes, it is difficult to predict where liability will lie. Distortions or inaccuracies involving insignificant events, places, and dates are likely to be safe, provided the errors are not pervasive. However, false statements pertaining to significant aspects of someone's life are more likely to result in liability, particularly if they involve highly personal and sensitive matters. The crucial question is whether the false portrayal would be offensive to a reasonable person in the position of the person portrayed. A false-light publication might be objectionable to the reasonable person for a number of reasons. As a result of the publication, the plaintiff might be humiliated, estranged from friends or family, or simply embarrassed. In *Carlisle*, the plaintiff was not able to prove that the false information was offensive or objectionable because the biographical inaccuracies were infrequent and insignificant. In *Spahn*, on the other hand, although it is doubtful that the plaintiff suffered any humiliation or estrangement, it is reasonable to suppose that he would have been highly embarrassed by the glorified, largely inaccurate version of his life.

FALSE LIGHT AND DEFAMATION: SIMILARITIES AND DIFFERENCES

In addition to proving an objectionable portrayal in a false-light case, the plaintiff might also have to prove malice—as is necessary in defamation. The false-light theory of invasion of privacy and defamation have much in common, so that as the law evolves with respect to one, the other is also affected. In 1964, the Supreme Court in *New York Times Co.* v. *Sullivan* articulated a new requirement for liability in defamation cases: Where the plaintiff is a public figure, public official, or otherwise newsworthy, and where the defendant is a member of the media, the plaintiff must prove that the allegedly defamatory statement was made with malice.[29] Malice is shown if the defendant knew the statement was false or if the defendant published the statement with reckless disregard for its truth or falsity. The Court felt that an unreasonable limitation on First Amendment freedoms would result if liability was imposed for mere negligence or failure to use due care in ascertaining the truth or falsity of publications.

The *New York Times* rule was at first limited to defamation cases. It thus was fairly easy for a newsworthy plaintiff to avoid the more stringent proof-of-malice requirement by couching the complaint in terms of invasion of privacy rather than defamation. If a cause of action for invasion of privacy could be maintained, the plaintiff could prevail over the media defendant by simply proving negligence.

This rather obvious means of circumventing the *New York Times* rule was done away with three years later in *Time, Inc* v. *Hill*.[30] The Supreme Court took the opportunity to extend the rationale of *New York Times* to false-light cases of invasion of privacy. A few years earlier, a family named Hill had been held hostage by escaped convicts, and the incident was subsequently portrayed in a play which differed in many material respects from the actual incident. After the play was written, *Life* magazine published a story on the incident which identified the Hills by name and stated as fact some of the fictionalized and dramatized parts of the play. In the Hills' suit, the Court required proof of malice even though the action was for invasion of privacy rather than defamation. As a result, newsworthy plaintiffs suing media defendants either for defamation or for invasion of privacy based upon public portrayal in a false light must prove that the defendant published with malice.

Although defamation and false-light cases are substantially similar, they do differ in several respects. First, the nature of the injury is different. Defamation is injury to the plaintiff's reputation within the community. False light is more inclusive, extending to injuries to the plaintiff's sensibilities caused by personal embarrassment, humiliation, estrangement of loved ones, and the like. Second, truth is an absolute defense for defamation, whereas it may not be for a false-light claim. For example, statements that might in fact be true may be published out of context so that they place the plaintiff in a false light. Finally, the rule of *New York Times* has been limited by *Gertz* v. *Robert Welch, Inc.*[31] In that case, the Supreme Court ruled that media defendants will be held liable for mere negligence, rather than malice, where the plaintiff is a private person who, by circumstances beyond his or her control, is thrust into the public eye. The *Gertz* ruling was limited to defamation cases, so the rule of *Time, Inc.* v. *Hill* apparently remains intact for false-light cases. In other words, in false-light cases, all newsworthy plaintiffs, whether or not they have voluntarily assumed their public role, must prove malice on the part of a media defendant.

COMMERCIAL APPROPRIATION OF ANOTHER'S NAME OR LIKENESS

Commercial appropriation of someone's name or likeness as an invasion of privacy bears little resemblance to cases based upon wrongful intrusion, public disclosure of private facts, or portrayal in a false light. In all of these other situations, the plaintiff must prove that the defendant's words or conduct caused the plaintiff to suffer humiliation, embarrassment, or loss of self-esteem, focusing on the injury to the plaintiff's sensibilities. In contrast, the law against appropriation is designed to protect someone's proprietary interest in one's own name or likeness. Athletes, movie stars, authors, and other celebrities obviously receive a considerable amount of their income from the controlled exploitation of their names or likenesses. The monetary benefits from such exploitation would be minimal without some legal protection.

In order to bring a suit for this type of invasion of privacy, one need only prove that the defendant wrongfully appropriated the plaintiff's name or likeness for commercial purposes. "Appropriation" in this sense means use. The fact of appropriation is rarely at issue in these cases, since the use will be obvious. However, the purpose of the use must be commercial, or expected to bring profits, either directly or indirectly. A purely private use will not result in liability for wrongful appropriation.

As with the other kinds of invasion of privacy, any use that is considered newsworthy will not be actionable as a commercial appropriation, even though some commercial gain might result from the use. As you might suspect, whether a use is newsworthy is often difficult to determine.

Rand v. *Hearst Corp.* concerned a book written by Eugene Vale and published by Hearst.[32] A review of the book appearing in the *San Francisco Examiner* maintained that Vale wrote with the same "mystique analysis" as author Ayn Rand. This excerpt comparing the two authors was printed on the front cover of Vale's book. Rand did not object to the original review since it was clearly privileged as being newsworthy, but she did object to the defendant's use of her name to advertise Vale's book. A lower court ruled for Rand, holding that the reviewer's privilege could not be extended to protect Hearst's appropriation. However, on appeal, the lower court's decision was reversed. The appellate court, in ruling that the publisher was privileged to quote from the review, stated that "a review concerning a book offered for sale is a matter of great public interest," at least to the extent that the review is of public interest and informative. Thus, although the defendant's use of Ayn Rand's name was clearly motivated by a desire to increase sales, the use was nevertheless privileged as being newsworthy.

Namath v. *Sports Illustrated* involved the use of a celebrity's likeness in an advertisement.[33] *Sports Illustrated* magazine published an article about the 1969 Super Bowl game that included some photographs of Joe Namath. One of those photographs was subsequently used in an advertisement promoting the magazine. Namath sued, alleging that the use of his photograph was a wrongful commercial appropriation. The court held for the magazine, maintaining that its use of Namath's picture was primarily informative because it indicated the general content and nature of the magazine as well as what subscribers could expect to receive in the future. Commercial benefits were only incidental. However, if *Sports Illustrated* had used Namath's picture in such a way that it appeared that Namath endorsed the magazine, the use would have been actionable, since the commercial purpose could not be said to be incidental to the dissemination of information.

It is clear from *Namath* v. *Sports Illustrated* and *Rand* v. *Hearst Corp.* that use of someone's name or likeness in solicitation or advertisement may not be actionable either because the use is newsworthy or because the advertising is incidental to informational purposes.

Courts appear to be less inclined to find a use newsworthy where the appropriation is of a performing artist's act in its entirety. In *Zacchini* v. *Scripps-Howard Broadcasting Co.*, a television station filmed and aired Mr. Zacchini's entire performance, in which he was shot from a cannon.[34] Zacchini sued, alleging wrongful commercial appropriation. The broadcasting company argued that the use was privileged since the performance was newsworthy. Although the Ohio Supreme Court ruled in favor of the broadcaster, the decision was reversed by the U.S. Supreme Court, where the majority held that the First Amendment freedom of the press and the public's right to know do not extend to the appropriation of a performer's entire act. Had the TV station merely aired a portion of Zacchini's act or merely offered an oral description of it, the use would have been privileged. But to show the entire performance was in effect to deny Zacchini his livelihood as a performer. This time the individual's right of privacy was stronger than the right of the press to fully report what was unquestionably a newsworthy event.

A commercial appropriation will not be actionable if the person portrayed has consented to the use. If you as a writer plan to use someone's name or photograph for endorsement or for any other commercial purpose, you should, clearly, try to get written consent. Consent could take the form of a licensing agreement or a release. It is important that you clearly define the terms of any consent in order to avoid accidentally exceeding its scope. It is equally important that you not rely on a third party such as a photographer or illustrator to get that consent. In *Cohen* v. *Hallmark Cards, Inc.* the defendant publisher, Hallmark, used some photographs of Cohen, the plaintiff, in one of its publications and relied on the photographer's statement that he had secured a release from the plaintiff.[35] In fact, no release was ever obtained. Cohen sued and the publisher was held liable. Hallmark was not permitted to raise as a defense its reliance upon the photographer's word. The publisher might have prevailed in a subsequent suit against the photographer, but a considerable amount of time and money could have been saved had the publisher verified at the outset that the consent had actually been granted. You as a writer could find yourself either in the position of the publisher, by relying on a photographer's or illustrator's word and including someone's name or likeness in a book without consent, or in the position of the photographer, by giving a publisher the go-ahead before consent is formally received. In fact, to avoid such problems, book publishers customarily require written statements from authors regarding releases from third parties, and delivery of the actual signed releases before any books are published.

A final question is whether a lawsuit based upon commercial appropriation can be brought after the death of the person whose name or likeness was used. There is considerable controversy over this issue.

In a 1984 case in New York, *Southeast Bank, N.A.* v. *Lawrence*, the court denied the defendants the right to name their theatre after playwright Tennessee Williams without his estate's consent.[36] The court held that New York recognizes a common-law *right of publicity*, which is the right to sue for unauthorized commercial appropriation. In this case the court ruled that the right of publicity survives death and descends to the deceased's heirs.

In a similar case involving the Elvis Presley estate, the plaintiff, Factors Etc., Inc., had acquired the exclusive right to market the name and likeness of Elvis Presley. It was undisputed that this license was valid and enforceable during Presley's lifetime. The issue was whether the license remained effective after Presley's death.

In *Factors Etc., Inc.*, the plaintiff sued, after Presley's death, to prevent Pro Arts from distributing posters bearing Presley's image.[37] The federal court, sitting in New York and applying New York law, ruled in favor of Factors, holding that when a party has the right to exploit a name or likeness during the lifetime of the subject, the right survives that person's death. Since Factors had exploited its exclusive license during Presley's life, the license remained valid and enforceable after Presley's death.

In another case involving the same license and essentially the same facts, but decided in the state of Tennessee under Tennessee law, the court reached the opposite opinion.[38] The Memphis Development Foundation had solicited money from the public for purposes of erecting a statue of Presley. A donation of twenty-five dollars or more entitled the contributor to an eight-inch pewter replica of the statue. The foundation sought a court ruling on whether the exclusive license of Factors Etc., Inc. to Presley's likeness was still valid. This time the court heid that a cause of action based upon commercial appropriation will under no circumstances survive the death of the person portrayed.

Since then the Tennessee legislature has passed a statute which explicitly states that the right to publicity *will* survive death and pass to the heir of the person whose name or likeness is commercially appropriated. Several other states, including California, Florida, Oklahoma, and Virginia, have passed similar laws. Such statutes guarantee the survival of such a right regardless of whether the person's name was commercially exploited during life. However, some states, while recognizing that the right to publicity can survive death, maintain that it will do so only if it was commercially exploited during life.

The latter position raises a difficult question by excluding the heirs of those famous individuals who chose not to exploit their names and faces while alive. In *Martin Luther*

King Jr. Center For Social Change, Inc. v. *American Heritage*, Coretta Scott King persuaded the court to enjoin the defendant, American Heritage, from selling plastic busts of Dr. King even though Dr. King had not commercially exploited his fame during life.[39] The court reasoned that "requiring lifetime exploitation would be to say that celebrities and public figures have the right of publicity in their lifetime, but only those who contract for bubble gum cards, posters and T-shirts have a descendable right of publicity upon their deaths."[40]

Since the law is unsettled on whether the right to sue for commercial appropriation survives death, it is difficult to make a general statement about the scope of such a right. Perhaps the most that can be said currently is that more and more courts and legislatures are recognizing that death should not automatically extinguish a right as meaningful and valuable as the right to control the use of a person's name or likeness. Many legal commentators approve this trend.

Since the legal concepts discussed in this chapter are still evolving, and since their treatment varies from state to state, you as a writer would be well advised to work closely with a lawyer when a question arises regarding invasion of a right to privacy.

11

The Writer's Estate

Many writers aspire to achieve a kind of immortality through their work. Yet even the most successful writers need to recognize their mortality, and careful estate planning is crucial to ensure disposal of their assets according to their wishes, while minimizing tax consequences to their beneficiaries. Proper estate planning will require a knowledgeable lawyer and perhaps also a life insurance agent, an accountant, or a bank trust officer, depending on the nature and size of the estate. In this chapter we will consider the basic principles of estate planning. This discussion is not a substitute for the aid of a lawyer experienced in estate planning. Rather, it is to alert you to potential problems and aid in preparing you to work with your estate planner.

THE WILL

A will is a legal instrument by which a person directs the distribution of property in the estate upon death. The maker of the will is called the *testator*. Gifts given by a will are referred to as *bequests* or *devises*. Certain formalities are required by state law to create a valid will. About thirty states require that the instrument be in writing and signed by the testator, in the presence of two or more witnesses. This requirement varies from state to state, and some states require three witnesses. In those states, the witnesses affirm by their signatures that the will is genuine and was indeed signed by the testator. The rest of the states also permit unwitnessed wills, known as holographic wills, if they are entirely handwritten and signed by the testator.

A will is a unique document in two respects. First, if properly drafted it is *ambulatory*, meaning it can accommodate change, such as applying to property acquired after the will is made. Second, a will is *revocable*, meaning that the testator has the power to change or cancel it before death. Even if a testator makes a valid agreement not to revoke the will, he or she will still have the power to revoke it, though liability for breach of contract could result.

Generally, courts do not consider a will to have been revoked unless it can be clearly shown that the testator either (1) performed a physical act of revocation, such as burning or tearing up a will, with intent to revoke it; or (2) executed a valid later will which revoked the previous will. Most state statutes also provide for automatic revocation of a will in whole or in part if the testator is subsequently divorced.

To change a will, the testator must execute a supplement, known as a *codicil*, which has the same formal requirements as those for creating a will. To the extent that the codicil contradicts the will, those contradicted parts of the will are revoked.

Before the property in a will can be distributed, all outstanding debts and taxes must be paid. When the property owned by the testator at death is insufficient to satisfy all the bequests in the will after all debts and taxes have been paid, some or all of the bequests must be reduced or even eliminated entirely. The process of reducing or eliminating bequests is known as *abatement*, and the priorities for reduction are set according to the category of each bequest. The legally significant categories of gifts are generally as follows: *specific* bequests or devises, meaning gifts of a particular kind or uniquely identifiable items ("I give to X all the furniture in my home"); *demonstrative* bequests or devises, meaning gifts which are to be paid out of a specified source unless that source contains insufficient funds, in which case the gifts will be paid out of the general assets ("I give to Y $1,000 to be paid from my shares of stock in ABC Corporation"); *general* bequests, meaning gifts payable out of the general assets of an estate ("I give Z One Thousand Dollars"); and finally, *residuary* bequests or devises, or gifts of whatever is left in the estate after all other gifts and expenses are satisfied ("I give the rest, residue and remainder of my estate to Z").

Intestate property, or property not disposed of by the will, is usually the first to be taken to satisfy claims against the estate. (If the will contains a valid residuary clause, there will be no such property.) If this property is not sufficient, residuary bequests will be used. If more money is needed, general bequests will be used and, lastly, specific and demonstrative bequests will be taken together in proportion to their value.

If the testator acquires more property in the time between the execution of the will and death, the disposition of such property will also be governed by the will, which, as we have seen, is ambulatory in nature. If the will contains a valid residuary clause, such after-acquired property will go to the residuary legatees. If there is no such clause, such property will pass outside the will to the persons specified in the state's law of intestate succession.

When a person dies without leaving a valid will, this is known as dying *intestate*. When a person dies intestate, his or her property is distributed according to the state law of intestate succession, which specifies who is entitled to what parts of the estate. An intestate's surviving spouse will always receive a share, generally at least one-third of the estate. An intestate's surviving children likewise always get a share. If some of the children do not survive the intestate, the grandchildren of the intestate may be entitled to a share by representation. *Representation* is a legal principle which means that if an heir does not survive the intestate, but has a child who does survive, that child will take the non-surviving heir's share in the estate. In other words, the surviving child stands in the shoes of his or her dead parent in order to inherit from a grandparent who dies intestate.

If there are no direct descendants surviving, the intestate's surviving spouse will take the entire estate or share it with the intestate's parents. If there are neither a surviving spouse nor any surviving direct descendants of the intestate, the estate will be distributed to the intestate's parents, or if the parents are not surviving, to the intestate's brothers and sisters by representation. If there are no surviving persons in any of the above categories, the estate will go to surviving grandparents and their direct descendants. In this way the family tree is constantly expanded in search of surviving relatives. If none of the persons specified in the law of intestate succession survive the decedent, the intestate's property ultimately goes to the state. This is known as *escheat*.

State law will often provide a testator's surviving spouse with certain benefits from the estate even if the spouse is left out of the testator's will. Historically, these benefits were known as *dower*, in the case of a surviving wife, or *curtesy*, in the case of a surviving husband. In place of the old dower and curtesy, modern statutes give the surviving spouse the right to "elect" against the will, and thereby receive a share equal to at least one-fourth of the estate. Here again, state laws vary; in some states, the surviving spouse's elective share is one-third. The historical concepts of dower and curtesy are in large part a result of the law's traditional recognition of an absolute duty on the part of the husband to provide for the wife. Modern laws are perhaps better justified by the notion that most property in a marriage should be shared because the financial success of either partner is due to the efforts of both.

ADVANTAGES TO HAVING A WILL

Now that we have some background as to what a will is and what happens without one, we can begin to look at some of the benefits in having a will. Wills are especially important to writers because of the unique nature of property rights in written works. Authors will want to ensure that the ownership of their works after their death will end up in safe and knowledgeable hands. Note, however, that the right to renew a copyright under the 1909 Copyright Act cannot be willed if the writer's spouse or children are still living, because the rights will pass to the spouse or children by law.

The writer may wish to limit certain rights within the copyright, such as the right to publication, completion, or display. A will affords the opportunity to direct distribution of all these rights and to set out limitations by making gifts conditional. For example, if a writer wishes to donate certain manuscripts to a library or museum, but only if certain conditions are adhered to, a will can make such conditions a prerequisite to the donation.

In any event, a will does permit a writer to nominate an executor to watch over the estate. If no executor is nominated by the will, the court will appoint one. It is often a good idea for writers to appoint joint executors, one with publishing or writing experience, the other with financial expertise. In this way economic decisions after the author's death will be considered from at least two perspectives. If joint executors are used, it will be necessary to make some provision in the will for resolving any deadlock between the two. For example, a neutral third party might be appointed as an arbitrator, who is directed to resolve any impasses after hearing both sides. It is also advisable to define the scope of the executor's power by detailed instructions. A lawyer's help will be necessary to set forth all of these important considerations in legally enforceable, unambiguous terms. It is essential to avoid careless language in a will which might be subject to attack by survivors unhappy with the will's provisions. A lawyer's help is also crucial to avoid making bequests which are not legally enforceable because contrary to public policy.

In addition to giving the writer significant posthumous control over his or her works, a carefully drafted will can greatly reduce the overall amount of estate tax paid at death. Because valuations of written works for estate tax purposes are not precise, estate taxes may turn out to be significantly higher than might have been anticipated. Thus, it is very important for authors to attempt to reduce their taxable estate as much as possible. The following information on taxing structures is applicable to federal estate taxation. State estate taxes often contain similar provisions, but state law should always be consulted for specifics.

THE GROSS ESTATE

The first step in evaluating an estate for tax purposes is to determine the so-called "gross estate." The *gross estate* includes all property in which the deceased had an ownership interest at the time of death and before the will is put into effect.[1] The key element in determining ownership is control. Thus, the gross estate will include all property over which the deceased retained significant control at the time of death. Examples would include life insurance proceeds, annuities, jointly-held interests, and revocable transfers.

Under current tax laws, the executor of an estate may

elect to value the property in the estate either as of the date of death or as of a date six months after death. The estate property must be valued in its entirety at the time chosen. However, if the executor elects to value the estate six months after death and certain pieces of property are distributed or sold before then, that property will be valued as of the date of distribution or sale.[2]

Fair market value is defined as the price at which property would change hands between a willing buyer and a willing seller, when both buyer and seller have reasonable knowledge of all relevant facts. Such a determination is often very difficult to make, especially when writings or other types of artwork are involved. Although the initial determination of fair market value is generally made by the executor when the estate tax return is filed, the Internal Revenue Service may disagree with the executor's valuation and assign assets a much higher fair market value. For example, in 1979 the IRS claimed that writer Jacqueline Susann's diary had an estate tax value of $3,800,000 as a literary property.[3] The diary, which neither Susann nor her executor had considered particularly valuable, had been destroyed by the executor pursuant to Susann's directions.

When the Internal Revenue Service and the executor (or whoever represents the estate) cannot agree upon a valuation, the matter will be litigated. By far, the majority of these sorts of cases are settled out of court. Thus, there is very little case law dealing with the valuation of artistic or literary properties for estate tax purposes. *Estate of David Smith*[4] is the case most often cited as an example of valuation of artistic assets for estate tax purposes. While the decedent in this case was a sculptor and the controversy was over valuation of his creations, the same types of problems would arise in the attempt to value manuscripts in a writer's estate.

When the sculptor, David Smith, died, there were 425

works in his estate. The market for his sculptures was limited, since most pieces were large and abstract. Nevertheless, prior to Smith's death, each of the 425 pieces had been photographed and marked with an estimated sales price. When the executors of the estate figured fair market value of the pieces, they first reduced the figure representing the sum of all the estimated prices ($4,284,000) by 75 percent in an attempt to account for the effect of the sudden availability of so many sculptures on the limited market. They then reduced that figure by one-third to account for the gallery's commission as set out in the agency contract between the deceased and the gallery which had exclusive right to sell the artist's work. Thus, the executors' final figure representing fair market value on the tax return was $714,000.

The Internal Revenue Service, on the other hand, determined fair market value for the sculptures by simply adding up the "one-at-a-time" prices in Smith's gallery contract, claiming that the simultaneous-availability factor would have no adverse impact on the market value. The IRS thus set the total valuation at the $4,284,000 figure and sued the estate for the tax deficiency.

When the case went to court, the estate first argued that the number and nature of the sculptures, coupled with the limited scope and vagaries of the market, made valuation as of the date of death impossible. Thus, the only permissible valuation would be zero. The court rejected this argument, noting that difficulties such as limited markets should be taken into account, but that such difficulties do not bar the valuation process.

The court allowed a 50 percent reduction for sudden availability, and refused to deduct the gallery's commission, holding that the measure of value is the amount *received*, not retained, from a sale. Thus, the court's final figure was $2,700,000, a compromise between the executors' listed value of $714,000 and the IRS figure of over

$4,000,000. Notwithstanding the reduction, the estate tax was devastating.

Mauldin v. Commissioner is another case in which the Internal Revenue Service claimed a tax deficiency based on disagreement over the value of artistic assets.[5] This case involved valuation of an original manuscript and sketches for gift-tax purposes. However, it is likely that the reasoning in *Mauldin* will be applicable to estate-tax valuations as well.

The plaintiff in *Mauldin* claimed a charitable deduction on his income taxes in the amount of the estimated value of original materials he donated to the Smithsonian. The plaintiff's cartoons and drawings had received national attention as commemorating the American soldiers in World War II. After numerous requests from the Smithsonian, Mauldin eventually made two donations, giving a series of cartoons in 1966 and an original manuscript and sketches in 1967. The Internal Revenue Service disputed the value of the donations and Mauldin brought suit for judicial determination.

The cartoons Mauldin donated in 1966 were valued by his experts (as of the date of contribution) at $10,500 to $20,000 each. The original manuscript and sketches he donated in 1967 were valued at $7,270 and $1,600, respectively. The government experts valued the six cartoons donated in 1966 at between $25 to $75. Mauldin introduced evidence at trial of sales of similar cartoons in 1972 at $600 to $900 each. Mauldin's experts explained their higher values as attributable to the donated cartoons being the first and last in a series, making the series illustrative of the artist's progression and thus more valuable. The government made no effort to explain the discrepancy between its values and the 1972 sales.

The court agreed with Mauldin's valuations, citing the plaintiff's far-reaching fame as a factor and also emphasizing the fact that the plaintiff's expert had been selected by the Smithsonian, which is a federally-chartered museum. The court explained that when one government agency (the Smithsonian) makes an appraisal in order to induce a charitable donation, another government agency (the IRS) should not attack or ignore that appraisal after the contribution has been made. Similarly, the court approved a valuation of the manuscript and sketches donated in 1967 that was comparable to plaintiff's estimates.

In addition to valuing actual drawings or manuscripts, the executor of a writer's estate will need to make some effort to value copyrights and other intangible assets owned by the decedent. There is no hard and fast rule for valuing copyrights. The method most widely used is the sinking-fund method which uses a formula known as Hoskin's formula. Hoskin's formula basically involves determining the present value of future earnings from the copyrighted material.

As mentioned earlier, when an executor and the Internal Revenue Service disagree as to valuation, the court will decide the matter. In most cases, the burden will be on the taxpayer to prove the value of the copyright. Thus, expert testimony and evidence of the sale of the same or similar properties will be helpful, as in cases involving original manuscripts and drawings. In general, courts are reluctant to accept valuation by formula as determinative.

It is extremely difficult to determine a fair market value for a manuscript or the literary rights connected to a manuscript. The cases demonstrate that there is no guarantee court evaluations will necessarily be fair. Even a compromise approach by the court can result in artificially high valuations, which inflate a writer's gross estate and thus can lead to higher taxes. An estate thus may face real hardship in paying administration and tax costs when estate assets are not easily convertible to cash. Generally, estate taxes must be paid when the estate tax return is

filed within nine months of the date of death, although arrangements may be made to spread payments out over a
number of years if necessary.[6] It is not uncommon for executors to be forced to sell properties for less than full
value in order to pay taxes. This can be avoided by writers
obtaining insurance policies, the proceeds of which can be
set up in a trust. (For an explanation of a trust, see the section "Distributing Property outside of the Will," below.)

The law allows a number of deductions from the gross
estate to arrive at a figure representing the taxable estate.
The *taxable estate* is the basis upon which to compute the
tax owing. The following section gives you a closer look at
some of the key deductions used to arrive at a figure representing the taxable estate.

THE TAXABLE ESTATE

Figuring the taxable estate is the second major step in
evaluating an estate for tax purposes, after determining
the gross estate. Typical deductions from the gross estate
include funeral expenses; certain estate administration
expenses; debts and enforceable claims against the estate;
mortgages and liens; and, perhaps most significant, the
marital deduction and the *charitable deduction*.

The marital deduction allows the total value of any interest in property which passes from the decedent to the
surviving spouse to be subtracted from the value of the
gross estate. The government will eventually get its tax on
this property, when the spouse dies, but only to the extent
such interest is included in the gross estate. This deduction may occur even in the absence of a will making a gift
to the surviving spouse, since state law generally provides
that the spouse is entitled to at least one-fourth of the
overall estate regardless of the provisions of the will.

Charitable deduction refers to the tax deduction allowed upon the transfer of property from an estate to a recognized charity. The charitable deduction is especially significant to the writer. Although income-tax benefits from donating copyrights and manuscripts are negligible (see the section on charitable deductions near the end of Chapter 2), estate tax benefits are substantial. In effect, the fair market value of donated works is excluded from the taxable estate. Although leaving the work in the estate will pass some value to those inheriting, at a high rate of taxation that value will be considerably less than the tax-free value of the work donated to a charitable institution. Since the definition of charity for tax purposes is quite technical, it is advisable to insert a clause in the will which provides that if the institution specified to receive the donation does not qualify for the charitable deduction, the bequest will go to a substitute qualified institution at the choice of the executor.

Once deductions are figured, the taxable estate is taxed at the rate specified by the Unified Estate and Gift Tax schedule. The unified tax imposes the same rate of tax on gifts made by will as on gifts made during life. It is a progressive tax, meaning the percent paid in taxes increases with the amount of property involved. The rates rise significantly for larger estates, i.e., from 18 percent, where the cumulative total of taxable estate and taxable gifts is under $10,000, to 55 percent, where the cumulative total is over $3,000,000. Tax credits are provided by year according to the tax schedule. Federal estate tax is also reduced by state death-tax credit or actual state death tax, whichever is less. Tax credits result in a $600,000 exemption, which is available to every estate. This exemption, combined with the previously discussed unlimited marital deduction, allows most estates to escape estate taxes altogether. Thus, only very wealthy writers' estates will be subject to significant taxation.

Distributing Property outside the Will

Property can be distributed outside of the will by making *intervivos* gifts (gifts between living people), or by placing the property in trust prior to death. The main advantage to distributing property outside of the will is that the property escapes the delays and expense of probate, the court procedure by which a will is validated and administered. It used to be that there were also significant tax advantages to making intervivos gifts rather than gifts by will, but since the estate and gift tax rates are now unified, there are few remaining tax advantages. One remaining advantage to making an intervivos gift is that if the gift appreciates in value between the time the gift is made and death, the appreciated value will not be taxed. If the gift were made by will, the added value would be taxable since the gift would be valued as of date of death (or six months after). This value difference can represent significant tax savings for writers and artists who have recently realized fame and whose works are rapidly gaining in value.

The one other remaining advantage to making an intervivos gift involves the yearly exclusion. A yearly exclusion of $10,000 per recipient is available on intervivos gifts. For example, if $15,000 worth of gifts were given to an individual in 1985, only $5,000 worth of gifts would actually have been taxable to the donor (who is responsible for the gift tax). A married couple can combine their gifts and claim a yearly exclusion of $20,000 per recipient. Gifts made within three years of death used to be included in the gross estate on the theory that they were made in contemplation of death. Recent amendments to the tax laws, however, have done away with the three-year rule, for most purposes. The three-year rule is still applicable to gifts of life insurance and to certain transfers involving stock redemptions or tax liens; the rule also retains relevance in certain valuation schemes, the details of which are too complex to discuss here.

Gift-tax returns must be filed by the donor for any year where gifts made exceed $10,000 to any one donee. It is not mandatory to file returns when no gift to any one donee amounts to less than $10,000. However, where it is possible that valuation of the gift will become an issue with the IRS, then it may be a good idea to file a return anyway. Filing the return starts the three-year statute of limitations running. Once the statute of limitations period has expired, the IRS will be barred from filing suit for unpaid taxes or tax deficiencies due to higher government valuations of the gifts. If a taxpayer omits includible gifts amounting to more than 25 percent of the total amount of gifts stated in the return, the statute of limitations is extended to six years. There is no statute of limitations for fraudulent returns filed with the intent to evade tax.

In order to qualify as an intervivos, or living, gift for tax purposes, a gift must be complete and final. Control is an important issue. For example, if a writer retains the right to revoke a gift, the gift may be found to be testamentary in nature, even if the right to revoke was never exercised. The gift must also be delivered. An actual, physical delivery is best, but a symbolic delivery may suffice if there is strong evidence of intent to make an irrevocable gift. An example of symbolic delivery is when the donor puts something in a safe and gives the intended recipient the only key.

Another common way to transfer property outside the will is to place the property in a trust which is created prior to death. A *trust* is simply a legal arrangement by which one person holds certain property for the benefit of another. The person holding the property is the *trustee*; those for whose benefit it is held are the *beneficiaries*. To create a valid trust, the writer must identify the trust property; make a declaration of intent to create the trust; transfer property to the trust; and name identifiable beneficiaries. Failure to name a trustee will not defeat the trust, since if no trustee is named, a court will appoint one. The writer may name himself or herself as trustee, in which case segregation of the trust property satisfies the delivery requirement. Trusts can be created by will, in which case they are termed *testamentary trusts*, but these trust properties will be probated along with the rest of the will. To avoid probate, the writer must create a valid, intervivos, or living, trust.

Generally, in order to qualify as an intervivos trust, a valid interest in property must be transferred before the death of the creator of the trust, or the *settlor*. For example, if the settlor fails to name a beneficiary for the trust or make delivery of the property to the trustee before death, the trust will likely be termed testamentary. So designated, the trust will be deemed invalid unless the formalities required for creating a will were complied with.

A trust will not be termed testamentary simply because the settlor retained significant control over the trust, such as the power to revoke or modify the trust. For example, when a person makes a deposit in a savings account in his or her own name as trustee for another, and reserves the power to withdraw the money or revoke the trust, the trust will be enforceable by the beneficiary upon the death of the depositor, providing the depositor has not in fact revoked the trust.[7] Many states allow the same type of arrangement in authorizing joint bank accounts with rights of survivorship as valid will substitutes. Property transferred under one of these arrangements is thus passed outside the will and need not go through probate. However, even though such an arrangement escapes probate, since the settlor retains significant control, the trust property will likely be counted as part of the gross estate for tax purposes. In addition, if the deceased settlor created a revocable trust for the purpose of decreasing the statutory share of a surviving spouse, in some states the trust will be declared illusory. The surviving spouse is then granted the legal share not only from the probate estate but from the revocable trust.[8]

Life insurance trusts can be used for paying estate taxes. The proceeds of a life insurance trust will not be taxed if the life insurance trust is irrevocable and the trustee is someone other than the estate executor.[9] But even where the trust is irrevocable and the trustee is a third party, the proceeds are taxed to the extent they are used to pay taxes to benefit the estate. The advantages to this arrangement, then, are not so much tax avoidance as guaranteed liquidity. This is especially important for writers and other creative people, since otherwise survivors can be forced to sell remaining works for much less than their real value in order to pay estate taxes.

CONCLUSION

All writers should give some thought to estate planning and take the time to execute a will. Without a will, there is simply no way to control the disposition of property, and posthumous control is especially important in the case of manuscripts and their attendant legal rights. Sound estate planning may include transfers outside of the will, since these types of arrangements escape the delays and expenses of probate. Certain types of trusts can be valuable will substitutes, but they may be subject to challenge by a surviving spouse. Since successful estate planning is complex, it is essential to work with a lawyer skilled in this field.

12

How to Find a Lawyer

Most writers expect to seek the advice of a lawyer only occasionally, for counseling on important matters such as contracting with a publisher. If you are a serious writer, you should establish an early relationship with an attorney who specializes in publishing law, so that when you find yourself ready to negotiate with a publisher, you will have confidence in your legal counsel.

An attorney experienced in publishing law should also be able to give you important information regarding areas of liability exposure unique to your work, such as portrayal of someone in a false light, invasion of privacy, pornography and obscenity, libel, copyright infringement, breach of the author-publisher contract, etc.

If employees assist you in research and writing, you should also have advice on your legal relationship with present and future employees. Ignorance of these issues can lead to inadvertent violation of the rules, which in turn can result in financially devastating lawsuits and even criminal penalties. Each state has its own laws covering certain business practices; thus, state laws must be consulted on many areas in this book. A competent local business attorney is, therefore, your best source of information on many issues which will arise in the running of your business.

What is really behind all the hoopla about "preventive legal counseling"? Are we lawyers simply seeking more work? Admittedly, as business people, lawyers want business. But what you should consider is economic reality: *Most legal problems cost more to solve or defend than it would have cost to prevent their occurrence in the first place.* Litigation is notoriously inefficient and expensive. You do not want to sue or to be sued, if you can help it. The expense is shocking; for instance, it can cost close to one hundred dollars per day simply to use a courtroom for trial. Pretrial procedures run into the thousands of dollars on most cases. The cost of defending a case filed against you is something you have no choice about, unless you choose to default, which is almost never advisable.

One of the first items you should discuss with your lawyer is the fee structure. You are entitled to an estimate, though unless you enter into an agreement to the contrary with the attorney, the estimate is just that. Business and publishing lawyers generally charge by the hour, though you may be quoted a flat rate for a specific service such as incorporation or review of an author-publisher contract.

If you do not know any attorneys, ask other writers and publishers whether they know any good ones. You want a lawyer who specializes in copyright and/or publishing law. Finding the lawyer who is right for you is like finding the right doctor; you may have to shop around a bit. Your city, county, and state bar associations may have helpful referral services. A good tip is to find out who is in the Intellectual Property Section of the state or county bar association, or who has served on special bar committees dealing with intellectual property law. It may also be useful to find out whether any articles covering the area of law you are concerned with have been published in either scholarly journals or continuing legal-education publications, and if the author is available to assist you. Your state or county law librarian can assist you here.

It is a good idea to hire a specialist or law firm with a number of specialists rather than a general practitioner. While you may pay more per hour for the expert, you will not be funding his learning time. The specialist's experience will be worth the higher hourly rate.

One aid in finding a lawyer who represents writers is the Martindale-Hubbell Law Directory, which can be found in your local county law library. (However, not all lawyers are listed in the directory. The mere fact that a particular attorney's name does not appear in the book should not give you cause for concern, since there is a charge for being included and some lawyers choose not to pay for the listing.)

After you have obtained some names, it would be appropriate for you to talk with several attorneys for a short period of time to evaluate them. Do not be afraid to ask about their background and experience, and whether they feel they can help you.

Once you have completed the interview process, select the lawyer with whom you are most comfortable. The rest is up to you. Contact your attorney whenever you believe you have a legal question.

I encourage my clients to feel comfortable about calling me at the office during the day or at home in the evening. Some lawyers, however, may resent having their personal time invaded. Some, in fact, do not list their home telephone numbers. Learn your attorney's preference early on.

You should feel comfortable when confiding in your attorney and feel that whatever information you pass on will be held in confidence. Disclosure of your confidential communications, under most circumstances, would be considered an ethical breach which could subject your lawyer to professional sanctions.

If you develop a good relationship with the right attorney, you may find that your increased confidence in understanding your legal situations actually increases your effectiveness as a writer.

Organizations
That Offer Help

Always, your best source for finding the professional who can help you is a friend whose needs have been the same as yours. Chapter 12 offers suggestions for ways of finding a lawyer; in addition to those sources, consider asking the journalism department of your local college or university for the names of people or groups who might be of help. Then there is *The Literary Market Place* (the LMP), available at any major library, with a wide variety of listings that include agents, writers' conferences, editors, fellowships and grants, and a host of other useful categories.

WRITERS' ORGANIZATIONS

The following are some of the best-known and largest of the writers' organizations. The LMP will provide you with the names of more specialized associations such as translators or writers on black, medical, or regional subjects—to name only the beginning. *The Writer's Resource Guide*, with its wider breakdown of writers' associations, is even more comprehensive.

American Society of Journalists &
 Authors (ASJA)
1501 Broadway, Suite 1907
New York, NY 10036

The Authors League of America
234 West 44th St.
New York, NY 10036

Canadian Authors Association
24 Ryerson Ave.
Toronto, ONT M5T 2P3
Canada

International Women's Writing Guild
Box 810, Gracie Sta.
New York, NY 10028

Media Alliance
Fort Mason
San Francisco, CA 94123

National Writers Club
1450 S. Havana, Suite 620
Aurora, CO 80012

National Writers Union
13 Astor Pl.
New York, NY 10003

PEN American Center
568 Broadway
New York, NY 10012

Poets and Writers Inc.
201 West 54th St.
New York, NY 10019

Society of Children's Book Writers
Box 296, Mar Vista Sta.
Los Angeles, CA 90066

Writers Guild of America East
555 W. 57th St.
New York, NY 10019

Writers Guild of America West
8955 Beverly Blvd.
Los Angeles, CA 90048

VOLUNTEER LAWYERS FOR THE ARTS

Volunteer Lawyers for the Arts—the VLA—was founded in New York City in 1969 to provide artists and arts organizations with the legal assistance they needed but were not able to afford. Today, New York alone has approximately 900 lawyers volunteering their time and help, and most states have a VLA chapter and there is one in Toronto as well.

Each VLA chapter is different; some offer seminars, conferences, and news letters; others provide accounting and business advice; some have financial requirements for eligibility; and some charge minimal fees for services. Contact the VLA nearest you to find out more about it or, for a directory listing all the VLAs and all the services they provide, write to the New York City VLA, including $2 to cover postage ($1 for subsequent copies).

Bay Area Lawyers for the Arts
  (BALA)
Fort Mason Center, Bldg. C
San Francisco, CA 94123

Los Angeles VLA
P.O. Box 57008
Los Angeles, CA 90057

San Diego Lawyers for the Arts
1295 Prospect St., Suite C
La Jolla, CA 92037

Canadian Artists Representation
  Ontario (CARO)
345-67 Mowat Ave.
Toronto, ONT M6K 3E3
Canada

Colorado Lawyers for the Arts
  (COLA)
770 Pennsylvania
Denver, CO 80203

Connecticut Volunteer Lawyers for
  the Arts (CTVLA)
Connecticut Commission on the Arts
190 Trumbull St.
Hartford, CT 06103-2206

D.C. Lawyers Committee for the Arts
  (LCA)
Volunteer Lawyers for the Arts
918 16th St. N.W., Suite 503
Washington, DC 20006

D.C. Washington Area Lawyers for
  the Arts (WALA)
2025 I St. N.W., Suite 608
Washington, DC 20006

Volunteer Lawyers for the Arts
  Program
Pinellas County Arts Council
400 Pierce Blvd.
Clearwater, FL 33516

Broward Arts Council
100 So. Andrews Ave.
Fort Lauderdale, FL 33301

Business Volunteers for the
  Arts/Miami
c/o Greater Miami Chamber of Commerce
1601 Biscayne Blvd.
Miami, FL 33132

Liaison to the Entertainment and
  Arts Law Committee
Public Interest Programs
Florida Bar Association
600 Appalachee Parkway
Tallahassee, FL 32301-8226

Georgia Volunteer Lawyers for the
  Arts (GVLA)
32 Peachtree St., Suite 521
Atlanta, GA 30303

Lawyers for the Creative Arts (LCA)
623 So. Wabash Ave., Suite 300-N
Chicago, IL 60605

Volunteer Lawyers for the Arts Committee
Cedar Rapids/Marion Arts Council
424 1st Ave. N.E.
Cedar Rapids, IA 52407

Barry Lindahl
622 Dubuque Building
Dubuque, IA 52201

Dee Peretz
Lexington Council of the Arts
161 No. Mill Street
Lexington, KY 40507

Community Arts Council
609 W. Main St.
Louisville, KY 40202

Louisiana Volunteer Lawyers for the
Arts (LVLA)
c/o Arts Council of New Orleans
ITM Bldg., Suite 936
2 Canal St.
New Orleans, LA 70130

Maine Volunteer Lawyers for the Arts
Project
Maine State Commission on the Arts
& the Humanities
55 Capitol St.
State House Station 25
Augusta, ME 04333

Maryland Lawyers for the Arts
c/o University of Baltimore Law
School
1420 No. Charles St.
Baltimore, MD 21201

The Arts Extension Service (AES)
Division of Continuing Education
University of Massachusetts
Amherst, MA 01003

Lawyers & Accountants for the Arts
The Artists Foundation
110 Broad St.
Boston, MA 02169

Michigan Volunteer Lawyers for the
Arts (MVLA)
1283 Leeward Dr.
Okemos, MI 48864

Minnesota Volunteer Lawyers for the
Arts (MVLA)
c/o Fred Rosenblatt
100 So. 5th St., Suite 1500
Minneapolis, MN 55402

St. Louis Volunteer Lawyers & Accountants for the Arts (SLVLAA)
c/o St. Louis Regional, Cultural &
Performing Arts
Development Commission
329 N. Euclid Ave.
St. Louis, MO 63108

Montana Volunteer Lawyers for the
Arts
c/o Joan Jonkel
P.O. Box 8687
Missoula, MT 69807

Volunteer Lawyers for the Arts of
New Jersey
A special project of the Center for
Non-Profit Corporations
36 W. Lafayette St.
Trenton, NJ 08608

Volunteer Lawyers for the Arts
Program
Albany League of Arts
19 Clinton Ave.
Albany, NY 12207

Arts Council in Buffalo & Erie County
700 Main St.
Buffalo, NY 14202

Huntington Arts Council
213 Main St.
Huntington, NY 11743

Volunteer Lawyers for the Arts (VLA)
1560 Broadway, Suite 711
New York, NY 10036

Dutchess County Arts Council
    (DCAC)
12 Vassar St.
Poughkeepsie, NY 12601

North Carolina Volunteer Lawyers
    for the Arts (NCVLA)
P.O. Box 590
Raleigh, NC 27602

Cincinnati Area Lawyers & Accoun-
    tants for the Arts
ML003
University of Cincinnati
Cincinnati, OH 45221

Volunteer Lawyers for the Arts
    Program
c/o Cleveland Bar Association
Mall Bldg.
118 St. Clair Ave.
Cleveland, OH 44114

Arnold Gottlieb
421 North Michigan Street
Toledo, OH 43624

Betty Price
State Arts Council of Oklahoma
Room 640
Jim Thorpe Bldg.
Oklahoma City, OK 73105-4987

Philadelphia Volunteer Lawyers for
    the Arts (PVLA)
251 So. 18th St.
Philadelphia, PA 19103

Ocean State Lawyers for the Arts
    (OSLA)
96 Sachem Rd.
Narragansett, RI 02882

South Carolina Lawyers for the Arts
    (SCLA)
P.O. Box 10023
Greenville, NC 29603

Bennett Tarleton
Tennessee Arts Commission
320 6th Ave. No.
Nashville, TN 37219

Austin Lawyers & Accountants for the
    Arts (ALAA)
P.O. Box 2577
Austin, TX 78768

Volunteer Lawyers & Accountants for
    the Arts (VLAA)
1540 Sul Ross
Houston, TX 77006

Utah Lawyers for the Arts (ULA)
50 So. Main, Suite 900
Salt Lake City, UT 84144

Washington Lawyers for the Arts
    (WVLA)
428 Joseph Vance Bldg.
1402 Third Ave.
Seattle, Wa. 98101

Notes

2. KEEPING TAXES LOW
1. *See e.g.*, Economos v. C.I.R., 167 F.2d 165 (1948), *cert. denied*, 335 U.S. 826, *reh'g denied*, 335 U.S. 905; Fletcher v. C.I.R., 164 F.2d 182 (1947), *cert. denied*, 333 U.S. 885.
2. Treas. Reg. § 1.183-2(b).
3. Chaloner v. Helvering, 69 F.2d 251 (D.C. Cir. 1934).
4. Howard v. Commissioner, 41 T.C.M. 1554 (1981).
5. Weissman v. Commissioner, 47 T.C.M. 520 (1983), *rev'd*, 751 F.2d 512 (2d Cir. 1984).
6. Moskovit v. Commissioner, 44 T.C.M. 859 (1982).
7. Frankel v. Commissioner, 82 T.C. 318 (1984).
8. Treas. Reg. § 1-263(a)-1.

3. WHAT YOU SHOULD KNOW ABOUT CONTRACTS
1. Lake Wales Publishing Co., Inc. v. Florida Visitor, Inc., 335 So. 2d 335 (Fla. Dist. Ct. App. 1976).
2. Carpel v. Saget Studios, Inc., 326 F. Supp. 1331 (E.D. Pa. 1971).
3. Mallin v. The University of Miami, 354 So. 2d 1227 (Fla. Dist. Ct. App. 1978).
4. Cardozo v. True, 342 So. 2d 1053 (Fla. Dist. Ct. App. 1977).
5. Philip Freund v. Washington Square Press, 34 N.Y.2d 379, 314 N.E. 2d 410 (1974).

4. CONTRACTS WITH BOOK PUBLISHERS AND MAGAZINES
1. *Judge Sustains Lawsuit by Authors against Addison-Wesley*, Publishers Weekly, Feb. 7, 1986 at 18, col. 2.
2. Freund v. Washington Square Press, Inc., 41 A.D.2d 371, 343 N.Y.S.2d 401 (N.Y. App. Div. 1973), *modified*, 34 N.Y. 379, 314 N.E.2d 419, 357 N.Y.S.2d 857 (1974).
3. Harcourt Brace Jovanovich, Inc. v. Goldwater, 532 F. Supp. 619 (S.D.N.Y. 1982).
4. Dell Publishing Co. v. Whedon, 577 F. Supp. 1459 (S.D.N.Y. 1984).
5. *Id.* at 1461 (1984).
6. Doubleday & Co. v. Curtis, 763 F.2d 495 (2d Cir.), *cert. dismissed*, 106 S. Ct. 282 (1985).
7. *Id.* at 500 (1985).
8. *See* Fowler, Mark, "The 'Satisfactory Manuscript' Clause in Book Publishing Contracts," 10 Colum.-VLA J.L. & Arts 119 (1985).
9. Van Valkenburg, Nooger & Neville, Inc. v. Hayden Publishing Co., 30 N.Y.S.2d 329 (1972), *cert. denied*, 409 U.S. 875 (1972).

10. Wolf v. Illustrated World Encyclopedia, Inc., 34 N.Y.2d 834, N.E.2d 342, 359 N.Y.S.2d 59 (1973).
11. *Publishers Weekly*, April 9, 1979, pp. 18, 19.
12. Harper & Row Publishers, Inc. v. Nation Enterprises, 105 S. Ct. 2218 (1985).

5. FINDING A PUBLISHER AND DEALING WITH AGENTS
1. Janklow, "The Lawyer as Literary Agent," 9 Colum. J. Art. & L. 407 (1985).
2. RESTATEMENT (SECOND) OF AGENCY § 1 (1953).
3. Wilck v. Herbert, 78 Cal. App. 2d 392, 178 P.2d 25 (1947). *See also* RESTATEMENT OF THE LAW, AGENCY § 449, comment 6 (1933).
4. Clews v. Jamieson, 182 U.S. 461 (1901). *See also* RESTATEMENT, SECOND, AGENCY § 88 (1953).

6. ALTERNATIVES TO LARGE BOOK-PUBLISHING HOUSES
1. Stellema v. Vantage Press, 411 N.Y.S.2d 191 (1978).
2. Exposition Press and Edward Uhlan v. Federal Trade Commission, 295 F.2d 869 (1961).

7. COPYRIGHT LAW
1. *See, e.g.*, American International Pictures, Inc. v. Foreman, 576 F.2d (5th Cir. 1978).
2. 17 U.S.C. § 201(a) (1976).
3. 17 U.S.C. § 201e (1976) as amended by § 3413 of Pub. L. No. 95-598 (1978).
4. Schroeder v. William Morrow Co., 566 F.2d 3 (7th Cir. 1977).
5. Mitchell Brothers Film Group v. Cinema Adult Theater, 605 F.2d 852 (5th Cir. 1979).
6. Harcourt, Brace & World Inc. v. Graphic Controls Corp., 329 F. Supp. 517 (S.D.N.Y. 1971).
7. Eltra Corp. v. Ringer, 579 F.2d 294 (4th Cir. 1978).
8. Warner Bros. Pictures, Inc. v. Columbia Broadcasting System, Inc., 216 F.2d 945 (9th Cir. 1954).
9. Detective Comics v. Bruns Publications, 111 F.2d 432 (2d Cir. 1940).
10. Walt Disney Productions v. Air Pirates, 345 F. Supp. 108 (N.D. Cal. 1972).
11. Alfred Bell & Co. v. Catalda Fine Arts, Inc., 191 F.2d 99 (2d Cir. 1951).
12. 17 U.S.C. § 101 (1976).
13. White v. Kimmel, 193 F.2d 744 (9th Cir. 1952).
14. *Id.*
15. Rushton v. Vitak, 218 F.2d 434 (2d Cir. 1955).
16. 1*Nimmer on Copyright*, 4-69, § 4. 3[B] (1982).
17. 17 U.S.C. § 407 (1982).
18. 17 U.S.C. § 408 (1982).

19. 17 U.S.C. § 405 (1982).

20. Nichols v. Universal Pictures Corp., 45 F.2d 119 (2d Cir. 1930).

21. Sony Corporation of America v. Universal Studios, Inc., et al., 464 U.S. 417 (1984), *reh'g denied* 465 U.S. 1112 (1984).

22. Columbia Pictures Industries, Inc. v. Professional Real Estate Investors, Inc., Case No. 83-2594 (C.D. Ca. Jan. 15, 1986).

23. Columbia Pictures Industries, Inc. v. Aveco, Inc., 612 F. Supp. 315 (M.D. Pa. 1985); Columbia Pictures, Inc. v. Redd Horne, Inc., 749 F.2d 154 (3d Cir. 1984).

24. Maxtone-Graham v. Burtchaell, 231 USPQ 535 (2d Cir. 1986).

25. *Id.* at 541.

26. Meeropol v. Nizer, 560 F.2d 1061 (2d Cir. 1977).

27. *Id.* (1977).

8. CENSORSHIP AND OBSCENITY

1. Near v. Minnesota, 283 U.S. 697, 713 (1931).

2. *See, e.g.*, Bantam Books, Inc. v. Sullivan, 372 U.S. 58 (1963).

3. New York Times Co. v. United States, 403 U.S. 943 (1971).

4. *Id.*

5. United States v. The Progressive, Inc., 486 F. Supp. 5 (W.D. Wis. 1979).

6. *See* "The Progressive," Vol. 43, No. 11, Nov. 1979.

7. Nebraska Press Association v. Stuart, 427 U.S. 539 (1976).

8. *Id.* at 563.

9. Virginia State Board of Pharmacy v. Virginia Citizens Consumer Council, 425 U.S. 748 (1976).

10. *See, e.g.*, Freedman v. Maryland, 380 U.S. 51 (1965).

11. A Quantity of Copies of Books v. Kansas, 378 U.S. 205, 224 (1964).

12. Near v. Minnesota, 283 U.S. 697, 713 (1931).

13. *Id.*

14. Bethel School District No. 403 v. Fraser, ____ U.S. ____ (1986).

15. Doubleday & Co. v. New York, 297 N.Y. 687, 77 N.E.2d 6 (1947), aff'd, 335 U.S. 848 (1948)

16. Commonwealth v. Gordon, 66 Pa. D.C. 101.

17. Roth v. United States, 354 U.S. 476, *reh'g denied*, 355 U.S. 852 (1957).

18. Regina v. Hicklin, L.R. 3 Q.B. 359 (1868).

19. *Roth, supra* note 16, at 489.

20. Jacobellis v. Ohio, 378 U.S. 184 (1964).

21. A Book Named "John Cleland's Memoirs of a Woman of Pleasure" v. Attorney General of Massachusetts, 383 U.S. 413 (1966).

22. *Id.* at 418.

23. Kois v. Wisconsin, 408 U.S. 229 (1972).

24. *Id.* at 231.

25. Miller v. California, 413 U.S. 15 (1973), *reh'g denied*, 414 U.S. 881 (1973).

26. *Id.* at 23.
27. *Id.* at 24-25 (citations omitted).
28. Hamling v. United States, 418 U.S. 87, 105-06 (1974).
29. Jenkins v. Georgia, 418 U.S. 153, 157 (1974).
30. Smith v. United States, 431 U.S. 291 (1977).
31. Blucher v. United States, 581 F.2d 244 (C.A. 10th Cir. 1978), *jud.* vacated, 439 U.S. 1061 (1979).
32. *Miller, supra* notes 24-25.
33. *Smith, supra* notes 28, 153.
34. *Roth, supra* notes 16, 476.
35. Brockett v. Spokane Arcades, Inc., 472 U.S. 491 (1985).
36. Butler v. Michigan, 352 U.S. 380 (1957).
37. *See, e.g.,* Mishkin v. New York, 383 U.S. 502 (1966); Hamling v. United States, 418 U.S. 87 (1974); Lakin v. United States, 363 A.2d 990 (1976); and Ward v. Illinois, 431 U.S. 767 (1977).
38. Ginzberg v. United States, 383 U.S. 463 (1966).
39. Hamling v. United States, 418 U.S. 87 (1974).
40. Kingsley International Pictures Corp. v. Regents of New York University, 360 U.S. 684 (1959).
41. *Id.* at 685.
42. Manual Enterprises v. Day, 370 U.S. 478 (1962).
43. New York v. Ferber, 458 U.S. 747 (1982).
44. Advocates for the Arts v. Thompson, 532 F.2d 792 (1976).
45. *Id.* at 798.
46. American Council for the Blind, et al. v. Daniel J. Boorstin, Librarian of Congress, 644 F. Supp. 811 (D.C. 1986).
47. Carole S. Vance, Porn in the U.S.A., The Meese Commission on the Road, *The Nation*, Aug. 2/9 (1986) at 78.

9. DEFAMATION AND LIBEL

1. New York Society for the Suppression of Vice v. MacFadden Publications, 260 N.Y. 167, 183 N.E. 284, 86 A.L.R. 440 (1932).
2. Buckley v. Vidal, 327 F. Supp. 1051 (S.D.N.Y. 1971).
3. Reported in the *London Times* on the 26th and 27th of November, 1878 and discussed in B. Hollander, *The International Law of Art* (1959).
4. Lanford v. Vanderbilt University, 44 Tenn. App. 694, 318 S.W.2d 568 (1958).
5. 376 U.S. 254 (1964).
6. *Id.* at 270.
7. Sharon v. Time, Inc., 599 F. Supp. 538 (1984).
8. Westmoreland v. CBS, 596 F. Supp. 1170 (1984).
9. Rosenblatt v. Baer, 383 U.S. 75, 85 (1966).
10. Rosenbloom v. Metromedia, Inc., 403 U.S. 29 (1971).
11. Gertz v. Robert Welch, Inc., 418 U.S. 323 (1974).
12. *Id.* at 345; *see also* Wolston v. Reader's Digest Ass'n., Inc.. 443 U.S. 157 (1979).

13. Gertz v. Robert Welch, Inc., 418 U.S. 323, 345 (1974).
14. Time, Inc. v. Firestone, 424 U.S. 448 (1976).
15. Philadelphia Newspapers, Inc. v. Hepps, 54 U.S.L.W. 4373 (U.S. Apr. 21, 1986).
16. Dun & Bradstreet Inc. v. Greenmoss Builders, Inc., ___ U.S. ___, 105 S. Ct. 2939 (1985).
17. Goldwater v. Ginzberg, 414 F.2d 324 (2d Cir. 1969), *cert. denied*, 396 U.S. 1049 (1970).
18. Burnett v. National Enquirer, No. C157213 (Cal. Super. Ct. 1981).

10. THE RIGHT OF PRIVACY

1. *The Right to Privacy*, 4 HARV. L. REV. 193 (1890).
2. *Id.* at 195-96.
3. Pavesich v. New England Life Ins. Co., 122 Ga. 190, 50 S.E. 68 (1905).
4. *Id.* at 194, 50 S.E. at 69.
5. N.Y. [Civil Rights] LAW §§ 50, 51 (McKinney 1980); N.Y. [Penal] Law § 250 (McKinney 1980); OKLA. STAT. ANN. tit. 21, §§ 839-840 (West 1958); 76 UTAH CODE ANN. §§ 7609-401 to -406 (1953); VA CODE §§ 2.1-377 to -386 (1979); CALIF. CIV. CODE §§ 1798 *et seq.*
6. Milner v. Red River Valley Pub. Co., 249 S.W.2d 227 (Tex. Civ. App. 1952); Brunson v. Ranks Army Stores, 161 Neb. 519, 73 N.W.2d 803 (1955); Henry v. Cherry & Webb, 30 R.I. 13, 73 A. 97 (1909); Yoeckel v. Samonig, 272 Wis. 430, 75 N.W.2d 925 (1956).
7. Bowers v. Hardwick, ___ U.S. ___, 106 S. Ct. 2841 (1986).
8. Dieteman v. Time, Inc., 284 F. Supp. 925 (D.C. Cal. 1968) *aff'd*, 449 F.2d 245 (9th Cir. 1971).
9. Galella v. Onassis, 353 F. Supp. 196 (D.C.N.Y. 1972), *aff'd in part*, rev'd in part, 487 F.2d 986 (2d Cir. 1973).
10. *Id.* at 223.
11. Dodd v. Pearson, 279 F. Supp. 101 (D.C.D.C. 1968), *aff'd in part*, *rev'd in part*, 410 F.2d 701 (D.C. Cir. 1969), *cert. denied*, 395 U.S. 947 (1969).
12. Cox Broadcasting Corp. v. Cohn, 420 U.S. 469 (1975).
13. Sidis v. F-R Publishing Corp., 113 F.2d 806 (2d Cir. 1940), *cert. denied*, 311 U.S. 711 (1940).
14. *Id.* at 807.
15. *Id.* at 809.
16. *Id.*
17. Melvin v. Reid, 112 Cal. App. 285, 297 P. 91 (1931).
18. *Id.* at 291, 297 P. at 93.
19. Briscoe v. Reader's Digest Association, Inc., 4 Cal. 3d 529, 93 Cal. Rptr. 866, 483 P.2d 34 (1971).
20. Friedan v. Friedan, 414 F. Supp. 77 (S.D.N.Y. 1966).

21. Rinaldi v. Village Voice, Inc.,
22. Estate of Hemingway v. Random House, Inc., 23 N.Y.2d 341, 244 N.E.2d 250 (1968).
23. *Id.* 244 N.E.2d at 258 (1968).
24. Lord Byron v. Johnston, 2 Mer. 29, 35 Eng. Rep. 851 (1816).
25. Leverton v. Curtis Publishing Co., 192 F.2d 974 (3d Cir. 1951).
26. Cantrell v. Forest City Publishing Co., 419 U.S. 245 (1974)
27. Carlisle v. Fawcett Publications, Inc., 201 Cal. App. 2d 733, 20 Cal. Rptr. 405 (1962).
28. Spahn v. Julian Messner, Inc., 21 N.Y.2d 124, 233 N.E.2d 840, 286 N.Y.S.2d 832 (1967).
29. New York Times Co. v. Sullivan, 376 U.S. 254 (1964).
30. Time, Inc. v. Hill, 385 U.S. 374 (1967).
31. Gertz v. Robert Welch, Inc., 418 U.S. 323 (1974).
32. Rand v. Hearst, 31 A.D.2d 406, 298 N.Y.S.2d 405 (N.Y. App. Div. 1969), *aff'd* 26 N.Y.2d 348, 257 N.E.2d 895 (1970).
33. Namath v. Sports Illustrated, 48 A.D.2d 487, 371 N.Y.S. 2d 10 (N.Y. App. Div. 1975), *aff'd* 39 N.Y.2d 897, 386 N.Y.2d 397, 352 N.E.2d 584 (1976).
34. Zacchini v. Scripps Howard Broadcasting Co., 433 U.S. 562 (1977).
35. Cohen v. Hallmark Cards, Inc., 58 A.D.2d 770, 396 N.Y.S.2d 397 (N.Y. App. Div. 1977), *rev'd on other grounds*, 45 N.Y.2d 493, 410 N.Y.S.2d 282, 382 N.E.2d 1145 (1978).
36. Southeast Bank, N.A. v. Lawrence, 483 N.Y.S.2d 218, 104 A.2d 213 (1984) *reh'g denied*, 486 N.Y.2d 299 (1985).
37. Factors Etc., Inc. v. Pro Arts, Inc., 579 F.2d 215 (2d Cir. 1978), *cert.* denied, 440 U.S. 908 (1979).
38. Memphis Development Foundation v. Factors, Etc., Inc., 616 F.2d 956 (6th Cir. 1980), *cert. denied*, 449 U.S. 953 (1980).
39. Martin Luther King, Jr. Center For Social Change, Inc. v. American Heritage, 250 Ga. 135, 147, 296 S.E.2d 697, 706 (1982).
40. *Id.*

11. THE WRITER'S ESTATE

1. Treas. Reg. §§ 20.6151-1, 2-.6075-1.
2. I.R.C. § 2032 (1982).
3. The Wall Street Journal, Aug. 29, 1979, at 1, col. 5.
4. Estate of David Smith, 57 T.C. 650 (1972), *aff'd*, 510 F.2d 650 (1972).
5. Mauldin v. Commissioner, 60 T.C. 749 (1973).
6. I.R.C. § 2522(a) (1982); Treas. Reg. § 25. 522(a)-1(a).
7. Matter of Totten, 179 N.Y. 112, 71 N.E. 748 (1904).
8. Newman v. Dore, 275 N.Y. 371, 9 N.E.2d 966 (1937).

Commonly Used Legal and Publishing Terms

Since an exhaustive list of legal and publishing words and phrases is not practical, this glossary includes only some of the most generally used words and phrases—those that are likely to come up in preliminary conversations with a lawyer or publisher. More specific terms are covered in appropriate sections of the book.

Accelerated depreciation or **accelerated cost recovery (ACR)**. A method of recovering, through tax deductions, investment in business equipment such as a car, machine, or building. This method allows the taxpayer to take larger deductions in the earlier years of the life of an asset. For example, under straight-line depreciation, for a machine that costs $1,000 and is to be depreciated over ten years, you could deduct $100 per year. But with accelerated depreciation you might deduct $250 the first year, $200 the second year, $100 the third year and decreasing amounts thereafter. You should consult a CPA, tax attorney, or tax consultant to determine whether an item is eligible for accelerated depreciation.

Advance against royalties. A payment, in effect, of anticipated royalties before they are earned.

Assign (verb). To transfer one's rights and obligations to another party.

Assign (noun) or **assignee**. The person or business to whom rights and obligations are assigned.

Auditing clause. A clause in an author/publisher contract allowing the author to examine the publisher's books and records.

Author. In copyright terms, the person who created a work, or the employer for whom an employee created a work within the scope of employment.

Bailment. Rightful possession of another's property. For example, parking your car in a parking lot establishes a bailment.

When a publisher agrees to keep your manuscript for you, a bailment has been established.

Bequest (noun). Property left in a will.

Bequest (verb). The act of leaving property by will. Generally "devise" refers to real property and "bequest" refers to personal property.

Capitalizing a cost. Spreading out, over a period of years, the deductions being taken (for tax purposes) for depreciation of a capital expenditure—as for a word processor, for example.

Chilling effect. A term relating to the effect that certain laws or regulations might have on particular actions or works. Most commonly used in connection with censorship.

Codicil. A supplement to a will.

Common law. The body of law developed by the courts, independent of statutes.

Condition (in regard to contracts). A fact or event that, once it occurs, creates a duty to perform. If the condition does not occur, the duty to perform is extinguished.

Consideration (in regard to contracts). A payment or detriment incurred; an advantage that gives another party a reason for entering into an agreement.

Contingency fee. A payment that will occur only if a certain event occurs. Attorneys sometimes take law suits on a contingency-fee basis, which means they will not be paid unless they are successful in litigation or settle a suit in favor of the client. If they do not win or settle they are not paid.

Contingency waiver. The intentional relinquishment of a known right that someone is entitled to by contract. This phrase is common in contracts. If the party with whom you have signed a contract does not do something the contract requires, such as pay within 30 days, and you do not terminate the contract as you are entitled to do, this does not mean that you cannot terminate the contract the next time the party is late.

Copyright. The right granted to the creator of an original work of authorship that has been reduced to tangible form to prevent others from copying that work. A copyright is intellectual property (intangible property as distinguished from tangible property) that protects works such as books, art, or music.

Corporation. A hypothetical legal person created by the state for the purpose of carrying on a business. It may be created for the purpose of generating a profit or as a not-for-profit organization. It is separate and distinct from its owner(s)/shareholder(s).

Covenant. An absolute, unconditional promise to do something.

Crime of moral turpitude. Something that is immoral in itself, such as rape or murder, aside from the fact that it is punishable by law.

Devise. A bequest, or a gift given under a will. See Bequest (verb).

Distribution. Division of assets or money.

Employee at will. An employee who has not been hired for a set length of time and can be let go at any time.

Estoppel. A legal action that prevents someone from claiming a right that is detrimental to another person if the second person has relied upon the conduct of the first. For example, if a supplier says you do not need to pay your bill this month because he understands you are in a cash-flow crisis and then learns that you are paying some other bills with the money that was earmarked for him, the supplier may be stopped from immediately suing you for the amount due, because you relied on his statement.

Execute. To perform the necessary formalities of a contract such as signing and dating.

Exempted use. Use of another's copyrighted work whether or not the copyright owner's permission has been obtained for such use. Exempted uses are permitted because they are deemed to be in the public interest: for example, a library copying an out-of-print book for archival purposes.

Fair market value. The price at which property would change hands between a willing seller and a willing buyer.

Fair use. The reasonable use of a copyrighted work that does not require the permission of the copyright holder. Fair use is a defense which may be used to justify what might otherwise be considered a copyright infringement.

First-option clause. The clause in an author-publisher contract in which the author grants the publisher first option to accept the author's next manuscript(s) and make an offer on it.

Good and valuable consideration. A common contractual term promising that you will be compensated in money and/or in some other way.

Gross estate. All property in which the deceased had an ownership interest at the time of death, and before the will is put into effect. It is determined before deducting any amounts.

Holographic will. A will written wholly in the handwriting of the person who has signed it.

Injunction. A court order to do or stop doing something. If someone is copying your copyrighted work you can get an injunction ordering that person to stop copying. An injunction is commonly granted when a legal remedy like monetary damage is insufficient to compensate you for your injury.

Instrument. A document.

Integration. The inclusion of one agreement into another one.

Intellectual property. A product of the mind such as a copyright, trademark, or patent.

Intervivos gift. One made while the giver is alive (rather than given by will).

Intestate. Having made no legal will.

Investment tax credit. A federal tax incentive program to encourage businesses to invest in equipment by allowing a percentage of the purchase price to be subtracted from the business taxes due. This is not simply a deduction.

Letters patent. A document issued by the federal government granting a patent to the patent owner.

Libel. A defamatory statement that is *written*.

Libel per se and **libel per quod.** Libel per se: libel in which the defamatory meaning is apparent from the statement itself. Libel per quod: libel in which the defamatory meaning is apparent only in conjunction with other statements.

Limited partnership. A hybrid form of business organization containing elements of both the partnership and the corporation. It is created by statute and must have one or more general partners and one or more limited partners. See Chapter 1.

Mass-market paperback. A paperbound book of smaller size than a trade paperback book. Mass-market paperbacks are usually sold in racks in grocery stores, discount stores, and drugstores, although bookstores also sell them.

Moral turpitude. See Crime of moral turpitude.

Multiple submission. A manuscript or proposal submitted to more than one publisher at a time.

Negotiable instrument. A legal term for a promise to pay that meets specific conditions. It must (1) be in writing and signed by the maker, (2) contain an unconditional promise, (3) state a set sum of money to be paid, (4) indicate that payment will be on demand or at a specific time, (5) show that payment is to the bearer or to "order," and (6) contain no other promise. A check is an example of a negotiable instrument.

Nonrecognition of gain. A tax term referring to the rule that allows the taxpayer to defer the payment of tax when a principal residence is sold for profit and another residence of at least the same value is purchased within two years.

Option contract. One in which the offeror agrees not to revoke the offer for a given or indefinite length of time.

Out of print. No longer available (pertaining to a published book). However, at what point a book is out of print can be difficult to determine. See "Termination and Reversion" in Chapter 4.

Partnership (as defined by most state laws). An association of two or more persons to conduct, as co-owners, a business for profit. Sometimes referred to as a general partnership. See Chapter 1.

Patent. The right to prevent others from copying an invention. It is granted by the federal government and may take several forms: for example, mechanical patents, design patents, and application patents.

Preliminary injunction. An injunction granted before a hearing on the merits. It is used to preserve the status quo until the final hearing is complete.

Primary right (as opposed to subsidiary rights). The first right to publish and sell a work, usually in book form. Subsidiary rights are any conceivable other rights: for example, serial, reprint, book club, foreign-language, TV or film rights.

Principal (in regard to the author-agent relationship). The person an agent represents.

Prior restraint. Censorship *before* publication.

Publish. To make something known to the general public by putting it into circulation or making statements about it. In the copyright sense this means to distribute copies to the public.

Recitals. Statements at the beginning of a contract or other agreement that explain the reasons for the transaction.

Remaindering. Selling books at a greatly reduced price to dispose of the remainder or residue of the books on hand.

Representation. 1. Statements of fact made to cause another person to enter into an agreement. 2. A term used in inheritance when an heir to a will is no longer alive but has living children who will receive the heir's share.

Reserve. Royalties due the author but held back by the publisher to cover anticipated returns of books reported as sold.

Right of publicity. The right one has in one's own name or likeness.

Royalty. Money paid to an author out of the proceeds of the sale of the author's work.

Savings clause. A clause which permits the retrieval or salvaging of certain rights or property: for example, the clause in the 1976 Copyright Act that makes it possible to save the copyright in certain cases where a work has been published without proper copyright notice.

Secured party. Someone who holds a security interest in property: for example, a mortgage lender or a person who sells an automobile pursuant to an installment contract.

Security interest. Security in collateral used to secure a debt. A mortgage creates a security interest in real estate by permitting the holder of the mortgage (if payments are not made) to foreclose the mortgage and sell the property to recover the amount of the outstanding loan.

Self-publishing. Book publishing done by the author.

Serial rights. First serial rights: the right to publish a work, in part or in entirety, in a specific periodical before it is published anywhere else. Second serial rights: the right to publish all or part of a work after it has already appeared elsewhere.

Severability. Capable of being divided. If a contract has a severability clause and part of the contract is found to be void or illegal, the void or illegal parts may be taken out without destroying the rest of the contract.

Slander. A defamatory statement that is *spoken*.

Specific enforcement. Forcing the party who broke a contract to carry out the promised actions.

Statute of limitations. A rule that bars legal action after a certain period of time has passed.

Statutory damages. Financial compensation, the amount of which is determined not by the situation but by statute.

Straight-line depreciation. See Accelerated depreciation.

S Corporation (formerly known as a Subchapter S corporation). A designation under the tax laws which allows owners of a small corporation to elect to have the corporation taxed as a partnership, thus avoiding double taxation. Certain requirements must be met in order for a corporation to qualify for S corporation treatment.

Subsidiary rights. See Primary right.

Subsidy publishing. A publishing arrangement in which the author contributes money for the publishing of a book. The publishing house treats the book like any of its other books, giving it the usual editorial, design, printing, promotion, and distribution attention, and putting its logo on the book. This arrangement is often used in cases where the publisher feels the book deserves to be published but would have too small a market to be profitable.

Testator. The maker of a will.

Title. Ownership. If you hold the title to your car, house, or a work of art, it means you own it.

Tort. A wrongful act, damage, or injury, whether done intentionally or through negligence, but *not* involving a breach of contract.

Trade-book publishing. Publishing books intended to be sold through bookstores.

Trade paperbacks. Paperback books of higher quality and larger size than mass-market paperbacks, intended to be sold primarily through bookstores.

Trademark/service mark. A kind of intellectual property used by a merchant or manufacturer to identify his or her goods or services and distinguish them from those of anyone else.

Transferee. Umbrella term for either an assignee or licensee: one to whom something is transferred by assignment or license.

UCC (Uniform Commercial Code). A uniform series of laws governing commercial transactions (sales of goods and negotiable instruments, secured transactions, and other commercial transactions) that has been adopted in all states except Louisiana.

Unintended partner. Someone who, in the eyes of the law, is considered a partner in a business venture even though that was not the intention when that person became involved. See Chapter 1.

Vanity publishing. Entirely author-subsidized publishing. See Chapter 6.

Voidable contract. A contract that is valid until voided by the party that has that right. This is quite different from a contract that is *void*, and thus illegal and unenforceable from the outset.

Work for hire. A copyright term referring to work done while a writer was an employee of someone else or work which the parties have agreed, in writing, to be characterized as a work for hire—provided the work is of a type designated by the copyright law as capable of being a work for hire. Work done as a work for hire gives the employer, not the writer, the copyright.

Work of authorship. See Author.

Index